BROWN-ROA
A Division of Harcourt Brace & Company

Justice & Peace

JOSEPH STOUTZENBERGER

BROWN-ROA

A Division of Harcourt Brace & Company

O u r   M i s s i o n

The primary mission of BROWN-ROA is to provide the
Catholic and Christian educational markets with the
highest quality catechetical print and media resources.
The content of these resources reflects the best insights
of current theology, methodology, and pedagogical research.
The resources are practical and easy to use, designed to meet
expressed market needs, and written to reflect the
teachings of the Catholic Church.

Nihil Obstat
Rev. Richard L. Schaefer

Imprimatur
✠ Most Rev. Jerome Hanus, O.S.B.
Archbishop of Dubuque
August 11, 1998

The Imprimatur is an official declaration that a book or pamphlet is free of doctrinal or moral error.
No implication is contained therein that anyone who granted the Imprimatur agrees with the contents,
opinions, or statements expressed.

Photo credits appear on page 298.

Printed in the United States of America

ISBN 0-15-950448-1

10   9   8   7   6   5   4   3

Contents

Foundations for a Just World

Issues of Justice in our World

Creating a Peace-filled World

Dedication

To Timothy: I pray that God our Father and our Lord Jesus Christ will be kind and merciful to you. May you be blessed with peace (based on 1 Timothy 1:2). May compassion inspire you and your generation to work for justice and peace.

Acknowledgements

The following educators read through the manuscript of this text and provided valuable suggestions and observations:

Anne Marie Meehan and Jane Seminara
Arlington Catholic High School
Arlington, MA

Suzy R. Eyler
Bishop Eustace Preparatory School
Pennsauken, NJ

Elena Hoye PVBM
Diocesan Director of Catechesis and Catechist Formation
Sioux City, IA

Father John Bohrer assisted in the selection of prayers included in the text.

Erin Small provided a young person's perspective on early chapters.

CHAPTER 1

A Just World

The Christian Vision

The fundamental belief underlying this course is that Christian faith calls believers to do justice. Working for justice with God's grace, we create a community of compassion such as the one God intended. To begin our study of justice and peace, we need to identify elements of a just world. Since justice leads to becoming involved in the world, we also need to take note of characteristics in society that can influence our work for justice.

Major Concepts

A. A Just World Is a Sacred Place

Elements of a Christian vision of a just world

- Concern for basic needs
- Concern for personal dignity
- Concern for solidarity
- Concern for social structures

B. Culture and Countercultural: Reading the Signs of the Times

Cultural values that hinder justice

- Individualism
- Consumerism
- Fatalism

Countercultural values that encourage justice

- Interdependence
- Simple living
- Hope

Opening Prayer

Jesus, you inspire and challenge us to seek justice. May we always remember your hopeful message: Wherever two or three are gathered in your name, you are there in our midst. In this course we gather together to study justice and peace. Our faith assures us that as we come to know justice and peace more deeply, we are indeed growing in our knowledge of you. Bless our work this semester. Be with us always. We unite our prayer, our study, and our work with all those who need you and seek you. Amen.

Before we begin . . .

Complete the following sentences.

1. To me, justice means . . .

2. To me, injustice means . . .

3. One time I experienced an injustice was . . .

4. One time I stood up (or wish I had) for someone suffering an injustice was . . .

5. Three justice issues facing our world today are . . .

6. Three trends or movements that are helping to bring about justice today are . . .

The Good Samaritan

Just then a lawyer stood up to test Jesus. "Teacher," he said, "what must I do to inherit eternal life?" Jesus said to him, "What is written in the law? What do you read there?" He answered, "You shall love the Lord your God with all your heart, and with all your soul, and with all your strength, and with all your mind; and your neighbor as yourself." And Jesus said to him, "You have given the right answer; do this, and you will live." But wanting to justify himself, he asked Jesus, "And who is my neighbor?" Jesus replied, "A man was going down from Jerusalem to Jericho, and fell into the hands of robbers, who stripped him, beat him, and went away, leaving him half dead. Now by chance a priest was going down that road; and when he saw him, he passed by on the other side. So likewise a Levite, when he came to the place and saw him, passed by on the other side.

But a Samaritan while traveling came near him; and when he saw him, he was moved with pity. He went to him and bandaged his wounds, having poured oil and wine on them. Then he put him on his own animal, brought him to an inn, and took care of him. The next day he took out two denarii, gave them to the innkeeper, and said, 'Take care of him; and when I come back, I will repay you whatever more you spend.' Which of these three, do you think, was a neighbor to the man who fell into the hands of the robbers?" He said, "The one who showed him mercy." Jesus said to him, "Go and do likewise."

Luke 10:25–37

A Just World Is a Sacred Place

The Good Samaritan story teaches us about the interest for justice in a broken world. Too many of us find ourselves bleeding and abandoned by the side of a road, beaten down by poverty or limited opportunities, disabilities or discrimination. Our condition may strike us suddenly or weigh us down over a lifetime. Meanwhile, the rest of the world seems to be moving along the road, oblivious to our plight.

The story Jesus tells invites us to consider a different world. We know the hero of the story simply as a Samaritan—no one special, and not someone with whom the Jews hearing the story would want to associate. The Samaritan shows genuine concern for the suffering man's welfare. He sees someone in need and responds with compassion, one human being helping another. Jesus seems to suggest that the Samaritan is acting in a profoundly human way, while those who pass by without helping are damaging their own humanity.

A world filled with Good Samaritans is the human world at its best. By God's grace and with our cooperation, it also becomes a more sacred place. To be Christian means to participate in fashioning such a world. Today, the task looms large. Today, we realize that those in need are not simply on our own streets but are on the other side of the earth as well. Often they do not speak the language we speak. Typically, their suffering results from lacking even minimum necessities while others try to figure out how best to manage all of their wealth.

Nevertheless, isn't it true that we want a world such as the one fashioned by the cooperation of the Good Samaritan with God's kingdom? Its beauty strikes us as too alluring to dismiss. It mirrors the world that Jesus proclaimed and that we have prayed for since we were children: "Your kingdom come on earth as it is in heaven." In the words of the old movie, it is "the stuff that dreams are made of." Is a Good Samaritan world doomed to be merely an impossible dream, one that tantalizes us with its splendor, but lies always beyond our grasp?

Contrary to this fatalistic attitude, the Christian vision of justice affirms that with God's grace a world of caring and sharing is possible. With God's grace we can participate in making a just world an expanding reality, a gradual building up of a more holy place. This sacred world cannot be built alone or without hard work, pain, and sacrifice. Nevertheless, it can be built. How we can be a part of moving the human community toward becoming an even more sacred place is the subject of this course.◆

◆ The story of the Good Samaritan presents an image of a just world. In a song, painting, poem, story, collage, mime, or other art form, create your own image of a just world. To help you design your image, you might look ahead to the characteristics of a just world mentioned in this chapter.

Four Elements of a Just World

A just world is one in which families, friends, and strangers share their resources, care for one another's needs, and work out their differences for mutual benefit. In the next few chapters, we will see that such a world mirrors God's design, embodies the message of Jesus, and reveals the concerns of Church leaders and Christian saints throughout the ages. At the same time, as we will see, challenge and controversy accompany any move we might make toward justice. Taking the time to examine specific characteristics of a just world will give us a better idea of what that world is like and of the steps we can take to help build it.

Creation has its own goodness and proper perfection, but it did not spring forth complete from the hands of the Creator. The universe was created "in a state of journeying" (*in statu viae*) toward an ultimate perfection yet to be attained, to which God has destined it. (302)

1. Concern for Basic Needs

God destined the earth and all it contains for all people so that all created things would be shared fairly by all. . . .
—Vatican Council II, *The Church in the Modern World*, no. 69.

Christian teaching on justice declares that all people have a right to basic life goods. For instance, Pope John XXIII listed the following as *basic needs* that people have a right to have met:

- food
- shelter
- rest
- clothing
- health care
- social services

In addition, people have a right to the **means** to attain these basic life goods. These include:

- equal opportunity
- education
- employment

Affirmation that people should have basic needs met represents a bottom-line principle of justice. Saint Ambrose, an early Church leader, addressed this point in these words to the rich members of his community:

means

method or resources

You are not making a gift to the poor man from your possessions, but you are returning what is his. For what is common has been given for the use of all, [but] you make exclusive use of it. The earth belongs to all, not to the rich.

—John C. Haughey, *The Faith That Does Justice*, Mahwah, NJ: Paulist Press, page 128.

Jubilee Year

redistribution of property and wealth that took place according to Jewish law every fifty years in order to restore greater equality in possession of goods

Similar testimony to this principle of justice comes from our biblical roots. Ancient Jewish law called for a **Jubilee Year** every fifty years. The law required that land be returned to its original owners. Likewise, all debts were to be canceled. This special year was an attempt to insure a fair distribution of wealth and, thereby, prevent a widening gap between people who were rich and those who were poor.

The world produces enough for everyone's need but not everyone's greed.

Justice Versus Equality

Concern for meeting basic needs is not without controversy. Sometimes this concern actually appears to run counter to what we might consider fair—equal treatment for everyone. Consider the following scenarios:

A teacher discovers that one of her students suffers from dyslexia, a common reading impairment. She decides to give this particular student extra time to complete tests. Is this "fair" to the other students? Shouldn't all students be required to complete tests in the same amount of time?

A woman who has worked successfully for five years as a sales representative for a company takes time off to have a baby. When she returns to work, she requests that she be given a sales territory closer to her home and flexible working hours so that she can care for her child. Her supervisor tells her that it would be unfair to afford her preferential treatment just because she is now a mother.

Two young men are graduating from college. Because his parents are wealthy, one young man attends a prestigious college, has not worked during his college years so that he can concentrate on his studies, and with his good grades and a degree from a top-ranked university is destined to achieve a high level of economic and social success. The other young man has worked his way through a local community college, fitting his class schedule around the various jobs that he needed to keep in order to pay his tuition. Upon graduation he will take a middle-level job in order to pay off student loans and provide for himself. Since the first young man has higher grades from a more reputable university, it's only fair that he should end up in a higher-level profession, isn't it?

Anthony's brother is born with cerebral palsy, a condition that demands much attention from all family members. Anthony, who had been used to receiving his mother's exclusive attention, feels left out and cheated by the fact that his brother gets all the attention.

The child of migrant farmworkers, Jose Miguel has never attended school regularly. Soon he will be expected to pick crops to help support the family. Since he will not be receiving a high school diploma, Jose Miguel will never have anything other than menial jobs. ◆

◆ Role play each character's experience of equal treatment as depicted in the previous stories. Through the role playing define whose basic needs are being met. What arguments would each person present about what would be required for him or her to feel he or she is being treated fairly and justly?

After each role play discuss in terms of the first element of a just world, whether there is a difference between equal treatment and justice (meeting basic needs)? Explain.

As the previous scenarios indicate, people have different degrees of need and different types of needs. For instance, a student with dyslexia has different needs from other students in a classroom. A student who comes to school hungry has different needs from well-fed students. People who are homeless have needs that others do not. Therefore, meeting people's basic needs sometimes runs counter to "treating everyone equally"—a popular definition of justice.

Recent Church teaching about justice makes the following assertions about basic needs and our world today:

- The majority of the earth's population do not have basic needs met.
- Our present resources *could* provide for the basic needs of all people.
- More equal distribution of the earth's goods would move the human community along toward becoming a just world.

Review

1. How does the text distinguish between justice and equal distribution?
2. What three assertions about meeting basic needs today are made in recent Church teaching?

Discuss

A. Anthropologist Margaret Mead suggested that a basic human need is that someone is concerned when you don't come home at night. Do you agree? Do you believe that this is an actual concern in our culture today?

B. Besides physical needs what are some psychological and emotional needs that people have?

Giving with Dignity

A service club in a suburban Catholic high school decides to collect toys and clothing for children living in an urban parish. Club members plan on dressing up in Santa Claus outfits and personally distributing the gifts on Christmas Eve.

The pastor of the urban parish visits their club to speak to the students. "I appreciate your work on behalf of our children," he tells them, "but I can't have you delivering toys to the children themselves. Parents should be Santa Claus for their children, not wealthy young people from the suburbs. It would diminish the self-esteem of our parents if you brought the gifts to their children. Instead, I suggest that you bring the toys and presents to the church hall the week before Christmas. Then our parents can come and choose the things that they feel would be best for their children. In that way the children will receive gifts at Christmas, and the parents will also participate in the giving."

- Do you believe the pastor's concerns in the story are justified? Why?

2. Concern for Personal Dignity

Then God said: "Let us make humankind in our image, according to our likeness. . . ."

—Genesis 1:26

What is most striking about the story of the Good Samaritan is his recognition of the one beaten by the side of the road as a person of profound worth. The second component of a just world—a concern for personal dignity—considers the psychological dimension of people's basic needs as being on a par with their physical needs. All people not only share basic needs, but also possess *God-given worth and dignity.* Thus, people have a right to a sense of self-esteem and to develop their own capabilities, the ability to *give* as well as to receive. In other words they have a right to be fully human, subjects of their own destiny and not merely objects of someone else's kindness. The above incident illustrates this dimension of justice.

This second element of a just world requires that we work toward the **empowerment** of people. Perhaps you can recall what a thrill it was when as a child you were allowed to take responsibility for something—walking to a store by yourself, staying at home without a babysitter, spending your own money. Many people feel as though they lack power even over their own lives. If personal dignity is accounted for, then people who are currently far removed from the centers of power must be included in decision making. That is, they must gain power over their own lives and share power with others to shape the world and the human community.

We all know how much greater our sense of personal satisfaction is when we help to design or create something for ourselves. Conversely, we probably can recall science fiction stories about aliens from another galaxy who impose their idea of a "perfect" civilization upon earthlings. Looking back in history a few decades, we discover totalitarian governments such as those in China and Cambodia in the 1970s which imposed on people exactly how they were to live and make a livelihood. Because people have no say in its design, the perfect world ends up being an inhuman nightmare. A truly human world is not imposed from above but grows out of human creativity.

When I look at your heavens, the work of your fingers, the moon and the stars that you have established; what are human beings that you are mindful of them, mortals that you care for them?

Yet you have made them a little lower than God, and crowned them with glory and honor. You have given them dominion over the works of your hands; you have put all things under their feet, all sheep and oxen, and also the beasts of the field, the birds of the air, and the fish of the sea, whatever passes along the paths of the seas.

O Lord, our Sovereign, how majestic is your name in all the earth!

—Psalm 8:3-10

for

providing low-cost housing
soup kitchens
food pantries
clothing donations

with

Habitat for Humanity
providing garden plots
gleaning after crops
material to sew clothes

3. Concern for Solidarity

Solidarity helps us to see the "other"—whether a person, people, or nation—not just as some kind of instrument, with a work capacity and physical strength to be exploited at low cost and then discarded when no longer useful, but as our "neighbor," a "helper" (cf. Gen. 2:18–21) to be made a sharer, on a par with ourselves, in the banquet of life to which all are equally invited by God.

—Pope John Paul II, *On Social Concern,* no. 39.

Concern for **solidarity** means that working for justice involves working with, not working for. Solidarity among people with unequal power requires a redistribution of power. Therefore, this element of a just world corresponds with concern for personal dignity. For instance, in the Good Samaritan story, the hero gives no indication that he considers himself above or apart from the person in need. His welfare and that of his neighbor are not separate. The goal of his action is not to maintain a split between himself as powerful and the other as powerless but to empower the other, to bring the other back to life and vitality. In a similar way people concerned about helping people in need do not simply cry, "We must feed the poor." Instead, they also say: "We must learn from people who are poor how they can help us, as well as how we can help them help themselves. We need to give those who are voiceless a voice. We need to share important decisions among those who are rich and those who are poor."

solidarity

a spirit of unity and mutual concern; the quality of justice that breaks down barriers between people

At the age of ten, I was diagnosed with pre-leukemia. . . . I have greater compassion for those who are suffering, and a much greater respect for those who help them. This respect has made me think about becoming a doctor or nurse so that I can help people that are sick or dying. I want to be there for them, just like people were there for me. Maybe at the same time I would feel like I have started to repay those people who helped me.

—Ann Marie Hines, "From Isolation to Liberation," in *I Know Things Now: Stories by Teenagers 1*, Winona, MN: St. Mary's Press, pages 56–57.

Pope John Paul II has spoken frequently about solidarity, which he equates with interdependence and mutual responsibility:

> When interdependence becomes recognized . . . . the correlative response as a moral and social attitude, as a "virtue," is solidarity. This then is not a feeling of vague compassion or shallow distress at the misfortunes of so many people, both near and far. On the contrary, it is a firm and persevering determination to commit oneself to the common good; that is to say to the good of all and of each individual, because we are all really responsible for all.
>
> —On Social Concern, no. 38.

mutuality

the recognition that we need each other and that the good of one person matches the good of all people

Put simply, solidarity is that quality of justice that breaks down barriers between people: the powerful and the powerless, rich and poor, men and women, black and white, Asian and Western, Hispanic and Anglo-American, young and old, those in prison and those who are free. As we will see in the next chapter, Christians naturally lean toward solidarity since Jesus so radically identified with the suffering and joys of all people, especially of those who were penniless and voiceless. Solidarity implies a spirit of **mutuality**. ◆

◆ With a partner or small group, role play how you might address the following problems, first using a working-for approach, then using a working-with approach.

- A classmate is receiving failing grades.
- A friend develops a drinking problem.
- A neighborhood near you is in serious disrepair.
- Your local parish would like to help those leaving prison who have no place to go.
- Your grandmother is alone and homebound.

4. Concern for Social Structures

Society should be so structured that it is easy for people to be good.
—Peter Maurin, co-founder of the Catholic Worker Movement.

societal problems
problems that affect an entire community or nation

personal problems
an individual's concerns

The Good Samaritan story describes a one-to-one encounter. Often it is easier to act compassionately when operating on such a personal scale. However, justice also seeks to address problems on a larger scale, where "persons" merge into a faceless "society." And the fact is, **societal problems** are **personal problems,** even if we don't experience them as such.

For example, if a cousin's house burns down and she is suddenly homeless, chances are your family would take her in. On the other hand, if during a visit to an urban center, you came across a person who is homeless, you might feel uncomfortable but incapable of doing anything about it. Similarly, if the sole breadwinner of a family you know is out of work, you might contribute to a collection for temporary financial support. But on the other hand, you might remain unmoved when hearing that "unemployment in our state is at 10 percent"—even though behind that statistic are real mothers and fathers with real families to feed. ◆

The immenseness of social problems often seems to overwhelm our ability to respond. Part of the dilemma is that our society can be structured so that it either promotes or hinders justice. It can help either the majority of people or mostly a privileged few. It can either advocate attention to those most in need or shield others from ever encountering them. Concern for justice, then, includes concern for social structures.

◆ With a small group, think of another example of a problem that exists on a *societal* scale and that is a *personal* problem for someone who is experiencing this problem. Describe possible solutions that address the problem on a personal level and on a societal scale. Present your ideas to the class.

Social structures, a concept we will look at more closely in chapter four, refer to commonly accepted ways a society is organized. For instance, the way a society structures its educational system says a great deal about what a society values and even to a degree whom a society values. Indeed, the percentage of tax money spent on schools compared to other government spending reveals how much education itself is valued. Whether private cars or public transportation is the norm for a society makes a statement about priorities given to public, shared space versus private space. It also speaks to the types of human interaction expected in a society. (For example, people with cars can avoid interacting with people who don't own cars whereas people without cars more consistently share public space.) Similarly, a country's economic system can function more or less competitively and more or less directed toward the common good. In the words of the U.S. bishops:

> *Our economic activity in factory, field, office, or shop feeds our families—or feeds our anxieties. It exercises our talents—or wastes them. It raises our hopes—or crushes them. It brings us into cooperation with others—or sets us at odds.* —U.S. Catholic Bishops, *Economic Justice for All*, no. 6.

Here's an example to illustrate the importance of social structures in terms of meeting or failing to meet people's needs:

Requiring a wheelchair for transportation creates special problems. Yes, if we don't need a wheelchair ourselves, we might offer to help those who do by shopping for them or transporting them places. But what happens when we cannot be with them? What about those who require wheelchairs and have no one to assist them?

What changes could occur in a society that would help *all* people who use wheelchairs? With this question we address the issue of social structures. For instance, many communities build sidewalks with ramps at intersections so that people in wheelchairs can better travel by themselves. Special parking places and ramps to public buildings also help those in wheelchairs become more self-reliant. As you can imagine, such societal changes can do as much as many hours of volunteer help on the part of caring individuals. These changes also free people to have access to those things they need to be fully human.

Attending to social structures is an essential part of caring for people's basic needs, their self-esteem, and their solidarity. Concern for social structures is such an important consideration in working toward a just society that we will look at this element of justice throughout the course.

Review

3. What does empowerment mean as an element of justice?
4. Name and give an example to illustrate the four elements of a just world.
5. Give an example illustrating that "societal problems are personal problems."
6. Name three social structures that affect your daily living.

Discuss

C. Name some ways that people with less apparent power can help people with greater apparent power grow in understanding. For instance, what insights can poor people provide rich people; what might a blind person teach people with sight; what can adults learn from children?

Culture and Counterculture: Reading the Signs of the Times

You know how to interpret the appearance of earth and sky, but why do you not know how to interpret the present time? And why do you not judge for yourselves what is right?

—Luke 12:56–57

The 1997 film *Marvin's Room* tells about two adult daughters who have gone their separate ways. One daughter, Lee, left home to pursue her own dreams and aspirations. The other daughter, Bessie, remained home to care for her father, who is bed-ridden with a stroke, and her aunt Ruth, who is borderline senile. By the end of the movie, the two sisters are reconciled because Bessie, who had stayed home to care for her sick father and aunt, now is dying of leukemia herself.

In a poignant conversation near the end of the film, Bessie tells her sister, "I've had such love in my life. I look back and I've had such love." Lee responds by saying, "They love you very much." But Bessie then says, "I don't mean . . . I mean I love them. I am so lucky to have been able to love someone so much. I am so lucky to have loved so much. I am so lucky."

Precisely because she has spent most of her life giving to and caring for others, Bessie is dying with a sense of joy and peace. In that sense her entire life runs counter to what typically is presented in our culture as the way to happiness. According to the values of our culture, should we, like Lee, leave behind people who burden us and instead pursue our own dreams? Is it a shame that Bessie was saddled with caring for two helpless invalids, one physical and one psychological? When we think about "love" in our lives, don't we really mean that we want to *be* loved?

If we want to create a just world, then we need to develop our awareness of the "signs of the times"—that is, the current direction and values in our culture. Certainly, there is much that is good in our culture. However, certain cultural values work against the well-being of some or all members of a society. In fact, dominant cultural values can have both positive and negative effects on people.

Aboard the U.S.S. Earth

Here is one author's symbolic description of our world today. Admittedly, it paints a grim picture—especially of first-class passengers. However, before we reject the scenario as unreal, we would do well to consider whether characteristics of the ocean liner match characteristics actually at work in our world.

The earth is like an ocean liner with first-class, second-class, and third-class passengers. The first-class passengers, making up about one-fourth of the ship's list, have insisted on bringing along their automobiles, freezers, hair dryers, television sets, kitchen disposal units, and pets. They have indiscriminately filled a number of the ship's holds with empty cans, bottles, discarded plastic, old newspapers, and broken appliances—the residue of their excessive consumption. In other holds they keep cattle, which are periodically slaughtered to sustain their customary first-class eating habits. And in still other compartments, they keep grain reserved for feeding the cattle.

Those privileged passengers have some dangerous personal habits as well. They flush garbage down the toilets, blow smoke and gasoline fumes into the ship's ventilation system, and insist on unlimited use of the ship's limited electricity and water. Every once in a while they have a major brawl among themselves and threaten to sink the ship, and "just in case," they constantly improve their assorted bombs with which to do so.

The ship has no captain because the first-class passengers are afraid to give anyone authority to steer a new course or to change the ship's arrangements. Instead, there is a committee, which has no power and is not allowed access to the bridge. The committee is permitted only to discuss possible future directions and to make highly tentative suggestions.

—Adapted from Adam Daniel Finnerty
No More Plastic Jesus, pages 2–3.

- How true-to-life is this analogy of the world as an ocean liner?
- What actual conditions do you think the author is referring to?
- In what ways is the author on target in his description?
- Do you think he exaggerates or is inaccurate in any way?

Individualism Versus Interdependence

Human beings are a lot like crabgrass. Each blade of crabgrass sticks up into the air, appearing to be a plant all by itself. But when you try to pull it up, you discover that all the blades of crabgrass in a particular piece of lawn share the same roots and the same nourishment system. Those of us brought up in the Western tradition are taught to think of ourselves as separate and distinct creatures with individual personalities and independent nourishment systems. But I think the crabgrass image is a more accurate description of our condition. Human beings may appear to be separate, but our connections are deep and we are inseparable.

—Fran Peavey, *Heart Politics*, page 1.

Let's look at three of the characteristics implied in the ocean-liner image to determine whether they apply to our culture. In addition, let us name values that can serve as antidotes to unhealthy aspects of these characteristics in our society.

Western society, especially the North American branch of Western society, glories in its history of rugged **individualism**. "I've got to be me" and "every man for himself" are basic social themes. "Self-reliance" is practically synonymous with the North American spirit. At the political level, reliance on military power accompanies excessive individualism.

The 1985 study of North American values, *Habits of the Heart*, identifies individualism as a longstanding core theme in American life. The study describes moral individualism in these terms: "The ultimate ethical rule is simply that individuals should be able to pursue whatever they find rewarding, constrained only by the requirement that they not interfere with the 'value systems' of others" (6). The authors, Robert Bellah and his team, interviewed people from across the country to demonstrate this theme. A young man had this to say:

> *One of the things that I use to characterize life in California, one of the things that makes California such a pleasant place to live, is people by and large aren't bothered by other people's value systems as long as they don't infringe upon your own. By and large, the rule of thumb out here is that if you've got the money, honey, you can do your thing as long as your thing doesn't destroy someone else's property, or interrupt their sleep, or bother their privacy, then that's fine. (6–7)*

individualism

emphasizing personal independence and the rights of individuals over interdependence and concern for the common good

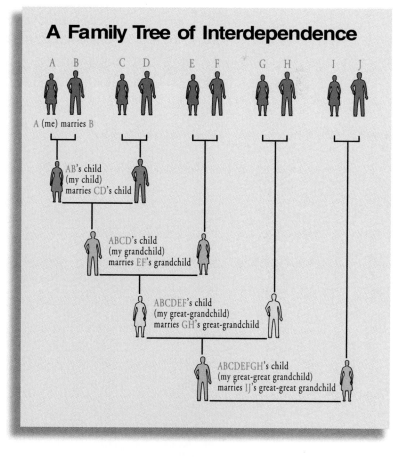

Interdependence can sound so abstract. One way to picture the concept more concretely is to think about the reality that your great-great-grandchildren will be direct descendants of fourteen people besides yourself who are living today. If you care about your own great-great-grandchildren and their children, shouldn't you also be concerned about the people around you today who may end up being their great-grandparents or great-great-grandparents?

The earlier ocean-liner story hints at the dangers of excessive individualism. Given the precarious nature of our world today, we either learn to live and work together or we perish together. Our world is a "global village" in which all segments are dependent upon one another. In that sense, a realistic description of our world acknowledges that we are neither independent nor dependent. Rather, we are **interdependent.**

interdependent

reliance on others for survival and well-being

Examples of global interdependence are not hard to find.

- When British cows or Taiwanese pigs are found to be diseased, the price of meat rises across the globe.

- An accident at a nuclear power plant anywhere on the earth affects levels of radioactivity everywhere.

- When oil prices go up, the cost of all consumer goods goes up.

- The U.S. heartland serves as the breadbasket of the world because it provides a large portion of the earth's grain. Drought in the U.S. leads to hungry people on the other side of the world.

- Brazil's enormous jungles act as the earth's oxygen tank, producing much of the oxygen we breathe. Destruction of rain forests damages the entire earth's air supply.

Clearly, stressing individual initiative and responsibility is valuable. Individualism has helped make our country great. However, it is important that we acknowledge how much we are interdependent. A spirit of cooperation is needed for our mutual survival.

Review

7. What potentially counter cultural message is contained in the movie *Marvin's Room*?

8. Define the concept of *moral individualism*.

9. Use an example to illustrate *interdependence*.

Discuss

D. What brings Bessie joy in the movie Marvin's Room?

E. Are Bessie's values the norm for women in our society but not for men? How do you feel about her choice? Explain.

F. Do you believe that the young man in the quote on page 15 speaks for most Americans?

G. In what sense does his attitude reflect your own?

H. In what sense does it not reflect your attitude?

I. Name ways, either positive or negative, that the moral individualism he talks about has an impact on justice in the world.

Consumerism Versus Simple Living

Christian faith and the norms of justice impose distinct limits on what we consume and how we view material goods. The great wealth of the United States can easily blind us to the poverty that exists in this nation and the destitution of hundreds of millions of people in other parts of the world. Americans are challenged today as never before to develop the inner freedom to resist the temptation to constantly seek more. Only in this way will the nation avoid what Paul VI called "the most evident form of moral underdevelopment," namely greed

—U.S. Catholic Bishops, *Economic Justice for All*, no. 75.

North Americans have had a long love affair with the frontier. Throughout most of our history, there was always more land available "out West." If one locality could no longer support more people, then it was always possible to move on. North America seemed to offer limitless land, limitless resources, and limitless opportunities. Even when the land was parceled out and some of our resources showed signs of running out, we put our faith in space as "the final frontier."

The ocean-liner image awakens us to a different reality—**the crisis of limits.** While we tend to bring an excessive number of possessions along with us on our life journeys, we need to heed experts on the future who are waving a yellow flag of caution. They warn us that if we continue to use up our resources at the current rate, we will be facing drastic shortages in the not-too-distant future. If we are to survive, we had better change our ways.

crisis of limits

the finite and irreplaceable nature of essential resources, such as oil and rainforests

In the quote which opened this section, the U.S. Catholic bishops identify a key problem contributing to the crisis of limits—**consumerism.** Think of TV commercials or magazine ads you have seen recently. Chances are that they tried to convince you how much better your life would be if you possessed whatever it is they are selling. Ads allure us into believing that our lives will be more comfortable, more interesting, more fun, or more rewarding if we possess this year's hot toy for children or adults. In the face of this allurement, the U.S. bishops associate three things with consumerism: blindness, lack of freedom, and moral underdevelopment.

consumerism

the distorted desire to possess things out of proportion to our needs or normal wants

All of us *consume* things; otherwise, we would be dead. However, consumerism is the distorted desire to possess things, all out of proportion to our needs or normal wants. Consumerism means allowing a passion for possessions to control us to the point that possessions become an end in themselves. Consumerism preaches that "we *can* buy happiness." ◆

◆ List purchases you have made over the past three months. Identify items on your list that are frequently advertised; that could be considered fads; that you could easily do without; that are a necessity.

What are some ways that consumerism manifests itself in your life? What are some ways that you attempt to counteract consumerism?

Pontius' Puddle

GOD QUICKLY CAME TO REGRET HIS MORE RELAXED *"ALL RIGHT, YOU CAN TAKE ONE THING WITH YOU"* POLICY.

Three Dangers of Consumerism

The ocean-liner story hints at the dangers of consumerism. Certainly, we need much more guidance about what to buy or not buy than what thirty-second commercials tell us. For one thing, excessive consumption takes needed resources away from third-class passengers. That is, money spent on a new car or the latest CD could be spent in ways that benefit people in greater need. Secondly, consumerism affects consumers as well. Namely, it equates happiness with *having* rather than with *being*. When we do buy the new car, the VCR, or the latest computer, we eventually find that we have more possessions but not necessarily more happiness. As news reports make clear, affluent persons sometimes commit suicide; and impoverished persons can struggle heroically to hang on to life in any way they can. Finally, consumerism can change people into commodities. Just as we may feel that we need to own a particular make of car, we may also feel compelled to wear a certain hairstyle or certain clothes, or to be seen with certain people. In this way consumerism makes commodities—consumer goods—of us and of the people around us. We package ourselves like any other consumer goods.

Side-by-side with the miseries of underdevelopment, themselves unacceptable, we find ourselves up against a form of superdevelopment, equally inadmissible, because like the former it is contrary to what is good and to true happiness. This superdevelopment, which consists in an excessive availability of every kind of material goods for the benefit of certain social groups, easily makes people slaves of "possession" and of immediate gratification, with no other horizon than the multiplication or continual replacement of the things already owned with others still better. This is the so-called civilization of "consumption" or "consumerism," which involves so much "throwing-away" and "waste." An object already owned but now superseded by something better is discarded, with no thought of its possible lasting value in itself, nor of some other human being who is poorer. ◆

—Pope John Paul II, *On Social Concern*, no. 28.

◆ Advertising reflects consumerism. Watch the ads on a typical evening of commercial television and list the possessions that the ads suggest lead to happiness. Also, describe techniques—such as being "cool," achieving status, or satisfying a manufactured need—that are used to sell these products. Make a video presentation to illustrate your conclusions.

Simple Living: An Antidote to Consumerism

We might conclude that in a consumer society people value material things. In fact, this is seldom the case. Instead, we may have so many things, and crave possessing other things, that we do not take time to value what we do have. As a result, a consumer society is a **throwaway society.** The things we craved yesterday become the junk of today. Like the ocean liner, our world can become overburdened with junk. If we apply the attitude of a throwaway society to the treatment of people, then we find in a consumer society that those who appear to be non-contributing members are relegated to human junkyards. That is, if we value only "beautiful people" or people useful to us, then "out of sight, out of mind" becomes the motto of society's attitude toward people confined to jails and mental institutions or trapped in pockets of poverty.

throwaway society
squandering of usable materials and products

The antidote to consumerism, then, is **simple living.** Simple living does not imply devaluing things. Rather, it means cultivating a spirit of reverence for both things and people. Simple living includes reducing the amount of energy and resources that we use in our daily living. It also suggests discovering ways to enjoy the many goods of the earth, including manufactured goods and the wonders of modern technology, in ways that are truly appreciative and not possessive.

simple living
buying and using only what is needed, out of respect for people and resources

Simple living makes sense because . . .

- It is an act of *solidarity* with all those who have little, not by choice but by circumstance.
- It is an act of *self-defense* against the dangers of over-consumption.
- It is a *celebration* of the true value of persons and things.
- It is a statement of *faith* in being, not having.
- It is an act of *resistance* against a high-pressure, achievement-oriented culture.
- It leads to greater *sharing* of public space and common goods.
- It *redirects our energy* away from satisfying artificially created wants toward an appreciation of truly valuable goods and services.

Reading the Gospels, we discover that Jesus speaks about the dangers of wealth and the lure of possessions more than about any other social issue. In addition to keeping the Commandments, Jesus tells the rich man in Mark's Gospel that if he truly seeks eternal life then he must give all that he has to the poor. When his followers are shocked at this teaching, Jesus repeats it—twice! If Jesus felt the need to stress the dangers of riches in his comparatively simple society, then how much more in our highly affluent society do we need to remain vigilant to the dangers of consumerism?

Fatalism Versus Hope

fatalism

the belief that the world is out of our control and in the hands of blind fate

hope

a virtue that envisions a better world and affirms that, with God's help, a better world is possible

To hope means to be ready at every moment for that which is not yet born, and yet not become desperate if there is no birth in our lifetime. . . . those whose hope is strong see and cherish all signs of new life and are ready every moment to help the birth of that which is ready to be born.

—Erich Fromm, "The Revolution of Hope," in *The Heart Has Its Seasons*, New York: Regina Press, 1971, page 247.

The ocean-liner story describes a world out of control. We can easily allow the many problems facing us to create a spirit of defeat. We may sense that the world and its problems are too big for us, that we can do little against the overwhelming powers of darkness filling our world. We seem to hear about a new crisis or trouble spot every week. What can we do? Where do we start? How do we counteract **fatalism**?

The antidote to fatalism is **hope.** According to Christian tradition, hope is a virtue. As a virtue, hope is a quality that we develop through practice. Too often we use the word *hope* only when things are out of our hands. For example, we might say, "That police officer just saw me driving way over the speed limit. I sure hope she doesn't give me a ticket."

Genuine hope is not throwing up our hands in despair but lending a helping hand where it is needed. As Erich Fromm says in the quote opening this section, hope means searching for signs of the birth of justice and being constantly ready to assist in that birth.

Reminding us of the power of hope, a modern monk notes that: "During the darkest periods of history, quite often a small number of men and women, scattered through the world, have been able to reverse the course of historical evolutions. This was possible only because they hoped beyond all hope." Hope affirms that all things are possible and challenges us to work to make them happen. In the words of Robert Kennedy: "Some men see things as they are and say, 'Why'? I dream things that never were and say, 'Why not?'" ◆

Simple living is not only good for the earth, it is also good for the human spirit.

◆ Choose one of the following activities on which to present a report to the class.

- Write a report describing a film, news story, song, or magazine article that contains a message of hope.
- Write a report on the life of a person who is a model of hope.

It would . . . be to give a one-sided picture, which could lead to sterile discouragement, if the condemnation of the threats to life were not accompanied by the presentation of the positive signs at work in humanity's present situation.

Unfortunately, it is often hard to see and recognize these positive signs, perhaps also because they do not receive sufficient attention in the communications media. Yet, how many initiatives of help and support for people who are weak and defenseless have sprung up and continue to spring up in the Christian community and in civil society, at the local, national and international level, through the efforts of individuals, groups, movements and organizations of various kinds!

—Pope John Paul II, *The Gospel of Life*, no. 26.

Review

10. Name one resource that has reached a *crisis of limits*.
11. What three dangers does the text identify with consumerism?
12. Define and give example of the term *throwaway society*.
13. Describe an action and an attitude associated with simple living.
14. Define *fatalism*.
15. What does it mean to say that hope is a virtue?

Discuss

J. Give concrete examples to illustrate what the U.S. bishops mean when they associate consumerism with blindness, lack of freedom, and moral underdevelopment.
K. Think of the last purchase you made. Was the product a *need* or a *want* on your part. If it was a *want* how could you have used the money to have benefited another? Was the happiness from the product short or long term? Did the purchase make you a commodity?
L. What problems would you encounter in trying to live more simply?
M. Do you think the world today is moving in a positive or a negative direction?
N. Do you see signs of hope that the world could become more of a community of justice? Give examples to support your position.
O. Can you recommend changes that would need to occur for a just world to be built?

In Summary: A Just World Is Possible

In this chapter we have laid out a vision of a just world and have identified some of the characteristics of contemporary culture. Obviously, we have powerful obstacles to overcome in creating a just world. As we move along in this course, we will examine in greater detail what justice involves. As we will continue to see, the journey toward justice and peace is challenging but hope-filled.

Before we conclude . . .

Let us pray . . .

God of justice and compassion, as we journey through this semester, help us to know you and to know our sisters and brothers with your mind and heart. May we remain attentive to these words of Saint Teresa of Avila:

"Christ has no body now but yours;
no hands, no feet on earth but yours.
Yours are the eyes through which he looks
with compassion on this world;
yours are the feet with which he walks to do good;
yours are the hands with which he blesses all the world.
Christ has no body now on earth but yours."
Amen.

For further study

1. List ways that you might foster the four elements of a just world in your personal life:

   - Concern for basic needs
   - Concern for personal dignity
   - Concern for solidarity
   - Concern for social structures

2. Research a project, organization, or group of people which fosters the four elements of a just world. Write a two-page report indicating how they foster each of the four elements.

3. In a small group, brainstorm ways that society might change to foster the four elements of a just world. Prepare a presentation for the class using a medium of your choice to present the ideas your group generated.

4. From the perspective of one of the groups listed below, prepare a presentation for the class on the following statement: *The wide gap that exists between the richest and poorest members of society is both unhealthy and unjust. We should take steps to insure greater equality both of wealth and of opportunity for all.*

   - CEOs of five leading companies on New York Stock Exchange
   - Members of a welfare-rights organization
   - Delegates to the United Nations
   - Catholic bishops of the United States
   - A union of peasant farmworkers in a poor country
   - Students at an elite Catholic prep school
   - Students at an inner-city Catholic high school

5. For each of the three assertions about people's basic needs listed on page 6, write a paragraph that expresses your viewpoint. Then write a paragraph explaining whether most people would agree with your viewpoints.

6. List other examples of how we are interdependent on personal, community, national, and global levels. Then answer the following questions. Give reasons for each answer.

   - Do you find that your school fosters more a spirit of interdependence or a spirit of individualism?
   - Do you believe that success in life depends more on individual achievement or on cooperation?
   - Does your family life indicate a high degree of interdependence?
   - Do you find the concept of interdependence frightening?
   - Do you believe that North American culture overemphasizes individualism?
   - Do you see signs of increased interdependence globally?

   Finally, part of the "culture wars" going on in the United States is between those who emphasize the value of individualism and those who emphasize interdependence. Debate the pros and cons of each position.

7. In light of the discussion about the three characteristics of North American culture, list ways that you might foster positive trends on a personal level.

8. Research a project, organization, or group which has fostered a positive trend in our society during the last year. In three to five paragraphs, describe this trend.

9. List ways that society might change to foster positive trends. Choose one of the trends you listed. Making two columns, indicate in the first column the advantages this trend could bring about; in the second column, indicate the difficulties that someone would face trying to implement this change.

10. Which of the reasons for choosing a simple lifestyle outlined on page 19 appeals to you most? In light of these reasons, can you identify ways that you and your family already practice simple living? Name other activities that you might do that would reflect the spirit of simple living.

CHAPTER 2

Scripture

The God Who Takes Sides

The Bible begins with creation of a world described as good and ends with the vision of a new heaven and a new earth. The writings in between tell about how the human community sags under the oppressive weight of injustices. More importantly, the Bible stories never let go of the hope that God, through the work of human hands, will transform the world into one where justice reigns. In this chapter, we will examine the key themes found in the Scriptures' call to justice.

Major Concepts

A. Choosing Sides in the Bible

- God especially cares for those who are poor and powerless

B. Genesis and Biblical Foundations for Justice

- The goodness of creation
- Stewardship
- In this together

C. The Exodus and Liberation

- Classic characters and themes related to liberation

D. The Prophets and Justice

- Religion
- Politics
- Social conditions

E. Jesus and Justice: Deepening and Broadening the Message

- Personal level
- Interpersonal level
- Political level

Opening Prayer

*God, throughout Scripture you reveal
yourself as a God who cares for those
who are poor, suffering, troubled, and
apparently hopeless. We praise you as
a God who loves your creation,
including those parts of it that we
ourselves might overlook or dismiss as
unimportant. We thank you for
showing us the way to true liberation
in the Exodus, and for using the
prophets to challenge us. Finally, we
stand in wonder before your Son,
Jesus, who not only preached justice
but lived justice. May we embrace
Scripture and make its call to justice
our own. Amen.*

Before we begin . . .

Answer **agree**, **disagree**, or **uncertain**
to the following statements. Explain
your answers.

1. I am quite familiar with
   Scripture already.

2. I believe that the Bible provides
   guidance for living.

3. I find the Bible's message to
   be comforting.

4. If I took the Bible seriously,
   I would live my life very
   differently.

5. I consider justice to be a central
   theme of Scripture.

6. What Jesus asks of us is
   unrealistic.

7. People who are poor or outcast
   are important in Scripture
   stories.

8. Those who are rich will have
   difficulty getting into heaven.

Team Player

Being the best, Martin and Alvin naturally chose the teams. In a ritual duplicated on playgrounds around the world, each one in turn picked the players to fill out his team. After everyone else was picked, Darnell and little Angelo remained. Seeing no other potential basketball players in sight, Martin reluctantly pointed to Darnell, leaving Angelo for Alvin's team. As the game began, Martin barked directions to Darnell, "Cover Angelo. Otherwise, stay out of the way."

- Have you ever been in a situation similar to either Martin's (someone who has power or who takes charge) or Angelo's (someone who lacks power and must depend on another)? Describe the situation. How did it feel?
- In a "just world" how would this story have looked?
- Have you ever been part of a similar situation that was handled justly?

Choosing Sides

Martin and Alvin are not cruel. In choosing sides for their basketball teams, they are merely mimicking the ways of the world. Of course, the best players should call the shots and be the center of attention. Those with lesser ability are troublesome; they should be passed over when they can be and merely tolerated when they can't. The Darnells and Angelos of the world may dislike the system, but it's not apt to change. It simply makes sense, doesn't it?

One coach had a vision of how basketball could be played differently. When Phil Jackson became coach of the Chicago Bulls in 1990, he inherited a talented team with perhaps the greatest player of all time. Nonetheless, this team had not been able to win an NBA championship. In his book, *Sacred Hoops*, Jackson talks about how he wanted his team to operate differently from what professional basketball had become—the glorified slam-dunk contest, with its emphasis on individual skills. He wanted to instill a philosophy of surrendering the me for the we. To do that he had to convince Michael Jordan that "the sign of a great player was not how much he scored, but how much he lifted his teammates' performance." He also had to convince all team members that their contributions were vitally important for the success of the team. To do that he made sure that all of his players received playing time, even during critical situations. Following this game plan, the Chicago Bulls won three straight NBA championships from 1991 to 1993 and three more in 1996, 1997, and 1998.

> *My idea was to use ten players regularly and give the others enough*
> *playing time so that they could blend in effortlessly with everybody else*
> *when they were on the floor. I've often been criticized for leaving backups*
> *on the floor too long, but I think the cohesion it creates is more than*
> *worth the gamble.*
>
> —Phil Jackson, *Sacred Hoops,* NY: Hyperion, page 99.

Choosing Sides in the Bible: God and the Anawim

The Bible offers a similar formula for a happy and wholesome world community. A successful community is not identified by how well those who are better off are doing. Rather, success is determined by how well those who would be picked last in the game of life are doing. The Hebrew word used in the Bible for this class of people is **anawim**. Among the anawim mentioned most often in Scripture are widows and orphans. In a society in which male householders were exclusively the means of a family's income, to be a widow or an orphan was like having a slow death sentence. Society was simply not set up to account for their needs. Foreigners also fit the description of anawim, and in Scripture God frequently reminds the Israelites that they once were foreigners themselves seeking hospitality and a home.

anawim
Hebrew word for the poor and the weak, those in special need of help

> *You shall not wrong or oppress a resident alien, for you were aliens in the*
> *land of Egypt. You shall not abuse any widow or orphan. If you do abuse*
> *them, when they cry out to me, I will surely heed their cry.*
>
> —Exodus 22:20–22

Throughout the Bible the message resounds: The true test about whether or not people are being faithful to God is how well the anawim are doing. In the Bible true prosperity comes only when those who are usually left out have their needs met and are appreciated for the contributions they make. Prosperity for a few at the expense of others is fleeting and ultimately unsatisfying. If the anawim are taken care of, everyone prospers.

In this sense we can say that the God of the Bible takes sides. By demanding special care for poor and other needy people, God is not against the non-poor. Instead, God is pointing out that true prosperity is mutual prosperity; the success of the team is measured by how well the least likely contributors are doing. Let's look at major sections of Scripture to see this recurring theme of God's special care for the anawim. ◆

◆ One author calls the *anawim* "God's nobodies." In small groups think of groups in your school, families, and society who might be labeled *anawim* today. Explain why these people are considered by society to be "nobodies." What are some ways that such groups could better be included in rather than excluded from their larger communities?

Genesis and Biblical Foundations for Justice

1. The Goodness of Creation

The first few chapters of Genesis, the first book of the Bible, contain accounts of creation and the fascinating story of Adam and Eve. Three foundations for a biblical view of justice surface in these early stories. These will continue to come into play throughout Scripture. Reading chapter one, we are immediately struck by the refrain, "God saw that it was good," following every step of creation. The first biblical foundation for justice, then, is God's affirmation of the basic goodness of all creation. To say that people and things have inherent goodness implies a way of viewing and treating them. It suggests that we show reverence for the earth and its creatures, including other people and ourselves. In the biblical refrain, God appears to be delighted and immensely pleased with creation. God's pleasure comes not from controlling or owning created things, as God could do, but from basking in their beauty and goodness. Similarly, we must first develop a sense of wonder, awe, and joy for all God's creatures if we are to act justly. We don't decide to help others crying out for justice because we are nice, but because we recognize the beauty in them that God sees.

2. Stewardship: Being Caregivers

The second foundation for justice exhibited in these stories is summed up in the word stewardship, a word meaning *caregiver*. The following passage describes this concept:

Then God said, "Let us make humankind in our image, according to our likeness; and let them have dominion over the fish of the sea, and over the birds of the air, and over the cattle, and over all the wild animals of the earth, and over every creeping thing that creeps upon the earth."

—Genesis 1:26

The word dominion here means stewardship, taking care of the earth as God cares for the earth. People are a reflection of God's image when they are co-creators of the earth, which of course includes human society. As the first foundation for justice invites us to see with God's eyes, so this second foundation summons us to act with God and for God. Being a steward means caring enough about people and other creatures to seek creative ways to overcome suffering and to cultivate a just world.

Every human life is holy;
every person mirrors the living God.

3. We Are All in This Together

The third biblical foundation for justice is demonstrated most clearly in the next Bible story, that of Cain and Abel. Driven by jealousy, brother kills brother. After the deed, Cain replies to God's inquiry about his brother Abel, "Am I my brother's keeper?" (Genesis 4:9). Looking at the story from the outside, we know the correct answer: "Yes, Cain, you are your brother's keeper, just as we all are responsible for one another."

Significantly, the same Hebrew word is used when God charges Adam to care for the earth as when God questions Cain about being his brother's keeper. In killing his brother, Cain decisively cuts himself off from the human community and becomes a friendless, homeless wanderer.

Implications for justice in this story are that we can never separate our relationship with God from our relationship with others. In God's eyes we are interconnected and thus responsible for one another. The third foundation for justice, then, states that we exist not in isolation but within an intricate web of relationships. As we journey through life or merely walk through the halls of our school, we touch others and they touch us. Together we make these encounters more or less life-giving, more or less deadly. The Cain and Abel story continues to be re-enacted today, but its outcome need not be repeated.

Review

1. What approach to team play did Phil Jackson employ in coaching the Chicago Bulls basketball team?
2. Who are the *anawim* referred to in the Bible?
3. In what sense can it be said that "the God of the Bible takes sides"?
4. Name the three foundations for a biblical view of justice.

Discuss

A. Name some actions that young people might take which can be life-giving for their friends, for their school community, and for their family. Explain your answers.
B. Name some actions that young people might take which would tend to be deadly for their friends, school community, or family.

The Exodus and Liberation

Think about some of the ways that you experience lack of freedom in your life. For example, at home you have to follow rules not of your choosing and far from your liking. If you had a choice, you might wish to skip a portion of your school experience. You dream about things you'd like to own, but because you don't have enough money, you are not able to purchase them. Maybe you have set your sights on a certain college, but SAT scores or class rank will prevent you from being accepted there. At a party, you meet "Mr. or Ms. Right," but your shyness keeps you from asking him or her for a date. ◆

The Exodus, the next great chapter in the biblical drama, is an epic tale about the struggle for freedom. In today's media-filled world, it seems as many people know the story through Hollywood as they do through the Bible itself. Exodus deserves Hollywood treatment. It combines universal themes with personal touches, such as the Hebrew women's and Pharaoh's daughter's trickery behind the scenes of political power to save the lives of children. Through vivid images, Exodus tells of injustice overcome, of a fearful journey through the wilderness, and of a prize won. While in the early stories of Genesis, God is Creator, in Exodus, God emerges as the compassionate Liberator:

> *"I have observed the misery of my people who are in Egypt; I have heard their cry on account of their taskmasters. Indeed, I know their sufferings, and I have come down to deliver them from the Egyptians, and to bring them up out of that land to a good and broad land, a land flowing with milk and honey. . . ."*
>
> —Exodus 3:7–8

If we examine the story symbolically, we can easily find parallels in our own stories of struggle, such as the examples of lack of personal freedoms listed above. When we shift our gaze to society at large, we can name many injustices experienced as lack of freedom. Today, too many people find themselves in "Egypt," that is, in the land of slavery. For instance, too many people even in North America are enslaved to homelessness without much hope of escape. Too many Americans find themselves in low-paying work with little hope of advancement, while even those with quality jobs are constantly fearful of losing them. Too many people in our world will go to bed hungry tonight. The Egypt of their hunger continues to enslave them. In other words, for too many people the slavery and oppression of "Egypt" are painful realities, not ancient history.

◆ Add to this list three ways that you experience lack of freedom in your own life. Based on your examples, how are *lack of freedom* and *injustice* either similar or dissimilar?

One group that found hope in the liberation message of Exodus were black slaves in pre-Civil War United States who converted to Christianity:

In their clandestine prayer meetings, held late at night in the slave quarters and hush harbors, the slaves participated in the transforming power of the age for which they hoped by petitioning God for deliverance from bondage. They believed that the same God who transformed the sinful status of their souls in the conversion experience would transform the sinful structures of the society. The God who had freed their souls from sin could certainly free their bodies from slavery.

—Cheryl J. Sanders, *Empowerment Ethics for a Liberated People,*
Minneapolis, MN: Augsburg Fortress, page 12.

Liberation and Justice

While the creation account affirms goodness, Exodus reminds us that our lives and our world are not completely what we want them to be. Too often we feel stuck and powerless. We are taught to distrust strangers. We are fearful to venture far from home at night. The amount of work that our society needs to make it better overwhelms us. We try not to think about people who slip through the cracks of our social services, who never feel cared for and lack opportunities to feel good about themselves.

liberation

the act of being set free

When faced with such painful realities, personal and societal, the Exodus language of **liberation** provides hope. The cry for liberation often arises from people seeking justice. In the 1960s and '70s, when women were seeking changes to better their lives, they formed what was called the "women's liberation movement." During that same time, Martin Luther King, Jr. joined with others seeking greater civil rights for African Americans and poor people. He often referred to the struggle for civil rights as a freedom movement. As a matter of fact, in his stirring speeches he frequently linked this movement with the story of the Exodus from Egypt to the Promised Land. On the night before he died, Dr. King said: "I have been to the mountaintop. And I've looked over, and I've seen the promised land. I may not get there with you. But I want you to know tonight that we as a people will get to the promised land."

From the moment of their Exodus from Egypt, the Israelites became God's chosen people, and God became their one God.

The language of liberation adds an essential component to a biblical understanding of justice. When we admit that all is not right with the world, we can gain inspiration from the characters in Exodus who fought against oppression in whatever ways they could. For instance, when the Egyptian Pharaoh orders midwives who assist at births of Hebrew women to kill all male babies, they refuse. The mother of Moses, seeking to save her child, schemes to place her son under the protection of Pharaoh's daughter and even manages to serve as her son's nursemaid. These heroines possess no apparent power. Yet, they follow God's law, not Pharaoh's, and use their ingenuity to set in motion events that lead the Hebrew people to liberation from slavery and entrance into the Promised Land. Their stories truly demonstrate the strength of the weak. Their stories give encouragement to the seemingly powerless who must face the troubles of modern life. ◆

Review

5. What image of God emerges in the Exodus story?
6. In terms of justice, what might Egypt symbolize in the Exodus story?
7. Give an example of a twentieth-century person or group who associated the idea of liberation with their movement.
8. Give an example of a character in Exodus who fought against oppression.

◆ Break into small groups to study the first fifteen chapters of the Book of Exodus. Describe how people in the chapters your group studied, people with little apparent power (midwives, Moses' mother, Moses' sister Miriam), do what they can to stand up to unjust power.

Name a group of people who possess little apparent power in today's society. Analyze possible ways that this group exhibits "the strength of the weak"; that is, how a people with little apparent power oppose or defeat unjust power. Present your work to the class.

The Prophets and Justice

Imagine that a group of friends you belong to begins to criticize some others harshly. They become increasingly bold in taunting and teasing these others. Could you stand up to your group and tell them, "No, this is not what we should be doing. We must stop it"? Would you have the courage to make such a statement even if it meant you would be dropped from the group, teased by them, and even be subject to underhanded tricks? Essentially, this describes the scenario faced by the next contributors to a biblical understanding of justice—the **prophets**.

Leaving Egypt, the Hebrew slaves do become free and enter the Promised Land. However, their moment in the sun is short-lived. Soon they acquire a system of government, military power, alliances with other countries, an established social system, and a king to rule over them. Unfortunately, they also acquire the quarrels, corruption, and injustices that accompany this culture. During this historical period of the Jewish people, a unique group of people arises who speak loudly a message of justice that still has an impact today.

prophet
one who speaks divinely inspired insights

The Hebrew word for prophet—*nabi*—means "mouthpiece." A prophet, therefore, is a person who speaks for God. For Jews, Moses most clearly speaks God's message. Jesus follows in the line of Jewish prophets. However, John's Gospel calls Jesus not simply one who speaks the words of God, but one who is himself the very Word of God. Although Moses and Jesus possess many characteristics in common with other Jewish prophets, for our purposes, we will focus on those prophets mentioned in the Scriptures who lived during the eighth and seventh centuries before Christ.

You can read about these prophets—most notably Amos, Hosea, Isaiah, and Jeremiah—in the books of the Bible that are named after them. In their preaching the prophets address the specific religious, political, and social problems of their time. Yet, their words can still challenge us today. To understand the prophets' unique vision of justice, we must first examine the kind of people they were.

> The meaning of the word **prophet** is so stretched today that it covers "reformers" and even "statesmen." Strictly speaking, the word denotes a person specially called to be a spokesperson for God. Israel's prophets were charismatic men and women like Miriam (Exodus 15:20–21) and Deborah (Judges 4:4). They had a deep experience of God, who called them to speak his word in trusting faith. Some report a vision of the heavenly court (Isaiah 6:1–13; Jeremiah 1:4–19, 1 Kings 22:19–22). These inspired poets, preachers, and teachers were not microphones. Even though they prefaced their message with expressions such as "The word of the Lord is," they brought to God's message their own personal, historical, and social images and terminology. They were masters of the art of symbolic communication. Their views, like ours, were affected by the conditions and limitations of their time and by the sources of knowledge to which they had access.
>
> —Timothy G. McCarthy, *Christianity and Humanism*, Chicago: Loyola Press, page 79.

Amos	a shepherd from the southern kingdom of Judah who speaks to the people of the northern kingdom of Israel. He is both a member of the peasant class and a foreigner!
Jeremiah	called by God to prophesy. He responds, "Truly, I do not know how to speak; for I am only a boy." (Jeremiah 1:6)
Hosea	being chosen a prophet rests upon his dubious distinction of having a wife, Gomer, who is constantly unfaithful to him.
Moses	difficulty speaking, so much so that he must bring along his brother, Aaron, to speak for him before the pharaoh.
Deborah and Esther	used their positions as judge and queen to save the Hebrew people from their enemies.

Characteristics of the Prophet: A Reluctant and Unlikely Mouthpiece

Prophets in the Bible are among the least likely people that we would expect to speak for God. At the time there were official "prophets" employed by the king. The official prophets were known for speaking the "smooth words" that the king and people wanted to hear, nothing that would disrupt their lives. The true prophets, the ones whose words became part of Scripture and have been quoted by Jesus and by Jewish, Christian, and Muslim leaders to this day, spoke "harsh words" that gave disturbing and unsettling messages. Thus, the true prophets were reluctant mouthpieces. They often did whatever they could to avoid speaking because they knew it would bring on scornful reactions from their audiences. In spite of probable rejection and hardship, however, the prophets spoke. The impact that the prophets had lies not in their personal traits or their influence but in the strength of their message. ◆

◆ In small groups, study the Book of Ezekiel and answer the following questions:

1. What verses display actions or words that would lead people to consider Ezekiel an extremist or a fanatic?
2. What verses relate Ezekiel's efforts to warn the people in Babylon about the destruction of Jerusalem?
3. What images are used by Ezekiel to prophesy the restoration of the Israelite nation?

The Message of the Prophets: Religion as Social Criticism

If you prefer a religion that doesn't bother you, then don't read the prophets. Their message tends always to bother people. Would you like a religion whose focus is a church building and a weekly Mass that you attend and then forget about religion the rest of the week? Then don't read the prophets. Would you prefer a religion that speaks about "spiritual" matters but doesn't get involved with politics and social problems? Then don't read the prophets. Are you comfortable with your lifestyle, with the amount of possessions you own, and with the direction of your life? Then don't read the prophets. The biblical prophets call people to conversion on both the personal and societal levels. They remind people that to do God's will means to do justice; the two can never be separated.

Thus, the prophets speak not only on behalf of God but also on behalf of those who have no voice in the usual political, social, and economic arrangements of society.

Just as God and the needs of poor and voiceless people cannot be separated, so the prophets despise any practice of religion that is not linked to working for justice. Consequently, they condemn the religious insincerity of their day. Amos, one of the earliest prophets, puts the case clearly:

> *I hate, I despise your festivals, and I take no delight in your solemn assemblies. Even though you offer me your burnt offerings and grain offerings, I will not accept them; and the offerings of well-being of your fatted animals I will not look upon. Take away from me the noise of your songs; I will not listen to the melody of your harps. But let justice roll down like waters, and righteousness like an ever-flowing stream.*

> —Amos 5:21–24

The prophets do not separate religion from politics or from the social conditions of their day. They recognize that many political decisions contradict God's call for justice:

> *Because you have trusted in your power and in the multitude of your warriors, therefore the tumult of war shall rise against your people, and all your fortresses shall be destroyed.*

> —Hosea 10:13–14

For the prophets, religion, politics, and social conditions are all matters of justice. Through the prophets, God calls for social, as well as personal, conversion:

> *Thus says the LORD of hosts, the God of Israel: Amend your ways and your doings, and let me dwell with you in this place. . . . For if you truly amend your ways and your doings, if you truly act justly one with another, if you do not oppress the alien, the orphan, and the widow, or shed innocent blood in this place, and if you do not go after other gods to your own hurt, then I will dwell with you in this place, in the land that I gave of old to your ancestors forever and ever.*

> —Jeremiah 7:3–7

The view of justice backed by the prophets is a highly challenging and controversial one. They were not interested in compromise or anything short of wholehearted commitment to correcting mistreatment of the downtrodden members of their society. Interestingly, even though they preach a sharply stinging message, the prophets always include a vision of a peace-filled community built on justice and hold out hope especially when circumstances seem particularly hopeless:

Is not this the fast that I choose: to loose the bonds of injustice, to undo the thongs of the yoke, to let the oppressed go free, and to break every yoke? Is it not to share your bread with the hungry, and bring the homeless poor into your house; when you see the naked, to cover them, and not to hide yourself from your own kin? . . .Then your light shall rise in the darkness and your

"Did not your father eat and drink and do justice and righteousness? Then it was well with him. He judged the cause of the poor and needy; then it was well. Is not this to know me?" says the LORD.
—Jeremiah 22:15–16

gloom be like the noonday. The LORD will guide you continually, and satisfy your needs in parched places, and make your bones strong; and you shall be like a watered garden, like a spring of water, whose waters never fail.

—Isaiah 58:6–7, 10b–11

As we will see, the firm commitment to justice found in the prophets of Israel continues in the mission and message of Jesus.

Review

9. What is the Hebrew word for *prophet*? What does the meaning of this word say about the biblical prophets?
10. Name two biblical prophets. Why were they considered prophets in their time?
11. Use an example to illustrate what the text means by saying that a biblical prophet was an "unlikely mouthpiece."
12. Describe and use an example to illustrate the difference between "smooth words" and "harsh words."
13. What do the prophets insist as the way to know God?
14. What type of positive message do the prophets include with their social criticism?

Discuss

Even today politicians and preachers, poets and song writers, can speak either "smooth words" (what people want to hear) or "harsh words" (what people need to hear).

C. Give examples of modern-day prophets who speak either "smooth words" or "harsh words."
D. What would be some of the "harsh words" that people today need to hear?

The Messiah Is Among Us

For years the old monk had lived in the woods near the monastery. Often, the other monks wanted to hear from this wise old man who in his youth had a reputation as a great teacher. However, they respected his desire to live alone and to keep his thoughts to himself.

Then one evening after a bitterly cold spell, one of the monks was sent to him to inquire about his provisions. When he arrived at the small hermitage, the monk found his colleague cheerful and welcoming. He was invited to join the older monk in a cup of tea. After sitting mostly in silence for some time, the younger monk risked asking the hermit, "In the monastery, all of us wonder what truth, what knowledge you have gained from your years in solitude with God. If there was one message that you would share with the other monks, what would it be?"

The old monk replied quickly and starkly, "The Messiah is among you."

The younger monk thanked him and returned to the monastery. He gathered the other monks in the chapel and told them of the message: "The Messiah is among us."

All of the monks looked upon their wise old brother with great reverence, so they treated his message very seriously. Yet, what could he mean? Did he mean that one of them was the Messiah? Could it be old Brother Jerome who took such loving care of the books in their sparse library? Could it be Brother Gregory who cooked their meals and kept the kitchen running smoothly? Could it be Brother Timothy, the one who smelled like the animals because he spent so much time caring for them?

Each monk pondered the old man's message and realized that any one of them could be the Messiah—indeed, even oneself! From that day on, every monk treated each of his brother monks as if he were the Messiah. People who visited the monastery marveled at the aura of holiness that emanated from these monks.

- Spend a day acting as if "the Messiah is among us." Assume that all the people you meet are holy and deserve profound respect. Don't tell anyone that you are treating them with this attitude. Let your actions speak for you.

Jesus and Justice: Deepening and Broadening the Message

Matthew sums up the importance of Jesus in the following famous passage from the first chapter of his Gospel:

"Look, the virgin shall conceive and bear a son, and they shall name him Emmanuel," which means, "God is with us."

—Matthew 1:23

In case we miss his message along the way, Matthew ends his Gospel with the same theme:

. . . I am with you always, to the end of the age.

—Matthew 28:20

Just as the old monk's message, "The Messiah is among us," leads the other monks to view themselves and one another with renewed reverence, so Jesus' message—that in him God is close at hand—leads us to view ourselves and one another differently today. Jesus does not depart from the core message of the earlier scriptural writings—the stories of Genesis and Exodus—or the radical teachings of the prophets. Yet, as God among us, Jesus embodies the biblical message of justice in his very being. He personalizes the foundations of justice that are proclaimed in the creation stories, demonstrated through the Exodus, and yearned for by the prophets.

To fully appreciate the radical nature of Jesus as "God among us," we would do well to read through the Gospels and take note of the amount of time that Jesus spends with people on the margins of society. By associating with the unclean of his day, Jesus himself becomes unclean. The lines between clean and unclean, healthy and sick, the righteous and the sinner were sharply drawn in Jesus' culture. Apparently, Jesus simply ignores these lines and thus steps out of the boundaries of proper society. As a result, Jesus is "God among us" in the form of the homeless person, the unwelcome foreigner, the incurably ill, and the child deprived of proper nourishment. As you can see, the biblical foundations of justice—inborn goodness, stewardship, and community—are broadened and deepened in Jesus. ◆

◆ Choose one of the four Gospels. Note words or deeds of Jesus that you feel have a message related to justice. Select one Gospel passage and write a paragraph describing the justice message that it contains. Create a poster or other work of art illustrating the message of the passage.

Jesus and God's Reign

Can you imagine a perfect world? Not just one where all of your needs are met, but one where the relationships among people are set right? Central to the teaching of Jesus is such a vision, called God's reign or the kingdom of God. Some of the ways Jesus describes this reign of God are as formidable today as they were when he first proclaimed them.

To the best of our knowledge, Jesus was a Jewish peasant who worked as a carpenter until he was about thirty. When he began his brief public life of preaching and healing, he went to his local synagogue and read the following passage from the prophet Isaiah:

> *"The Spirit of the Lord is upon me, because he has anointed me to bring good news to the poor. He has sent me to proclaim release to the captives and recovery of sight to the blind, to let the oppressed go free. . . . "*
>
> —Luke 4:18

This passage, which directly connects Jesus with the tradition of the prophets, also lays out his vision of what God's reign would be like. The three foundations of justice are all here in this brief passage. First, Jesus proclaims the basic goodness of groups of people who are frequently overlooked: poor, prisoners, and blind people. Secondly, Jesus expresses care for their plight. Thirdly, the underlying perspective is one of welcoming these forgotten ones back into *community*.

For Jesus, then, God's reign is inclusive and not an exclusive club. He welcomes into God's reign not only poor and outcast people but also those people typically considered "bad." Some other teachers of his day also speak of God's reign. However, their vision divides Jews from non-Jews, law keepers from lawbreakers, the wealthy from those who perform humble tasks, the good from the bad. In Jesus' vision of God's reign, every person has innate worth and dignity. ◆

◆ If you were to make a "proclamation of justice" such as Jesus did in his local synagogue, what would it sound like? What examples of injustice would you mention? How would you describe your vision of justice? Compare your proclamation with those of other class members and synthesize the various statements into one proclamation of justice for your class.

Jesus teaches the dignity of all people through both his actions and his words. Constantly, he seeks out the humble people of his day—lepers, tax collectors, prostitutes—with whom to share a meal or to spend some time. In fact, eating with diverse groups of people is a hallmark of his ministry, which is continued today in the Christian celebration of the Eucharist.

Jesus uses parables in striking ways to break through misconceptions about the worth of people. For instance, in the parable of the day laborers (Matthew 20:1–16), Jesus speaks approvingly about a vineyard owner who pays the same wages whether a person works a full day or a half day. The criterion for payment seems to be "what do these people need" rather than "what have they earned."

Elsewhere, Jesus describes the reign of God as a wedding banquet to which the invited guests do not come. Instead, unlikely guests are invited from the streets to enjoy the banquet: Servants went out into the streets and gathered all whom they found, both good and bad; so the wedding hall was filled with guests. (Matthew 22:10). Here again, in this simple story we see how Jesus broadens (everyone counts) and deepens (everyone shares even the intimacy of mealtime) the biblical message of justice.

God's Reign and the Kingdom of Heaven

We often equate God's reign with a heaven available to us only after we die. In fact, because of the Jewish reluctance to use the name of God, Matthew in his Gospel generally speaks of the "kingdom of heaven" when referring to God's reign. Yet, when we use this phrase, we may begin to think mistakenly that Jesus' vision is only *spiritual* in the otherworldly sense of the term. In truth, Jesus' vision of a kingdom is one that is within us and among us, as well as one that will see its fullness in the future. As recent Church statements have made clear, Christian hope in the "heavenly city" that awaits us in the next life actually inspires us and frees us for greater involvement in this life. As we pray in the Lord's Prayer, God's reign here and hereafter are intertwined.

> *"Far from diminishing our concern to develop this earth, the expectancy of a new earth should spur us on, for it is here that the body of a new human family grows, foreshadowing in some way the age which is to come." (1049)*

The Beatitudes: Portrait of the Christian Vocation

Blessed are the poor in spirit, for theirs is the kingdom of heaven.
Blessed are those who mourn, for they will be comforted.
Blessed are the meek, for they will inherit the earth.
Blessed are those who hunger and thirst for righteousness, for they
*   will be filled.*

Blessed are the merciful, for they will receive mercy.
Blessed are the pure in heart, for they will see God.
Blessed are the peacemakers, for they will be called children of God.
Blessed are those who are persecuted for righteousness' sake, for theirs
*   is the kingdom of heaven.*
Blessed are you when people revile you and persecute you and utter
*   all kinds of evil against you falsely on my account. Rejoice and be*
*   glad, for your reward is great in heaven.*

—Matthew 5:3–12

In the Sermon on the Mount, Matthew's Gospel summarizes key teachings of Jesus. The beginning section of that sermon contains a list of actions and attitudes that characterize the Christian life. Often studied by Catholics early in elementary school, the Beatitudes can sound so familiar, so taken-for-granted, that the depth of their message can become lost.

The Beatitudes are a prescription for joy. (Sometimes "blessed" is translated "happy," although happy is clearly not a forceful enough word for what the Beatitudes have in mind.) Think about the pursuit of happiness that occurs in our culture. Even more specifically, think about the way characters in popular television sitcoms pursue happiness. The most popular sitcom for much of the '90s was *Seinfeld*. When interviewed about the show, the comedian after whom the show is named points out that all the characters are losers whom no one would seriously want for friends. Typically, they pursue pleasure with little regard for anyone else. Although amusing, their lives are actually very shallow. No doubt the show sustained its popularity for so long because the characters were funny, and they reminded us of our own silly, but misguided, attempts at pleasure seeking.

The Beatitudes paint a very different picture of what brings true happiness, true joy. They speak about mourning, hungering and thirsting, enduring pain and persecution. Where's the joy in that? The answer lies in the word *passion*. As an agenda for Christian living, the Beatitudes encourage us to live life with passion. True passion for life must include compassion—that is, engaging in the struggles and sufferings of those around us. For example, if we have a true passion for music, we probably work very hard to master our instrument and become very excited when we learn a new piece of music. Even if we don't play an instrument, we might "hunger and thirst" for the latest CD by our favorite singing group. Similarly, according to the Beatitudes, the opposite of living a compassionate life is not a life of pleasure seeking but being apathetic, not caring, not getting involved, not looking beyond the narrow focus of our own viewpoints. In other words, the prescription for seeking justice and peace is to live a life of passion and compassion. Given our state of the world, both often entail suffering.

> *An event that often brings out the passion/compassion of the Beatitudes is the death of someone close to us. When friends lose someone they love through death, we are naturally drawn to share their suffering. In the words of one author, at such a time we feel compelled: to suffer with those who suffer, to mourn with those who mourn, to walk with those who are weary, to abide with those who are abandoned. Not that we can take their pain away or heal their wounds or bring their loved ones back to life, but rather to remind them by our presence, by our love, by our unspoken words, that they are not alone.*
>
> —Joseph Nassal, *The Conspiracy of Compassion*, Easton, KS: Forest Peace, page 55.

Review

15. How does Matthew's Gospel sum up the importance of Jesus?
16. Explain what it means to say that Jesus broadened and deepened the biblical foundations of justice.
17. How did Jesus begin his public life of preaching and healing?
18. What impact can hope in heaven have on a Christian's attitude toward this world?
19. In what sense are the Beatitudes a prescription for joy?
20. What is the opposite of living a compassionate life?

Discuss

E. Explain how Christian belief in heaven can encourage involvement in problems and concerns of this life.
F. Similarly, would faith in God make a difference in terms of getting involved in the world's problems? Explain.
G. Reflect on what you feel passionate about. Why do you think you are passionate about these things?
H. What could lead you to becoming passionate about matters of justice?
I. Do you believe that *passion for life* must go hand in hand with *compassion*, feeling intensely for and with others especially when they are suffering? Explain.

In Summary: In Scripture, Justice Means "Live Life to the Fullest"

In shaping our world, God created a masterpiece. Human beings are given the awesome responsibility of molding and shaping the world so that it reflects even more of God's design. Human beings must work together in this ongoing project of creation, either making the world better or destroying it. Unceasingly, Scripture reminds us that people suffer unnecessarily due to attitudes, actions, and social structures of our own making and that, trusting in God, these elements of injustice can be transformed. While suffering cannot be completely eliminated and differences among people abound, nonetheless reading Scripture as a call to justice can inspire us to live life passionately, compassionately, justly.

Let us pray . . .

Leader: To each description of Jesus, answer "give us your salvation."

Jesus, light of the world,

Jesus, prince of peace,

Jesus, who died to save us,

Jesus, friend to the lonely,

Jesus, hope for the suffering,

Jesus, healer of the sick,

Jesus, friend to the stranger,

Jesus, strength of the weak,

Jesus, justice for the oppressed,

Jesus, who welcomes outcasts,

Jesus, who suffers with us,

Jesus, who inspires us,

Jesus, who supports us,

Jesus, who forgives us,

Jesus, who brings us joy . . .

For further study . . .

1. Imagine that a friend of yours who is not taking this course picks up your textbook and reads the title of this chapter. How would you explain the title's meaning to your friend? Which of the following words or their opposites might you include in your explanation of the chapter title: *expected, challenging, unchristian, impassioned, heated, disturbing, legal, unusual, important, threatening, hurtful, just?*

2. Think back on an encounter you had with someone, an encounter that turned out to be transforming or life-giving for you. Write a letter to that person thanking her or him and explaining how she or he was life-giving for you. Mail the letter if you wish.

3. Often the meaning of a word comes to life when we think about its opposites. List all the possible antonyms that you can think of for the word creation. Demonstrate the theme "Creation and Its Opposites in My Life" in a work of art, poem, song, or essay.

4. *To us a single act of injustice—cheating in business, exploitation of the poor—is slight; to the prophets, a disaster. To us injustice is injurious to the welfare of the people; to the prophets it is a deathblow to existence; to us, an episode; to them, a catastrophe, a threat to the world.*

   —Abraham J. Heschel, *The Prophets,* New York: Harper Collins, page 4.

   In a one-page paper answer the following question: Are prophets extremist and fanatics, or are we lacking interest or concern?

5. Form two debate teams. One will defend, the other refute the following statement: Religion is about spiritual matters. Religious leaders should not address social problems or issues of politics and economics.

6. The text makes the comment about Jesus: "Constantly he seeks out the humble people of his day, lepers, tax collectors, prostitutes, with whom to share a meal or to spend some time." With this statement in mind, complete the following exercise: Describe in writing one activity that you imagine Jesus would do if he were to visit our world today.

   - Write an account of Jesus' activity from the perspective of a newspaper reporter.
   - Write an account of Jesus' activity from the perspective of someone who has been touched by him.

7. The text is clear that pleasure and joy are not opposites. Nonetheless, the two experiences can be distinguished. Identify in your own life one event that was pleasant and another one that was joyfilled. Using words or symbols, try to express how the two experiences differed.

CHAPTER 3

Church

The Community That Does Justice

The Bible lays out a foundation for justice. How has the
Church lived out this message? A look at history reveals that
Church members, individually and as a community, have
made justice a hallmark of what it means to be Christian.
This chapter examines four historical periods and the way that
the adventure called Christianity has responded with justice in
different settings.

Major Concepts

A. The Early Church: A Revolutionary View of Justice

• Emphasized love over law

B. The Medieval Church: Christendom as God's Kingdom

• Emphasized maintaining a well-ordered society

C. New World and New Challenges

• Emphasized creating an effective way of helping people in need

D. The Modern Era: Catholic Social Teaching

• Emphasizes the call for justice locally,
nationally, and globally

Opening Prayer

Jesus, your Church is a gift, rich in its history of doing justice and acting compassionately for others. We pray that we remain ever mindful of all who have gone before us seeking to do your will. As we study ways that your followers gave of themselves to bring about justice, may we humbly embrace the message: Today, we are Church. In union with all those, past and present, yearning to be your people we pray for the wisdom, the courage, and the compassion to create a future marked by justice for all. Amen

Before we begin . . .

1. Has your faith influenced you to be more sensitive to the needs of others? How?

2. Do you think that Christians have a special responsibility to work for justice? Why or why not?

3. Do you connect Catholicism with justice and compassion? Why or why not?

4. In what sense and to what degree is your local Catholic community known for justice and compassion?

A Lesson in Living

Ben looked at the course description: As a requirement for this course, students are expected to perform twenty hours of volunteer service. In the first place Ben thought, "If it's required, then I'm not really volunteering. Secondly, my parents are spending money for me to attend this Catholic school. The intention was to get a solid education so that I can get into a good college and succeed at the profession of my choice later in life. I'm taking high-level English, math, and science courses. My goal is to have a financially secure, comfortable life and provide nicely for a family when I grow up. I'm working hard, and I expect it to pay off. Isn't that an honorable goal? Why do I have to go out and 'serve others' as part of a religion course? It's bad enough that we have to take religion classes in the first place."

Ben pictured himself serving franks and beans to disgusting looking people at a soup kitchen for homeless people. Yuk! How about helping at the home for the elderly instead? Ben had been to such a home once when he was in grade school. He didn't care for the moaning sounds some of the old people made as he walked by their rooms, and the smell of urine mixed with heavy-duty cleansers was disgusting. Maybe he could join those students who are tutoring the young children at the grade school. The kids are bratty, but at least it's much less messy. There's the Special Olympics program for mentally challenged children and adults. That involves sports and may not be so bad. "I'll see what my friends are doing. There has to be a way to make this as painless as possible."

- What do you think about Ben's attitude toward Catholic education and his religion course requirements?
- Do you believe that Catholic schools should include a requirement for students to do service projects? Why or why not?
- Do you believe that, to a greater extent than other schools, Catholic schools should be noted for community service?

The Early Church: A Revolutionary View of Justice

Action on behalf of justice and participation in the transformation of the world fully appear to us as a constitutive dimension of the preaching of the Gospel, or, in other words, of the Church's mission for the redemption of the human race and its liberation from every oppressive situation.

—Synod of Bishops, "Justice in the World," *Vatican Council: More Conciliar Documents,* 1971, page 696.

Given the fact that its founder died disgracefully as a convicted criminal, that it had its beginnings in lowly Israel, and that its early development happened during a time of persecution of its members, how did Christianity end up controlling the Roman Empire? A major part of early Christianity's appeal lay in the way it valued and lived justice.

The Roman world in which Christianity bloomed valued *justice* greatly. It equated justice with law and with protection of rights. (The word *justice* itself is derived from the Latin word *ius,* meaning "law.") Principles of justice in the Roman tradition included doing no one harm, preserving the common good, and protecting personal property. Justice was identified with good order within society. Authority, rights, and duties were clearly defined, based on where one stood in the order of society. Being born in Rome, for instance, did not make one a citizen. Actually, most people who lived in Rome at the time were slaves. Men who owned property and who were the heads of households possessed greatest power, followed by free men who did not own land, such as artisans. In descending order there were freed slaves, slaves, and, beyond civilization itself, barbarians. Women and children, of course, also held secondary status to adult males. For Rome, then, justice meant its system of laws that maintained this proper ordering of society. Laws protected the power, rights, and property of those who had these things.

Ruins of the ancient Senate in Rome

Within this highly developed legal system of justice, the early Church proclaimed a radically different, indeed a revolutionary, understanding of justice. Here is how the Acts of the Apostles describes the new ordering of society that the early Christian community practiced:

> All who believed were together and had all things in common; they would sell their possessions and goods and distribute the proceeds to all, as any had need. Day by day, as they spent much time together in the temple, they broke bread at home and ate their food with glad and generous hearts, praising God and having the goodwill of all the people. And day by day the Lord added to their number those who were being saved.
>
> —Acts 2:44–47

Judging by the last line of this passage, evidently the re-ordering of society supported by Christianity was a principle cause of its popularity, despite persecution at the hands of the old order. Members of the newly formed Christian community viewed one another with a spirit of common concern and, in striking contrast to the Roman worldview, with a spirit of equality:

> . . . in Christ Jesus you are all children of God through faith. As many of you as were baptized into Christ have clothed yourselves with Christ. There is no longer Jew or Greek, there is no longer slave or free, there is no longer male and female; for all of you are one in Christ Jesus. And if you belong to Christ, then you are Abraham's offspring, heirs according to the promise.
>
> —Galatians 3:26–29

Communities of Compassion

Although the early Christian communities were not without their disputes, the concern that their members showed for one another and especially for those who were in need earns them the title *communities of compassion*. Early Christians viewed themselves as members of the Body of Christ, sharing in the joys and sorrows of all the other members. For example, John Chrysostom, the Archbishop of Constantinople as well as a famous preacher, warned his congregation against not caring for poor people, "Don't you realize that, as the poor man withdraws silently, sighing and in tears, you actually thrust a sword into yourself, that it is you who receive the more serious wound?"

The Christian spirit of compassion naturally held an appeal for the poor and outcast members of society. However, it also attracted a surprising number of rich and powerful individuals. These people saw in Christianity that:

It offered a new, vital form of justice—one based on mutual care instead of the protections of a legal system.

It provided deep joy which comes from sharing instead of the shallow pleasures of hoarding possessions.

It did not isolate people from those who were different.

It was a wellspring of communal religious experience rather than the lifeless formality of the official religion of the empire.

In short, the early Church communities discovered the essential Christian mystery and truth: Imitating Jesus, who shared meals with everyone and who served others even when it meant great personal sacrifice, leads to mutual joy and an ordering of society that reflects God's original intent.

Review

1. Describe the difference between a pre-Christian Roman understanding of justice and that of the early Church.
2. Who was Saint John Chrysostom? What message did he have for rich people in his congregation?
3. Who were drawn to the Christian spirit of compassion in the Roman Empire?

Discuss

A. What is the difference between the ancient Roman world order and the world order proposed by early Christianity?
B. Do you see evidence of either of these world orders at work today?
C. Saint John Chrysostom received his nickname—"Golden Mouth"—because he kept his congregations spellbound with his preaching. He was particularly concerned with the attitude of the rich toward the poor. He felt that poor people—servants, beggars, and circus performers, for instance—were viewed as non-persons and therefore abused. He spoke up for the dignity of all people. Twice he was sent into exile for his strong words.
  • Is there evidence today that poor people and people who perform certain tasks in our society are viewed as non-persons? Explain.
D. Have you ever been in a group that you could describe as a compassionate community? If so, describe the experience.

The Medieval Church: Christendom as God's Kingdom

Christendom

ruling powers and levels of society that existed in the empire were viewed as the way God intended them to be

The 1950s movie "Viva Zapata" tells the story of the Mexican rebel peasant Emiliano Zapata. Zapata leads a rebellion against a government that he believes to be insensitive to the needs of Mexico's peasants. Joining with other rebel leaders, Zapata succeeds in toppling the government and seizes power. As time progresses Zapata himself becomes caught in the workings of government, becoming more and more distant from peasants and their concerns.

In 313 AD, Roman Emperor Constantine pronounced the Edict of Milan, granting religious freedom to Christians. After centuries of living with persecution or with the threat of persecution, the formerly outlawed group now was an accepted, established organization. While earlier they were forced to live on the fringes of society, Christians soon moved under Constantine to the very center of Western civilization. After Constantine, Christianity became not an alternative to the established power but one with the dominant power itself. In short, Christianity became **Christendom**. "Christianity" and "civilization" were now one and the same.

Hierarchical Society Provides Order

civilization

the established social order

barbarians

people lacking refinement or culture

hierarchical

distinct levels of power and responsibilities

After Constantine, Christianity inherited the structures of the Roman Empire. The enemies to **civilization** were internal disagreements and, more importantly at first, the external threat of "uncivilized" **barbarians**. Society was seen as **hierarchical**. From lords to knights to serfs, every social group had its specified rights and duties. The nobility ruled by their inherited "divine right," just as serfs and their descendants were bound to the land because of their inherited positions. Although such a system obviously lent itself to abuses, it took a later age to question the structure itself. ◆

During the Middle Ages, then, Church leaders felt that God's justice was best served by maintaining the correct order of society and by assuring that rights were protected and responsibilities were carried out. The lord who did not provide protection for his serfs was judged irresponsible, and a serf who did not work productively in his lord's fields was disobedient and punished accordingly. As you can see, this social organization seems closer to the Greek and Roman view of society than to the vision held by early Christian thinkers.

Saint Francis of Assisi: The Flower of the Middle Ages

Into this world of kings, knights, and peasants, an exceptional person was born—a man who challenged the prevailing medieval view of justice. One historian has called Francis of Assisi (1181–1226) the greatest spiritual figure that Europe has ever produced.

◆ In small groups, draw a diagram that depicts the class structure of society during Constantine's reign. List the duties and expectations of society for each level of the hierarchy.

An exuberant and life-loving son of a wealthy Italian cloth merchant, Francis went off to war with a neighboring city outfitted with the finest knightly attire. Imprisoned in his first battle, Francis had time to think about his life and his values. He recognized that money, possessions, and power too often lead to corruption. To free himself, Francis did more than show compassion for the sick and poor people by sharing a portion of his wealth with them; instead, in his early twenties, Francis rejected his father's wealth and married "Lady Poverty." From that time on, he kept no possessions and urged his followers to do likewise. And so, in a radical and extreme manner, Francis went against the popular emphasis of his day on gaining wealth and material comforts.

Yet Francis' embrace of poverty was not life-denying or gloomy. Indeed, he sang with joy as he extended himself in compassion to all creatures and all people. He thought of himself and his followers as clowns of God, humbly celebrating the simple joys of life that can be overlooked when our focus is on accumulating wealth. Francis' unconventional decision to move from "riches to rags" actually reflects two surprising decisions at the very core of Christian faith: the decision of God to send his Son into the world of poverty and the decision of Jesus to die stripped of everything in order to show us the way to a new and glorious life.

An old and poor woman . . . once came to Saint Mary of the Angels to beg alms from Saint Francis. The saint went immediately to Brother Peter of Catania (who was the minister general at the time) and asked if there was anything to give the woman. . . . Brother Peter answered, "The only thing in the house is a copy of the New Testament, which we use to read the lessons during the night office." Saint Francis said to him, "Give her the Bible; it will be more pleasing to God that she should have it than we should read from it."

—Lawrence Cunningham,
Brother Francis, page 129

Francis was particularly concerned about the connection between possessions and warfare: "If we have possessions, we must have weapons to defend them, from which come quarrels and battles." He also saw that greed had a stranglehold on many people, diminishing their capacity to enjoy the simple things of life and preventing them from seeing the persons suffering around them.

Francis challenged his era by calling it back to the purity and simplicity of Christ's message. In a society in which budding cities offered new opportunities for wealth, Francis preached voluntary poverty. In a Church dominated by the power of the clergy, Francis refused priesthood for himself—once again demonstrating his commitment to "littleness." In a world in which Christians were fighting Muslims, Francis, seeking to end religious conflict, went to Egypt to speak personally with a Muslim leader.

Although he did not denounce the institutions and authorities of his day, Francis' example clearly pointed to their inability and unwillingness to care for the needy and to free people from their greed. Declared a saint only two years after his death, Francis inspired other grassroots reforms that continued to change the face of the Church as it left the Middle Ages behind. Perhaps the most universally popular saint of all time, Francis continues to inspire people today to work for justice, peace, and protection of the environment.

Review

4. Describe Emiliano Zapata's transformation.
5. Who initiated Christendom in the Middle Ages?
6. What does it mean to say that medieval society was hierarchical?
7. In what way did Saint Francis of Assisi go against the prevailing spirit of his day?
8. What did Francis say about the connection between possessions and warfare?

Discuss

E. In many ways the culture of Francis' day resembles our own. The decision by Francis to reject possessions and to delight in simple things was at first viewed as foolhardy. Yet Francis and his early followers, by their own choice "little brothers and sisters" or "clowns of God," spread such joy that they transformed both the Church and the Europe of their day.

In a circus, clowns are the little people who entertain between the big important acts. Clowns can be funny. They can also get under our skin.

- Can you see a sort of wisdom masked behind clowning?
- Are you or do you know a "class clown"? If so, do you or does this person serve an unusual but beneficial function in your group?

New Worlds and New Challenges

If one event marked the end of the Middle Ages for Christianity, it was the posting, in 1517, of Martin Luther's ninety-five theses on the church doors in Wittenberg, Germany. This event marked the beginning of the Protestant Reformation. The multiple abuses by the Church assured the eventual collapse of Christendom and the rise of **nationalism** that still characterizes the world today. Practically speaking, this meant that Europeans were beginning to identify more with their own nations (England, France, and Spain, for example) than with Christendom. Nationalism opened the door to new problems of justice and peace.

nationalism

promoting the interests of one's own country and culture over others

Accompanying nationalism was **colonialism**. European countries vied with each other to conquer territory either newly discovered by them or newly open to their control. The primary aim of colonialism was to benefit the conquering nation, which typically led to exploitation of the lands of America, Africa, and Asia. You might recall from history that some American colonists in Boston dumped tea from a British ship into Boston Harbor because they felt exploited by the excessive tax on tea at the time.

colonialism

one nation taking control of another nation by force

While nationalism and colonialism were on the rise, the feudal system was breaking down. Money was there to be made by a growing **middle class.** Wealth was no longer measured solely in terms of land. Producing, buying, and selling of goods created opportunities for amassing wealth separate from the feudal lord's power, which was centered on control of land. As a result, peasants had other means of making a living, although new types of labor also created new possibilities for injustice.

middle class

people of moderate income, distinct from wealthier people and those who are poor

Finally, the Protestant break with the Catholic Church further divided Europe along national lines. The stage was being set for the multiple international conflicts that have characterized the Western world for the past few centuries. ◆

Pontius' Puddle

Nationalism, colonialism, and the importance of the middle class continue to be dominant influences on the world today. In small groups, research one of the following issues and prepare to report your findings to the class. Use your library resources and/or the Internet to prepare your report.

- Advantages and disadvantages of nationalistic thinking. Your report should include concrete examples.
- Research a country that has a history of being colonized. Your report should include the effects that colonization has had on the country.
- What does the middle class of the United States look like? Your report should include numbers, and political, religious, and personal beliefs.

Christians Create New Responses for New Social Problems

While these changes brought new forms of human suffering, Church people emerged who boldly and effectively addressed these problems. The seventeenth to the nineteenth centuries were peopled with many saintly women and men who felt deeply the pain of those around them and who took steps to lighten their suffering. Examples abound, demonstrating how Christians creatively applied the gospel message of service to address emerging needs.

- In the 1600s in France, Vincent de Paul and Louise de Marillac founded orders of women that addressed the needs of the hungry and sick people crowded into cities of the time.

- John Baptist de La Salle (1651–1719) organized men to teach homeless boys and prisoners in Paris.

- In the 1800s, Elizabeth Ann Seton and other women began orders of women to teach the increasing Catholic population in the United States. Typically, Catholic immigrants to the U.S. were poor and poorly educated. Frequently, Catholic schools run by orders of religious sisters protected and nurtured immigrant children as they tried to settle into their new home.

- Katherine Drexel, a wealthy Philadelphia Catholic, saw a particular need to serve Native American and African American populations. She founded a religious order to work with these groups that were often overlooked.

- As Europeans conquered other lands, Christian missionaries were among the first to travel to these lands in order to introduce native people to the gospel. Sometimes missionaries were also exploiters of these groups. However, more frequently missionaries were the only voices demanding that these native Asians, Africans, and Americans be treated with respect and compassion.

> *Wherever the powerless were to be found, there he [Saint Vincent de Paul] went. Prison visiting and making demands for prison reform; dealing with delinquency; reaching for the abandoned in the midst of the rapidly expanding urban world; caring for the sick and the disabled—this whole world of social concern took over his life and absorbed his energies.*
>
> *Some have gone so far as to claim Vincent as the founder of what we today would call "social work." We must not claim too much for him in this regard, but there is evidence for such a claim.*
>
> —Austin Smith, CP, *The Radical Tradition*, ed. Gilbert Marcus, NY: Doubleday, 1993, pages 119–120.

The legacy of these efforts is seen in today's Catholic hospitals and schools, convalescent homes, hospitality centers for the hungry and homeless, and various other social service organizations. Even public school systems and community hospitals are by-products of works initiated by these and other reformers who believed that every person has a right to education, health care, and basic community services. Although Christianity emerged from this period split into Protestant and Catholic factions, nonetheless, individual groups of Christians in both traditions kept alive the Church's response to justice.

> *In the end people are saints for the way they love.*
>
> —Mary Reed Newland

Karl Marx Challenges Christianity's Stance on Justice

One of the shapers of the modern world, Karl Marx (1818–1883) deplored the effects of industrialization on working people in England and in his native Germany. He saw men, women, and even children and older people working long hours in inhuman conditions at less than living wages. Sometimes workers spent entire daylight hours in dark mines or factories. Marx observed that working class people lacked power; the wealthy few controlled the new industrial society. Workers were pawns in the hands of owners, who alone received the benefits from industrial production.

Marx also deplored Christianity, which he saw as supporting and maintaining this status-quo arrangement: "Religion is the sigh of the oppressed creature, the heart of a heartless world, the soul of soulless conditions. It is the opium of the people." In other words, Marx saw religion as a drug that kept people from facing the reality of their suffering and from working to better their lives. In his view Christian faith was a private affair between individuals and God that taught people not to seek change in this life and to expect happiness only after death. Marx therefore attacked religion as an instrument used by the powerful elite to keep the powerless workers from complaining or trying to better their conditions.

Marx proposed a radical restructuring of society. With his battle cry "Workers of the world, unite!" he called for an equalization of work and a sharing of resources. He wanted all people to be both workers and owners. In that way everyone would benefit equally from new technologies and new means of production. No one would be required to work excessive hours; everyone would be free to pursue cultural enrichments that were previously reserved for the wealthy few. In other words the world would become a workers' paradise.

Review

9. Following the Protestant Reformation what three changes in emphasis occurred that had an impact on justice?
10. Name two Catholic social reformers who emerged after the Reformation. Describe the work for which they were known.
11. Describe Karl Marx's view of the Christianity of his day.
12. What did Marx mean by a *workers' paradise?*

Discuss

F. Discuss the pros and cons of Karl Marx's critique of the society and Christianity of his day. (If you can, do further research on his views.) Do many people today still consider religion a private affair? Explain. Is Marx's idea of a "workers' paradise" appealing? Why or why not?

G. Marx referred negatively to religion as the "opium of the people." What symbol would you create that could be used to portray in a positive light the role of Christianity in the world? What saying or motto would you include to accompany your symbol, such as "Christianity, light of the world"?

The Modern Era: Catholic Social Teachings

The plight of workers concerned not only Marx but also Church leaders. In 1891, in the landmark papal letter *On the Condition of Labor* (in Latin, *Rerum Novarum*), Pope Leo XIII addressed the rights of workers in light of conditions produced by industrialization. This encyclical was the first of many modern Church documents to deal with the dignity of all humans. The United Nations Universal Declaration of Human Rights echoes the importance of the dignity of all human beings in the global community.

 1891

In the papal encyclical *On the Condition of Labor*, Pope Leo XIII strongly affirms the belief that the human person has basic rights, especially the rights to food, clothing, shelter, and a living wage. He also declares the rights of the poor must be "specially cared for and protected by the government."

 1931

In *The Reconstruction of the Social Order* and in *Divine Redemption*, Pius XI focuses on the right to life and to the economic means of existence, the right to follow one's path marked out by God, the right of free association, and the right to possess and use property.

 1942

Pope Pius XII, in his Christmas message, emphasizes the right to maintain and develop one's life in all ways, the right to work and freely choose one's state in life, the right to marry and have a family, and the right to material goods.

 1948

The United Nations, founded after World War II, adopts the *Universal Declaration of Human Rights* (UDHR), a vision statement with moral force that includes the rights to work; to health; to education; to such basic needs as food and shelter; to freedom of thought and expression; to freedom from slavery, torture, and illegal arrest; and to equality before the law.

 1963

In *Peace on Earth*, Pope John XXIII emphasizes that all human beings are "the children and friends of God," and so every human being, regardless of his or her culture or nationality, is entitled to civil, political, social, and economic services; the right to respect; the right to freedom in searching for truth, expressing opinion, and worshiping; the right to choose one's state in life, to marry and have a family; the right to work for a just wage in a safe environment. Also important are the rights to hold private property, to work freely for the common good, to move within one's own country, and to emigrate to other countries.

1965

The Second Vatican Council issues *The Church in the Modern World*, which notes the growing interdependence of the international human family and the importance of safeguarding every human's basic rights. The Council also issues *The Declaration on Religious Freedom*, which calls for the right to religious liberty.

 1966

The United Nations adopts the *International Covenant on Civil and Political Rights* (ICCPR). Known as "first generation rights," these include the right to life, to political participation, to free access to information, and to a fair trial, as well as to freedom of expression, assembly, and association. Also included is freedom from slavery; from torture; and from cruel, inhuman; or degrading treatments or punishment. Countries that sign this convention agree to implement it by 1976.

"The Universal Declaration of Human Rights is one of the highest expressions of the human conscience of our time."
Pope John Paul II, 1995

1966

The United Nations adopts the *International Covenant on Economic, Social and Cultural Rights* (ICESCR). Again, all countries that sign agree to implement it by 1976. Known as "second generation rights," these include the rights to work, to adequate food and shelter, to health care, and to education.

 1967

In *The Development of Peoples*, Pope Paul VI focuses on the economic rights and the economic well-being of all persons, noting we are all responsible for each other and that the economic development of the poor and the moral development of those with means are interlinked.

 1975

The Vatican's Pontifical Commission on Justice and Peace publishes *The Church and Human Rights*, supporting the UN Universal Declaration of Human Rights, reaffirming basic economic rights, and calling attention to the rights of women and ethnic, linguistic, and religious minorities.

 1979

The United Nations adopts the *Convention on the Elimination of all Forms of Discrimination Against Women* (CEDAW) to eliminate persistent social, cultural, and economic discrimination against women. It affirms women's right to political participation, nationality, and health; and also emphasizes marriage rights and the special needs of rural women.

 1986

The U.S. Catholic Bishops, in *Economic Justice for All*, reaffirm that the UDHR and internally accepted human rights standards "are strongly" supported by Catholic teaching. Human rights are "moral issues" because they are "all essential to human dignity and to the integral development of both individuals and society."

 1987

Pope John Paul II, in his encyclical *On Social Concern*, emphasizes that economic development must respect all the economic, social, political, and civil rights of every human being in every part of the global community.

 1989

The United Nations adopts the *Convention on the Rights of the Child* (CRC), emphasizing the right of children to be protected from the illicit use of narcotic drugs, from all forms of sexual exploitation and sexual abuse, from recruitment into the armed forces, from economic exploitation, and from hazardous working conditions.

 1989

Pope John Paul II, in his *Message for the 1990 World Day of Peace*, highlights the right to a safe environment.

—*Center of Concern*, "Catholic Social Teaching, the United Nations, and Human Rights", Washington, DC, 1998.

 1991

Pope John Paul II, in *On the 100th Anniversary of On the Condition of Labor*, declares that the right to ownership must be balanced with the common good of all, and affirms the right to share in work that makes wise use of the earth's resources. He also reaffirms the rights to life, to family, and to religious freedom.

 1993

Responding to human rights violations throughout the world, the United Nations World Conference on Human Rights adopts the *Vienna Declaration and Programme of Action.* It reaffirms a commitment to previously recognized human rights, with special recognition of the right to development and to economic, social, and cultural rights. It calls for an end to discrimination, poverty, and violence in all its forms.

 1994

The United Nations drafts the *Declaration on Human Rights and the Environment,* which focuses on the rights to a healthy environment and to safe and healthy food and water, and on the right to benefit from nature.

 1998

Pope John Paul II declares in his *World Day of Peace Message* that the United Nations Universal Declaration of Human Rights, "one of the UN's principal titles to glory," must be "observed integrally, both in its spirit and letter," and that social, economic and cultural rights must be fully observed.

The Church Challenges Socialism

encyclical
official papal letter

socialism
government ownership and administration of the production and distribution of goods

capitalism
individual ownership and administration of the production and distribution of goods

Rerum Novarum criticized the socialism preached by Karl Marx. The **encyclical** condemned **socialism** because it gave to the state the rights belonging to the individual and family. For this reason, socialism can jeopardize the dignity of the individual. Pope Leo's fear was borne out by the loss of personal liberties in the Communist countries that were established after 1900.

Although socialism was condemned by Pope Leo, his encyclical shocked many political leaders and owners of industries of the time because he also strongly criticized aspects of **capitalism**. According to capitalism, people who invest money (capital) in industry or farmland should determine what is produced and the conditions under which it is produced. Today, we take for granted that workers also have a say in determining working conditions because of the existence of trade unions and the right to strike. However, in the late 1800s, these practices were considered disruptive to the established order. Yet, *Rerum Novarum* supported the right of workers to form unions and to strike; it also advocated fair wages and decent working conditions.

Later popes felt strongly enough about Pope Leo's call for economic justice that they wrote their own social encyclicals on subsequent anniversaries of his 1891 letter. A reading of these encyclicals and other related Church documents makes it clear that the Church of the past century has been very concerned about human suffering due to social and economic conditions. In giving shape to modern Catholic social teaching, popes and other Church leaders have not shied away from taking strong positions on controversial issues. As a result the Church has been one of the most consistent voices in the world today speaking on behalf of poor people.

Catholic social teaching developed by Church leaders did not stay on the level of theory. It had an impact on Catholics faced with addressing issues related to industry and commerce. For instance, in Europe many political parties sprang up that embraced the Church's social teachings. Also, workers' unions and other labor organizations based on Christian principles became popular. The current face of European politics still reflects somewhat these Church-led developments. ◆

◆ Spend some time looking through a Catholic document on justice or peace. Write a paragraph explaining what you found surprising or significant about a certain passage.

Dorothy Day and the Catholic Worker Movement

The story of Dorothy Day and the Catholic Worker Movement presents an enlightening saga about the power and appeal of Catholic social teaching. She recounts her journey toward faith in her autobiography, *The Long Loneliness*. In her teenage years Dorothy was drawn to involvement with the poor but dismissed religion as a potential instrument leading to such involvement:

> *Children look at things very directly and simply. I did not see anyone taking off his coat and giving it to the poor. I didn't see anyone having a banquet and calling in the lame, the halt and the blind. And those who were doing it, like the Salvation Army, did not appeal to me. I wanted, though I did not know it then, a synthesis. I wanted a life and I wanted the abundant life. I wanted it for others too. I did not want just the few, the missionary-minded people like the Salvation Army, to be kind to the poor, as the poor. I wanted everyone to be kind. I wanted every home to be open to the lame, the halt and the blind, the way it had been after the San Francisco earthquake. Only then did people really live, really love their brothers. In such love was the abundant life and I did not have the slightest idea how to find it.*
>
> —Dorothy Day, *The Long Loneliness,* Harper San Francisco, page 39.

The picture she had of religious people was very different from what she thought it should be: "I knew the rich were smiled at and fawned upon by churchgoers. This is all that I could see" (39). In college, this negative impression of religion deepened for Dorothy: "When we were at the university together, we never met anyone who had a vital faith, or, if he had one, was articulate or apostolic" (70).

At the time those who demonstrated most concern for poor people were Marxists. Thus, Dorothy became a socialist. Dorothy was drawn to the masses of poor people living simple lives as best they could in run-down sections of big cities. However, she also noted that great numbers of poor people were not attending socialist meetings, but in every city she visited, they were pouring out of churches on Sunday mornings. She was coming to realize that the Catholic Church was where the poor people were—the very masses of poor people whom she claimed to want to help.

> *My very experience as a radical, my whole make-up, led me to want to associate myself with others, with the masses, in loving and praising God. Without even looking into the claims of the Catholic Church, I was willing to admit that for me she was the one true Church. She had come down through the centuries since the time of Peter, and far from being dead, she claimed and held the allegiance of the masses of people in all the cities where I had lived. They poured in and out of her doors on Sundays and holy days, for novenas and missions. What if they were compelled to come in by the law of the Church, which said they were guilty of mortal sin if they did not go to Mass every Sunday? They obeyed that law. They were given a chance to show their preference. They accepted the Church. It may have been an unthinking, unquestioning faith, and yet the chance certainly came, again and again, "Do I prefer the Church to my own will," even if it was only the small matter of sitting at home on a Sunday morning with the papers? And the choice was the Church (139).*

Church: The Community that Does Justice 61

Dorothy converted to Catholicism but kept up her radical identification with street people and laborers. With Peter Maurin, she began *The Catholic Worker* newspaper, so called to offer an alternative to Communism and to emphasize that Catholicism indeed can serve as inspiration and instigation for involvement with poor people. Peter and Dorothy opened up a house of hospitality for homeless people in New York. In a haphazard but steady progression, others, combining Catholicism and compassion, opened similar houses in major cities throughout the United States. Even though Dorothy died in 1980, *The Catholic Worker* newspaper and movement continue to be an active presence where Catholics are committed to helping people who are the poorest of the poor.

Catholic Social Teaching Today

Since the time that Pope Leo issued *Rerum Novarum*, the modern Church has focused increasing attention on justice-related concerns. During this period, the geographical center of Christianity in general, and of Catholicism in particular, has been changing. For example, Latin America contains the largest concentration of Catholics in the world today. Africa now rivals the United States in numbers of Catholics. For a few years, the breakdown of the former Communist bloc nations in the early 1990s led to increased religious freedom where it formerly had been suppressed.

Catholicism's shift from being predominantly a European religion to one of truly global dimensions has created new questions in regard to justice. Because its presence is now worldwide, extending beyond the interests of one country or one continent, the Church is uniquely suited to speak on global justice-related issues. The documents ratified by Catholic bishops during the Vatican Council II (1962–1965) signaled the Church's desire to make justice and concern for human suffering keys to its stance toward the world today: "The joy and hope, the grief

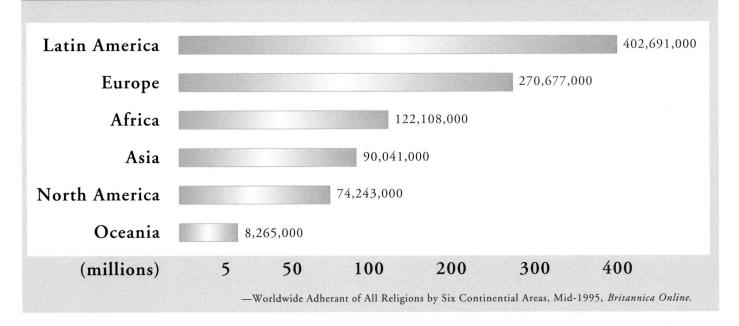

Roman Catholics by Six Continental Areas Mid-1995

Latin America	402,691,000
Europe	270,677,000
Africa	122,108,000
Asia	90,041,000
North America	74,243,000
Oceania	8,265,000

(millions)   5   50   100   200   300   400

—Worldwide Adherant of All Religions by Six Continental Areas, Mid-1995, *Britannica Online*.

and anguish of the [people] of our time, especially of those who are poor or afflicted in any way, are the joy and hope, the grief and anguish of the followers of Christ as well. Nothing that is genuinely human fails to find an echo in their hearts" (*Gaudium et Spes*, no. 1).

In other words, as Dorothy Day and other Catholics committed to justice affirmed, the Church has responded strongly to critics like Karl Marx by insisting that it has been called by Jesus to speak about justice. The Church does not offer a brand of religion that numbs people to present injustices with the promise of salvation after death. On the contrary, the salvation after death that was promised by Jesus cannot be separated from people's liberation from injustice now:

> *In their pilgrimage to the heavenly city, Christians are to seek and relish the things that are above: this involves not a lesser, but rather a greater commitment to working with all [people] towards the establishment of a world that is more human.*

> —*Gaudium et Spes*, no. 57.

Review

13. Describe Pope Leo XIII's contribution to Catholic social teaching.
14. What led to Dorothy Day's journey from socialism to Catholicism?
15. Why was *The Catholic Worker* newspaper so named?

Discuss

H. Do you understand the teenage Dorothy Day's desire to associate herself with "the masses"? How would following her example change your life?
I. How strongly are "Catholicism" and "compassion" linked in the perception of most people today?
J. Are they linked in your perception? Explain.

In Summary: The Church Proclaims the Gospel of Life

Throughout this book you will read passages from recent Church documents. Granted, they are not written with a teenage audience in mind. Nonetheless, they echo what Pope John Paul II calls the "Gospel of life" and, therefore, deserve the attention of those concerned about justice.

In the words of the pope, "every threat to human dignity and life must necessarily be felt in the Church's very heart" (*The Gospel of Life*, no. 3). He continues:

> *It is above all the "poor" to whom Jesus speaks in his preaching and actions. The crowds of the sick and the outcasts who follow him and seek him out find in his words and actions a revelation of the great value of their lives and of how their hope of salvation is well-founded* (no. 32).

In other words, the gospel message of Jesus proclaims our own dignity and also challenges us to confront every attack on the dignity of others. This gospel of life has been and continues to be the Church's mission of justice.

Before we conclude . . .

Let us pray . . .

It is truly right to give you thanks,
it is fitting that we offer you praise,
Father of mercy, faithful God.
You sent Jesus Christ your Son among us
as redeemer and Lord.
He was moved with compassion
for the poor and the powerless,
for the sick and the sinner;
he made himself neighbor to the oppressed.
By his words and actions
he proclaimed to the world
that you care for us
as a father cares for his children.

Keep your Church alert in faith
to the signs of the times
and eager to accept the challenge of the gospel.
Open our hearts to the needs of all humanity,
so that sharing their grief and anguish,
their joy and hope,
we may faithfully bring them the good news of salvation
and advance together on the way to your kingdom.

Open our eyes to the needs of all;
inspire us with words and deeds
to comfort those who labor
and are burdened;
keep our service of others
faithful to the example and command of Christ.
Let your Church be a living witness
to truth and freedom, to justice and peace,
that all people may be lifted up
by the hope of a world made new.

—Selections from *Eucharistic Prayers for the Mass for Various Needs and Occasions*, Totowa, NJ: Catholic Book Publishing Co., pages 49, 44, and 56.

For further study . . .

1. Identify and report on specific ways that the Church, Church organizations, and Christian communities promote or could promote justice. Remember that "the Church" is as local as you and your classmates and as universal as the international organization that spans the globe. In completing this assignment think about the Church as it exists locally, nationally, and internationally. There are web sites on the Internet that can provide you with information about various Catholic justice efforts and organizations.

2. Read each of the following statements. Chose the one you most closely agree with and prepare an argument to support your stand.

   - The early Christian re-arrangement of society is unrealistic. It would never really work. The Roman arrangement more realistically represents "the way of the world."
   - The early Christian re-arrangement of society should remain an ideal to strive for, even though it's not likely to be achieved.
   - The early Christian re-arrangement of society describes the world as I would like it to be.
   - I would be willing to work to help create the Christian ideal of a just world.

3. Imagine that you will be debating the topic "power corrupts," but you do not know whether you will be defending the pro or the con position. Prepare a statement on the topic from each point of view.

4. Listen to the music from the show "Godspell," in which Jesus is portrayed as a clown, or view the film "Brother Sun, Sister Moon" based on the life of Saint Francis. Each presents justice-related messages masked in child-like simplicity. Act out or illustrate a scene from one of these shows and present it to your class.

5. During troubling times of history, saints inspired by the gospel message have often come along to challenge popular trends that hurt people. Name some of the "saints" who are working for change today as reported in the news or as you know them in your personal life. Describe the saintly work or message of one of them in a report for the class. Try to find the source of inspiration that motivated them to help others in need or fight for change, maybe even at personal sacrifice.

6. The teenage Dorothy Day noticed that after a disaster such as the San Francisco earthquake, people tend to be particularly helpful to those in need. In your experience have you found this to be true? Research a recent national or local disaster. What groups, organizations, and individuals pitched in to help? What kind of help did they offer? Did they work with the people or for the people?

7. One country that has claimed the lives of Christian martyrs for justice is El Salvador. Read about and write a report on one of the following:

   - Archbishop Oscar Romero
   - Jean Donovan, Sisters Dorothy Kazel, Maura Clarke, and Ita Ford
   - The seven Jesuit martyrs

CHAPTER 4

Guidelines For Action

Doing Justice, Living Justly

Justice requires action. But what kinds of activities would be most beneficial in helping transform the world into a community of compassion? In this chapter we will look at two key ways to address problems in our world today—mercy and social action. Then, using compassion as our starting point, we will look at what living justly involves.

Major Concepts

A. Justice Through Direct Aid
- Works of Mercy

B. Justice through Changing Social Structures
- Social action

C. Living Justly, Living Compassionately
- Personal actions
- Life choices
- Prayer

Opening Prayer

Jesus, model of courage, your words and actions teach us how to live justly and compassionately. At this momentous time marking a new millennium, may we witness through our lives that your message still brings joy to the world and peace on earth. May we embrace a Christian lifestyle in our personal lives, and search for ever new ways to make the world a more perfect reflection of your boundless love. Amen.

Before we begin . . .

1. What are three ways that you think people are hurting in our world today?

2. What causes these hurts? Divide the causes into those related to individual decisions and those which exist because of the way society and its institutions are structured.

3. List three organizations that are involved in trying to help these people. Describe the work the organizations do. Are their solutions geared to helping the individuals or to changing the institutions that cause the problems?

Must We Choose?

Once upon a time there was a small village on the edge of a river. The people there were good, and life in the village was good. Then one day a villager noticed a baby floating down the river. The villager quickly jumped into the water and swam out to save the baby from drowning.

The next day this same villager was walking along the river bank and noticed two babies in the river. He called for help, and both babies were rescued from the currents. The following day, four babies were seen caught in the turbulent waters. And then eight, then more, and still more.

The villagers organized themselves quickly, setting up watch towers and training teams of swimmers who could resist the swift waters and rescue babies. Rescue squads were soon working twenty-four hours a day. But each day the number of babies floating down the river increased.

The villagers organized themselves efficiently. The rescue squads were now snatching many children each day out of the water. Groups were trained to give mouth-to-mouth resuscitation. Others prepared formula and provided clothing for the chilled babies. Many people were involved in making clothing and knitting blankets. Still others provided foster homes and placement.

While not all the babies could be saved, the villagers felt that they were doing well to save as many as they could. Indeed, their priest blessed them in their good work. And life in the village continued on this basis.

One day, however, one villager raised the question, "But where are all these babies coming from? How are they ending up in the river? Why? Let's organize a team to go upstream and discover the source of the problem." The seeming logic of the elders countered: "And if we go upstream, who will operate the rescue operations? We need every concerned person here."

"But don't you see," cried the one lone voice, "if we find out why they are in the river in the first place, then we might be able to stop the problem and no babies will drown. By going upstream, we could eliminate the cause of the problem."

"Our job is saving babies," decided the elders, "not expeditions upstream. We must continue our good work."

And so the number of babies in the river increases daily. Those saved increase, but those who drown increase even more.

—adapted from Inter-Religious Task Force for Social Analysis, *Must We Choose Sides?* pages 114–15.

This story can serve as an analogy for contemporary society. Think about the problems you listed in the opening activity.

- Identify ways that this story could be applied to these contemporary problems.
- Are the organizations that are addressing these problems doing so more in the style of the village elders or in that of the lone voice?

Justice Through Direct Aid
Works of Mercy

A starting point for doing justice is asking the question: How are people hurting? The answer to that question varies widely. Likewise, the way we help people can vary. The introductory story uses a shocking image—drowning babies—to make a case for expanding our vision of how we normally address people's problems.

No one escapes pain and suffering. Some hurts are related to **personal causes**. Other pain is brought about by **underlying causes**. In modern Christian tradition, two approaches to easing people's suffering emerge: **works of mercy** and **social action**. Appreciating the strengths and weaknesses of each approach gives us a better sense of how we can help people who are hurting in our local and global communities.

When we see people hurting, our heart cries out to help. The empty bowl held by a starving child begs to be filled. The sudden illness of a classmate calls for a visit or some other sign of care. When a natural catastrophe strikes a neighboring community, we pool our resources to help. By directly helping people in need, we are performing works of mercy.

personal causes

individual actions that lead to problems

underlying causes

ways society is structured that affect people

works of mercy

charitable actions by which we come to the aid of our neighbor in physical and spiritual ways

social action

steps taken to change society's structures

Works of Mercy

Corporal Works	Spiritual Works
• feed the hungry	• counsel the doubtful
• give drink to the thirsty	• instruct the ignorant
• clothe the naked	• admonish the sinner
• visit the sick	• comfort the sorrowful
• shelter the homeless	• forgive injuries
• visit the imprisoned	• bear wrongs patiently
• bury the dead	• pray for the living and the dead

Such works have been espoused by Jesus and his Church since the beginning. ". . . and whoever gives even a cup of cold water to one of these little ones in the name of a disciple—truly I tell you, none of these will lose their reward" (Matthew 10:42). Jesus sent the disciples out to proclaim the kingdom of God and to heal (Luke 9:2). As noted in the last chapter, caring for widows and orphans, sharing bread with the hungry, and other acts of mercy set the early Christian communities apart from their neighbors. Today, through organizations such as hospitals and Catholic Charities, or through the acts of individual Christians, the Church continues to relieve suffering and to help people in need. Even Catholic schools are charitable institutions, aimed at helping young people in need of education.

"Hence, those who are oppressed by poverty are the object of a preferential love on the part of the Church which . . . has not ceased to work for their relief, defense and liberation through numerous works of charity which remain indispensable always and everywhere." (CDF, instruction, Libertatis conscientia, 68)

— *Catechism of the Catholic Church*, 2448.

Sometimes, young Christians do works of mercy reluctantly. A young woman from Farmington Hills, Michigan, whose sports career is interrupted by an accident, fills her time by getting involved in school service projects. A boy from suburban Philadelphia begins tutoring children at an inner-city center because his high school requires service hours. When his requirement is completed, he still continues to help out. Sometimes, involvement in service accompanies preparation for the Sacrament of Confirmation. At Thanksgiving or Christmas time, school clubs or organizations often run drives aimed at feeding hungry people or giving financial support to poor people. Whatever the motivation or circumstance, it is hard not to associate works of mercy with being Christian. ◆

Mother Teresa: A Model of Mercy

Mother Teresa of Calcutta won the Nobel Peace Prize in 1979. Her careworn face framed by a simple Indian veil became a universal symbol of mercy. In India, she was known simply as "Mother." Her speeches were so often punctuated with the word *love* that she would sound naively sentimental if her actions had not proclaimed love so strongly. Whether working among starving and homeless people in Calcutta, garbage pickers in Mexico City, oppressed aborigines in Australia, or lepers in Africa, Mother Teresa's followers embody mercy in its clearest form.

◆ Have you ever participated in a service project that involved a work of mercy? Describe the experience. How did it feel? What motivated you to participate in this work? Did you feel as though you were helping another person or group?

Appropriately, Mother Teresa's order of sisters is called the *Missionaries of Charity*. Works of mercy perfect the Christian virtue of charity. Missionaries of Charity take a vow of "wholehearted, free service to the poorest of the poor." They take Jesus at his word when he said, "Truly I tell you, just as you did it to one of the least of these who are members of my family, you did it to me" (Matthew 25:40). Mother Teresa saw the face of Christ in the face of every poor person she met. The work of her order bears witness to the dignity and worth of every human person.

Mother Teresa cared little about political action and changing social structures. She cared about people—helping the poorest of the poor and encouraging others to love in whatever capacity they are capable. She viewed her calling as working among the numberless people who fall between the cracks of social structures.

Did she, then, reject social action as inappropriate or worthless? In fact, Mother Teresa has said:

> *If there are people who feel God wants them to change the structures of society, that is something between them and their God. We must serve Him in whatever way we are called. I am called to help the individual; to love each poor person, not to deal with institutions.*

Through her untiring work of mercy, Mother Teresa symbolized the spirit of compassion that must characterize all Christian service. If questioned about how to help those in need, she would simply say: "What you can do, I can't do, and what I can do, you can't do, but together we can do something beautiful for God."

> *What we need is to love without getting tired. How does a lamp burn? Through the continuous input of small drops of oil. What are these drops of oil in our lamps? They are the small things of daily life: faithfulness, small words of kindness, a thought for others, our way of being silent, of looking, of speaking, and of acting. Do not look for Jesus away from yourselves. He is not out there; He is in you. Keep your lamp burning, and you will recognize Him.*

> —Mother Teresa, *No Greater Love*, Boston: Pauline Book and Media, page 22.

Review

1. List the corporal and spiritual works of mercy.
2. Describe Mother Teresa's approach to helping people.

Discuss

A. Mother Teresa's Missionaries of Charity have grown in great numbers worldwide since their humble beginnings a few decades ago. Describe the type of work her religious order performs. How do you account for the appeal of her order? Why do you think members of her order seem so joy-filled?

Justice Through Changing Social Structures

Social Action

long-term solutions

answers which provide on-going resolutions to problems

The story about the townspeople helping the drowning victims demonstrates mercy in action, but it also raises important questions about helping people who are hurting. Can we do more than show mercy to individuals in need of help who cross our paths? Might we discover underlying causes to immediate problems and seek **long-term solutions** to them? Are certain people hurting because of attitudes, values, and structures deeply embedded within a particular society? Babies floating downstream are relatively powerless, but what about other people who are hurting? Is it possible to engage them actively in their own care and cure?

As the lone voice in the story suggests, seeking to alleviate *causes* of a problem is appropriate action on behalf of people who are hurting. In this approach to justice, social structures are examined and changes to those structures explored. In the story, for example, if villagers had investigated the situation upstream, they might have discovered that the babies were victims of injustice. Perhaps food shortages in another village led to this drastic measure, or discrimination against an oppressed group resulted in their babies being disposed of so heartlessly. Perhaps extreme overpopulation instigated a bizarre social policy of disposing of all infants. Investigation of the causes of the problem would quickly lead to dealing with social structures, societal values, and perhaps government policies.

Examining underlying causes and social structures, along with seeking long-term solutions and shared involvement of people, is a social action approach to justice. Like works of mercy, social action is a work of justice and an expression of compassionate care. Although it tends to be more indirect in helping people, social action is concerned with meeting people's needs just as works of mercy are. It also recognizes that providing only immediate relief for people who are mired in long-term problems does not root out the real causes of their suffering. Also, when people are always on the receiving end of a relationship, they can develop a diminished sense of personal dignity. As a result, they might feel powerless to help themselves. By addressing the impact of social structures on people's suffering, long-term solutions to problems might be uncovered. ◆

> *Respect for the human person proceeds by way of respect for the principle that "everyone should look upon his neighbor (without any exception) as 'another self,' above all bearing in mind his life and the means necessary for living it with dignity." (GS 27§1)*
>
> —*Catechism of the Catholic Church*, 1931.

◆ If we examine the urban landscape, we discover that many buildings that served as productive factories decades ago have been torn down to build stadiums and shopping malls or transformed into condominiums. When hotels or other establishments open, a variety of jobs are created, but usually wages are less than factory wages were. Without looking at underlying causes of a problem such as urban poverty, we get a distorted picture of the problem.

- Identify other social concerns that require examining underlying causes in order to be understood. Explain why deep-seated causes have a substantial impact on these problems.

What Are Social Structures?

In chapter one, where "concern for social structures" is identified as one of four elements of a just world, social structures are defined as "ways a society is organized that are commonly accepted." Social structures are the rules, written and unwritten, that govern a society. They include customs, such as a father dancing with the bride at his daughter's wedding. They also include laws and social policies, such as a father being financially responsible for his children whether or not he is married to their mother. A social structure can be as simple as telephone etiquette or as complex as a nation's educational system or its method of providing health care.

For example, in the U.S., education is free or affordable up to the twelfth grade. After that, people can pay large amounts for further education. U.S. public education is structured so that children who live in wealthier areas tend to receive more expensive and thus higher quality educational services. As a result the social structure known as the U.S. educational system gives an advantage to wealthier people over poorer people both for elementary and secondary education, as well as for higher education.

The former director of Catholic Charities for the United States points out that there can be either **graced social structures** or **sinful social structures**. Graced social structures are "those which promote life, enhance human dignity, encourage the development of community, and reinforce caring behavior." Sinful social structures "destroy life, violate human dignity, facilitate selfishness and greed, perpetuate inequality, and fragment the human community" (Fred Kammer, SJ, *Doing Faithjustice*, page 174).

graced social structures
encourage and strengthen life, dignity, and the development of community

sinful social structures
discourage and weaken life, dignity, and the development of community

For instance, a nation's tax system is an example of a social structure. Taxation can be structured in ways that either promote community and care or facilitate selfishness and greed. Retail business and shopping patterns also fit the definition of a social structure. Some justice-related concerns associated with business and shopping would be: the impact of large chain stores on small local businesses, the use of children to manufacture items cheaply in economically poor countries, the trend of closing plants in one community and opening them where the cost of labor is cheaper. Even packaging goods—excessive use of paper or plastic, for instance—has justice implications.

"Power Over" Versus "Power With"

Unlike works of mercy, social action addresses the issue of power. In other words people engaged in works of mercy can "give till it hurts," yet they still choose when and to whom to give their help. For their part, people on the receiving end of charity have no say in the matter. Social action, on the other hand, seeks to share **decision-making power**. That is, a social action approach to problem solving involves people who need help as active and equal participants in making decisions that affect them. Therefore, social action includes a challenge not present in works of mercy—transfer of power. Social action transforms power *over* into power *with*.

decision-making power
ability to make choices regarding an institution or one's life

A homeless person begging for money on a street corner seeks help from people passing by who may or may not give him or her money. The homeless person may try different approaches to get people to give money: "It's not for me; it's for my children." "My car broke down. Could you spare some change for bus fare?" Ultimately, passersby with money have the power to give or to refuse to give. A social action approach to justice seeks ways to increase the power that the person begging on the street corner has over his or her life—for instance, by instituting policies making inexpensive housing available in the neighborhood or by providing job assistance programs for unskilled workers. ◆

Here is an illustration of changing the distribution of power to address a situation where people might be hurting.

> *A multinational corporation is a business that operates in more than one country. Having international operations offers a corporation increased power over its employees and over its competition. If workers in one country do not approve of the corporation's wage scale, then the business can threaten to move its plant to a country where workers will settle for lower wages. The corporation's workers, therefore, are rendered powerless, lacking control over wage scales and working conditions while living under the threat of unemployment.*

Steps could be taken to increase the power of employees of such a corporation. For one thing, workers might organize on an international level, in which case the workers of different countries would not be in competition with one another. (Obviously, in this era of global economy such a movement is proving to be extremely difficult.) Secondly, workers might gain some say in the actual running of the corporation. Or, workers might organize to seek passage of laws that would forbid the import of goods from companies that do not meet certain standards.

As you can imagine, change in power is threatening to those who already have greater power. Unlike works of mercy, social action aims to change the relationship between "haves" and "have-nots." The message "Teach people to fish" appears harmless. However, social action takes another step. It asks, "Who has access to the pond where there are fish? Who claims ownership of the pond? Can we tear down the fence that allows only a select few to fish and prevents others from fishing?" When these questions are added, it becomes clear that a change in power is at stake.

> *Those responsible for business enterprises are responsible to society for the economic and ecological effects of their operations. (Cf. CA 37) They have an obligation to consider the good of persons and not only the increase of profits.*
>
> —Catechism of the Catholic Church, 2432.

◆ The U.S. bishops offer the following questions to families concerned about their participation in the nation's economic system:

> *Reflect on the economic choices your family makes and consider how they promote or diminish economic justice. Do they contribute to our growing culture of consumption? Do you patronize companies that treat their workers fairly? —A Decade After Economic Justice for All, page 14.*

- How would you respond to the questions raised by the bishops?

- How do you justify your family's spending choices?

Martin Luther King, Jr.: Model of Social Action

What immediately comes to mind when you think of Montgomery, Alabama? Chances are that in grade school you learned about the Montgomery bus boycott begun unintentionally by Rosa Parks near the end of the era of the segregated South. This African American woman refused to give her seat on the bus to white passengers. However, it is interesting and appropriate that almost one hundred years before it became the site of the beginnings of the civil rights movement, Montgomery served as capital of the Confederacy. In the mid-1950s, across the square from the Confederate government building sat Dexter Avenue Baptist Church, whose pastor first gained fame by leading a boycott of the segregated public bus system. In 1964, that same pastor, Reverend Martin Luther King, Jr., received the Nobel Peace Prize for his work benefiting African Americans and poor people of the United States.

Were Rosa Parks and other black women and men who rode the buses hurting? When asked why she didn't get out of her seat on this particular day, Mrs. Parks simply replied, "My feet hurt." But no doubt the hurt of giving up a seat simply because of the color of her skin was the greater hurt. How did Martin Luther King, Jr. set out to help ease the hurting that existed in the black community of Montgomery? Along with other leaders, he called for a boycott of the buses. That is,

he urged local citizens to walk places rather than taking a bus. Then he realized that he had to rouse the people to remain steadfast in their boycott. In a sense he was inviting them to greater suffering, walking to work instead of riding a bus—even if it was the back of a bus. But the suffering he was offering people this time was their choice, a way for them to take greater control over their lives. This suffering was aimed at changing a long-standing social structure of the American South—forced segregation. In the end, changing the way that society was structured would lead to better living conditions for all people hurting under this unjust system.

In other words the civil rights movement, which we today associate with Martin Luther King, Jr. was a social action movement. Like works of mercy its aim was relieving suffering. And yet clearly it differs greatly from mercy in how it seeks to achieve the same goal. Together, works of mercy and social action can be called "the two feet of Christian justice." ◆

> ◆ *You know my friends there comes a time when people get tired of being trampled over by the iron feet of oppression. There comes a time my friends when people get tired of being flung across the abyss of humiliation where they experience the bleakness of nagging despair. There comes a time when people get tired of being pushed out of the glittering sunlight of life's July and left standing amidst the piercing chill of an Alpine November.*
>
> —Martin Luther King, Jr., in *The Preacher King*, by Richard Lischer, page 87.

- What do you think Martin Luther King means in this passage?
- What groups in our society today might be "tired" of being oppressed?

The Feet of Christian Justice

Works of Mercy	Works of Social Action
• are concerned with the present symptoms of injustice.	• are concerned with the underlying causes of injustice.
• focus on individual needs.	• focus on changing social structures.
• look for immediate solutions.	• look for long-term solutions.
• provide a direct service with temporary results.	• provide indirect help aimed at permanent change.
• involve "haves" sharing with "have-nots".	• involve "haves" and "have-nots" working together and sharing power.
• require no change in social structures.	• require working toward changes in social structures.

The Two Feet of Christian Justice

The works of mercy and of social action are often called *the two feet of Christian justice* because to walk in justice requires that we walk with both feet. For instance, some organizations collect funds to help children in need who live in poor countries—an act of mercy. Other organizations publicize when companies exploit poor children in their manufacture of athletic shoes, soccer balls, or other items. They use this information to mount a boycott of these companies—a social action. Both "feet" of justice seek to help poor children.

Above is an outline of the differences between works of mercy and social action.

Review

3. Define *social structures.*
4. What is the difference between *graced* and *sinful* social structures?
5. Describe Martin Luther King, Jr.'s approach to helping people.
6. List the "two feet" of Christian justice and explain how they differ.

Discuss

B. Describe a situation where you or someone you know possessed power or lacked power. Was there evidence of "power with" at work? Explain.
C. How do you tend to use power when you have it?
D. Can you name a situation where you feel power was abused?
E. What appeals to you about Martin Luther King, Jr.'s approach to lessening hurtful conditions? What "power" did he possess? How did he use it?
F. Describe the approach. How was power used or changed through the action?
G. What situations exist today that you think could be addressed through a social action approach? What approaches would you suggest? How would people be using their power in these suggested approaches?
H. Would you be more comfortable engaging in works of mercy or social action? Explain.
I. Do you believe that social action is more effective or less effective than works of mercy in dealing with problems?

Living Justly, Living Compassionately

Our liberation and salvation is bound up with those in our midst who are suffering, who feel separated, who hunger for food and thirst for justice. Our liberation begins when we recognize in the routine of our lives that there are people who live in poverty and pain every day of their lives. Our liberation begins when we allow their look to seep through the cracks of our own broken hearts and move us to compassion.

—Joseph Nassal, *The Conspiracy of Compassion,* page 82.

Twelve times in the Gospels, it is said that Jesus was "moved with compassion." The word used implies that he was moved "in his guts." Being moved with compassion, in the depth of our being, for people who are hurting is the starting point for getting involved in works of justice. At the same time, compassion brings us closer to God in that it is the most God-like of virtues. Use this section to meditate on compassion as the springboard for justice. ◆

One scene in the Gospels that shows Jesus overcome with sorrow is the time he hears that his friend Lazarus has died: *When Mary came where Jesus was and saw him, she knelt at his feet and said to him, "Lord, if you had been here, my brother would not have died." When Jesus saw her weeping, and the Jews who came with her also weeping, he was greatly disturbed in spirit and deeply moved. He said, "Where have you laid him?" They said to him, "Lord, come and see." Jesus began to weep. So the Jews said, "See how he loved him!"*

—John 11:32–36

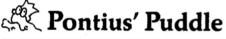 **Pontius' Puddle**

◆ Have you ever been "moved with compassion"? What were the circumstances? Did it lead to any action or to your getting involved with others? Did the event relate to justice in any way? If so, how?

Compassionate Action

Seldom are we moved by people at a distance. More typically, we get involved in struggles to overcome injustices, and in the midst of these struggles, we come to feel the pain of others and take it on as our own. In other words, action does not necessarily follow compassion. Instead, action and compassion go hand in hand. Works of mercy often start people off on the journey of doing justice. From there they might move to involvement in social action as well.

The word *compassion* is often associated with weakness, but true compassionate action is anything but wimpy. Compassion breaks down barriers between people. Isn't it true that there are plenty of people from whom we would like to be separated by large barriers? Compassionate action often pushes us beyond our usual comfort level, toward involvement with people with whom we may not initially feel comfortable being around. Compassionate action can lead us to look at people, problems, or parts of a city we might prefer to overlook. Compassionate action is courageous, heroic action.

Read the following descriptions of various actions. Identify each of them as an example of a *work of mercy* or *social action*. Be prepared to explain your choices. If you decide that an action fulfills both functions, mark both boxes. When you have categorized this list, think of your own examples of works of mercy and social action.

Christian Justice

	Works of Mercy	Social Action
1. A high school student government holds a canned-food drive for poor families before Thanksgiving Day.		
2. A high school pro-life club participates in a march held on the anniversary of the U. S. Supreme Court's decision legalizing abortion.		
3. A group of parents monitors TV programs for children and publishes ratings based on the amount of violence shown.		
4. A group of students visits a convalescent home for an hour a week to fulfill a requirement for their religion course.		
5. A student tutors a student from a foreign country in the English language.		
6. A student writes a letter to her local newspaper protesting the building of a nuclear power plant on a nearby river.		
7. An environmental organization lobbies members of Congress to pass legislation protecting clean air and water.		
8. A restaurant donates its surplus food to a local soup kitchen.		
9. The American Cancer Society raises funds to support research into the causes of cancer.		
10. A parish group holds protest demonstrations outside of a local movie theater that shows pornographic movies.		
11. A local parish converts its former convent into a drug rehabilitation center for drug-dependent teenagers.		
12. A group of citizens organize themselves into a town watch program to patrol neighborhood streets at night.		

Compassionate Speaking

When we see injustice happening, the compassionate response is to let others know about it. We can promote justice or support injustice through our speech. Compassionate speech accompanies compassionate listening. Compassion results when we listen to others and treat their stories with great reverence. To do that we must also hold our own stories in great reverence. Our experiences of hurting, then, are not an obstacle to compassion; but rather they serve as the very engine that propels us toward compassion for others. In other words in working for justice we are all "wounded healers." If we approach others with great reverence, then we will be very careful in how we speak about them. This is especially true for people about whom we normally would not speak very highly. ◆

Compassionate Choices

The term **life choices** simply refers to the choices we make that affect the way we live. For example, watching a few hours of television a night has become part of the typical North American lifestyle. Closing businesses for a few hours in the afternoon for a siesta (nap) is a traditional part of the lifestyle in Mediterranean countries. Compassionate life choices lead us to live in ways that are considerate of poor people and that keep us in touch with those who are hurting. For most Christians compassionate life choices do not mean living like the poorest of the poor, although some heroic Christians throughout history and in our present time have chosen to do so. It does mean that we question the style of life offered us by our culture.

The story on the next page illustrates how lifestyle can affect our view of what it means to be poor.

life choices

choices about living made by an individual or group

◆ Explain in your own words the following statements. Do you agree or disagree with them? Illustrate your position with concrete examples.

- The least compassionate response is not speaking up.
- Our own experiences of hurting help us to be compassionate.
- The way we speak about people is a matter of justice.
- Our liberation and salvation are bound up with those in our midst who are suffering.

A New Perspective

A priest from the midwestern United States invited a Venezuelan priest to visit him. The North American priest picked up his South American visitor at the airport in a late-model Oldsmobile sedan and drove him to his rectory in a nearby suburban parish. They arrived shortly before the evening meal, so they joined another priest living there for a drink followed by a delightful meal. After eating, they retired to an air-conditioned, carpeted lounge that contained a quality stereo system, a large-screen television capable of receiving numerous cable channels, and large comfortable chairs.

At the end of the evening, the North American priest asked his friend, "What do you think of our country so far?"

"So rich! So rich! I can't believe that you are so rich!" the Venezuelan replied.

"But we are not really rich," his friend laughed. "Everyone in our neighborhood lives as well as, if not better than, we do."

During their two-week visit together, the Midwestern priest tried to convince his friend that he was, in fact, not a wealthy person. For his part the South American always asked in amazement, "But living this way—how will you ever understand real poverty and those who are poor?"

• What answer would you give to the South American priest's question?

Compassionate Prayer

Most American teens say that they pray and that they value prayer. However, our current culture works against prayer. We live in what is often aptly called a "rat-race." Keeping busy is now a key characteristic of our lifestyle. Even when we slow down, seldom are we without the noise of TV or radio. "Taking a break" means playing solitaire on a computer.

Prayer is a different kind of presence, a different way of being. Through prayer we seek to keep company with God. We invite God into our inmost being and ask him to help us see ourselves and our world with his eyes. In that sense all praying is a prayer of compassion.

One aspect of prayer is always acceptance of ourselves as we are. Compassionate prayer directed toward ourselves is self-affirming, not guilt-inducing—unless, of course, a healthy dose of guilt nags at us to act justly in ways we have been trying to avoid. However, compassionate prayer is not simply a pat on the back. Jesus urged his disciples to love themselves and one another, as he assured them of his love. He also confronted them to take steps that must have overwhelmed poor uneducated fishermen and peasant women. If we actually take time to settle into prayer, searching for God's will, we are likely to be surprised at what God has in store for us.

Moreover, compassionate prayer is not a hopeless plea for God to make things better. Rather, it asks God to fill us with the hope, strength, and courage to know compassion and to act compassionately and justly. Since we need both inwardness and outwardness to experience God's presence, compassionate prayer includes both **solitary** and **communal** forms. In our rat-race world, the main thing is to make time for prayer and to cherish and honor those times faithfully.

Building Communities of Compassion

The film *Weapons of the Spirit* tells the little-known story of Le Chambon, a village in the south of France, whose residents sheltered thousands of refugees fleeing the Nazis. The citizens of this small town, which was comprised mostly of poor farmers, hid, fed, and housed thousands of Jews seeking to escape Hitler's holocaust.

The film documents how the town helped these people on their way to freedom from the Nazis. It contains interviews with many who were given sanctuary in Le Chambon and with villagers who opened their doors to those on the run. "There were scattered individuals who did this sort of thing everywhere in Europe, of course," one woman said, "but this was an entire community effort . . . by people so poor they had almost nothing to share, but shared it anyway—and risked everything to do so. I never heard of that happening anywhere else."

According to those interviewed in the film, five thousand Jews found sanctuary in this tiny village. "They risked their lives," one of the people who found refuge in Le Chambon said. "It was an unimaginable outburst of solidarity."

One of those who opened her doors to the Jewish refugees said, "It happened quite naturally. We can't understand the fuss. I helped simply because they needed help" (Joseph Nassal, *The Conspiracy of Compassion*, pages 106–107).

Le Chambon was a compassionate community. As one villager pointed out, the action they performed seemed natural. When people are hurting, compassion seems to be the natural response—certainly the human response. When an entire community is built on compassion, truly it becomes a "holy communion."

However, it is important to remember that communities of compassion might also be **communities of resistance**. As the citizens of Le Chambon mounted a campaign of resistance to Nazism, so compassionate communities resist movements, trends, and cultural practices and values that are harmful to people's well-being. Here again, it is important to recall that compassion in the form of resistance takes courage. It demands a price of individuals and of communities. What price does compassion ask of a community? What price does a community pay when it ignores compassion? What price would your school community pay if it ignored compassion? As you can see, compassionate communities seek answers to hard questions.

communities of resistance

groups who take a unified stand against an area of injustice

Avoiding "Compassion Fatigue"

In the late 1980s, a strange illness began striking a number of North Americans, many of them women. Symptoms varied, therefore, it was labeled a "syndrome" rather than a specific disease. A characteristic common to all sufferers was extreme fatigue, and thus "chronic fatigue syndrome" achieved its name.

We may feel drawn to getting involved in justice projects, but an initial spark of enthusiasm can easily fizzle into "compassion fatigue syndrome." Compassion fatigue refers to the combination of feelings that drains our energy and lessens our dedication, keeping us from giving ourselves to works of justice in any form. Serving meals at a homeless shelter can be a thankless task. Sometimes people who perform charitable works can even feel taken advantage of. Trying to change "the system" or parts of it through social action often appears hopeless or pointless. Martin Luther King, Jr. himself met failure in some of his projects, even after he won the Nobel Peace Prize and was a world-renowned figure.

No simple remedies for compassion fatigue syndrome exist. Many people who dedicate their lives to working for justice find that linking their engagement in justice with a strong religious faith keeps them going. The fire of love that sparks concern for people needs to be rekindled through a connection with a larger picture, such as the Christian story. Indeed, underlying this course is the belief that Christian faith does spark concern for justice and does provide a framework for setting an agenda for justice. That is, Jesus, who himself was moved to compassion two thousand years ago, continues to move people to act compassionately today.

For once you were darkness, but now in the Lord you are light. Live as children of light—for the fruit of the light is found in all that is good and right and true.

—Ephesians 5:8–9

7. What does the gospel term for *compassion* literally mean?
8. Why is compassionate action challenging?
9. What do compassionate life choices lead to?
10. What are the two forms of compassionate prayer named in the text?
11. What are the citizens of Le Chambon noted for?
12. What does it mean to say that communities of compassion must also be communities of resistance?
13. What experience is the author referring to by the term *compassion fatigue syndrome*?
14. What have many justice workers found to be helpful against compassion fatigue?

Discuss

J. What do you do to counteract the rat-race pace of modern society?
K. Pay attention to prayers said at your school or your parish church, such as the General Intercessions at Mass. Do they reflect concern for justice? Give examples
L. What people or groups do you like to keep at a distance? Why?
M. From the perspective of decades past, how do you think surviving citizens of Le Chambon feel about the choice they made to help Jews?
N. How do you think the children and grandchildren of Le Chambon villagers feel about the actions of their parents and grandparents?
O. How do you think they would feel today had they not helped people whose lives were in danger?

In Summary: Justice Is Compassionate Action

When people are hurting, change is called for. Change might be immediate, one-to-one, and short-term—a work of mercy. Or change might be long-term—social action directed toward identifying deep-seated causes of problems and aimed at changing social structures. Whichever path we choose to become involved in, when our passion for life blends with compassion for others, then the stage is set for beginning compassionate action.

Before we conclude . . .

Let us pray . . .

Lord Jesus, teach me to be generous;
teach me to serve you as you deserve,
to give and not to count the cost,
to fight and not to heed the wounds,
to toil and not to seek for rest,
to labor and not to seek reward,
except that of knowing that I do your will.

—Saint Ignatius of Loyola

For further study . . .

Some people seem to need to be pushed out of their nests. They have to learn that part of the solution to the problem lies within themselves. But until they can fly on their own, they will occasionally need the help of others. The ultimate goal is for people to fly on their own power, helping others and being helped when needed.

1. Reflecting back on this chapter to a situation where people are hurting, identify one type of charitable activity that you would find particularly meaningful. Identify one social change that you would be willing to work for. Describe one response that you could realistically make.

2. Plan a service project with a group of students. Report on the experience.

3. Interview someone who works in a service-related field. Based on the interview write a report on her or his motivation and experience as well as the joys and frustrations she or he encounters. Also, ask the person for recommendations about how young people might help people in need.

4. Another term for social structures is *institutions;* for example, health care, the criminal justice system, church, education, family, or the economy. Choose one of these institutions and answer the following questions:

   • What is its primary goal?
   • What are typical patterns of activities displayed in this institution?
   • What values are important in this institution?
   • What conflicts currently surround this institution?
   • Who benefits from the way this institution is structured? Do some groups benefit more than others?
   • Would you recommend any changes in this institution?

5. Make a list of what you consider to be characteristics of a North American lifestyle. (For example, shopping is a major form of recreation.) Evaluate each item on your list in terms of whether it helps us to be more or less compassionate.

6. In words or a work of art, compose a prayer of compassion.

7. *"What I'm saying is nobody feels sorry for anybody anymore, nobody even pretends they do. Not even the president. It's like it's become unpatriotic."*

   —Barbara Kingsolver, *The Bean Trees*, page 171.

   Form two debate teams who take opposite views on the following statement: Compassion is currently out of fashion.

8. In his book *Earth and Altar*, Eugene H. Peterson connects prayer with justice and compassion:

   The single most widespread American misunderstanding of prayer is that it is private. Strictly and biblically speaking, there is no private prayer. . . . Prayer, of course, has to do with God. . . . But prayer also has to do with much else: war and government, poverty and sentimentality, politics and economics, work and marriage. . . . Solitude in prayer is not privacy. The differences between privacy and solitude are profound. Privacy is our attempt to insulate the self from interference; solitude leaves the company of others for a time in order to listen to them more deeply, be aware of them, serve them. Privacy is getting away from others so that I don't have to be bothered with them; solitude is getting away from the crowd so that I can be instructed by the still, small voice of God, who is enthroned on the praises of the multitudes (pages 15–16).

   • What is the distinction that the author is making between solitude and privacy? Do you agree that it is an important distinction? Do you believe that most people's prayer typically includes a dimension of justice and compassion?

CHAPTER 5

Poverty in America

A Scandal We Can Overcome

We meet Jesus every day in those who are poor and in need. So if we wish to know Jesus better, we can learn about him from those in our midst who are homeless, hungry, chronically ill, out of work, unskilled, and underpaid. Jesus did not respond passively to people in need; rather, he took compassionate action to end their suffering. Applied to poverty Christian justice means poor and non-poor work together to overcome the scandal that poverty exists in a country with such vast riches and resources.

Major Concepts

A. *Poverty in America: Truths, Myths, and Misconceptions*
Recognizing and analyzing common perceptions
- Invisible to the rest of the population
- Viewed as being more "us" than "them"
- Viewed as being poor because of self-imposed shortcomings

B. *Homelessness: A Visible Symptom of the Depth of Poverty*
- Homeless and near homeless

C. *Migrants and Immigrants: A Continuing American Story*
- Immigration as affecting the U.S. economy
- Mexican immigration as a reflection of all immigration issues
- The Church's teachings on behalf of immigrants

D. *Christianity and Poverty*
- God's identification with those who are poor
- Catholic social teaching: to be anti-poverty means to be pro-child and pro-immigrant

E. *Responding to Poverty*
- Helping the poor who cannot help themselves
- Assisting the poor who can help themselves to become more self-sufficient

Opening Prayer

God of life, you filled the earth with good things and commissioned human beings to serve all. As we begin our study of poverty, help us to see all people through your eyes. We humbly accept the challenge before us, that poverty can be overcome. We pray for a fuller and deeper understanding of the gospel message, "Whenever you did it for any of my people, no matter how unimportant they seemed, you did it for me." Loving God, we unite our prayer with all who are poor, in body or in spirit. Amen.

Before we begin . . .

Answer **agree**, **disagree**, or **uncertain** to the following statements about poverty in the United States. Choose statements that you believe are most significant and explain your answers.

1. Most poor people in the U.S. live on welfare.

2. Taking care of poor people is better handled by private charities than by the government.

3. Because of special needs and disabilities, people beyond retirement age are more likely to be poor than younger people.

4. A major cause of poverty today is an increase among single-parent families.

5. Welfare keeps people from taking responsibility for their own lives.

6. Poor people are more likely to engage in drug use, promiscuous sex, theft, and violence.

7. Poverty is not a major problem in the U.S. Priority should be given to other concerns.

Poverty in America: Truths, Myths, and Misconceptions

The *Before we begin . . .* statements about poverty in the U.S. hint at how complex, confusing, and controversial the problem is. Some of the most deeply ingrained beliefs about poor people are completely false or are partial truths that cloud over the painful reality of poverty. For a number of decades now, a heated debate has been going on in the country about how best to address the problem of poverty. Approaches to solving the problem sometimes shift in emphasis with each national election. In order to put a human face on those who are poor in the U.S., let's first examine some common notions about poor people.

Poor People As Invisible

Today our most popular image of poverty is that of inner-city poverty, and for various reasons this image of the poor has found a place in our national consciousness. In the 1960s, the United States declared a "war on poverty," largely because of some heart-wrenching reports about the extent of poverty in the country and the harmful effects it was having on people. At the time rural poverty received much attention. Pockets of people lived in shacks or abandoned cars and buses on dirt roads out of sight from the majority of Americans. Rural poverty was invisible poverty; poor people living away from mainstream America were "out of sight, out of mind." However, for a number of reasons, poor people today continue to be largely "invisible." Why? Although rural poverty continues to be a problem, it seldom makes the news anymore. Secondly, more people who are poor are now living in the same neighborhoods as people who are not poor. They reside in small towns and suburbs, attending the same schools as their less-poor neighbors. On the surface they neither dress nor look any different from anyone else. And lastly, thanks to the build-up of suburbs, the relocation of jobs away from downtown areas, and highway systems that cut over or around older neighborhoods, the non-poor can for the most part avoid encountering the obviously poor who are living in clusters within major cities. The early 1990s movie *Grand Canyon* gives a clear picture of this third type of invisible poverty suddenly becoming visible. In the movie a suburbanite driving his luxury car home at night on a Los Angeles expressway pulls off the expressway when he begins having car trouble. He enters the world of a poor Los Angeles ghetto. Stranded, he contacts a local garage from his car phone. Before the pick-up truck arrives, a carload of teenagers pulls alongside the broken-down vehicle. The teenagers, carrying weapons, torment the man waiting with his car. When a garage mechanic arrives, he convinces the youths to spare the man and let the mechanic do his job. After the tense incident the mechanic movingly tells the wealthy suburbanite, "It's not supposed to be this way." Later, the mechanic and the driver become friends and travel to a place representing a simpler and healthier image of how America is supposed to be—the Grand Canyon. ◆

Poor People As "Us"

In fact, poor people are much more "us" than "them." There is no one "face" of poverty in America. Statistics that attempt to identify who is poor can overwhelm us. Members of all races are numbered among those who are poor. Most people who are poor are white; but a larger *percentage* of the African American, Latin American, and Native American populations are poor. Most of the people who are poor in the U.S. do not receive welfare. (Only about two-thirds of those eligible even apply.) A large number work full time or part time and still are poor. In fact, on average, people labeled as poor in the U.S. work much more than poor people in other Western countries. Even before recent changes limiting the time people can receive benefits, most welfare recipients received government help intermittently rather than continuously. This suggests that they worked for a time but, for various reasons, did not hold onto jobs. Studies of women on welfare indicate that most of them have appreciated programs aimed at helping them get off welfare and become gainfully employed. Finally, poor people are much more likely to be victims than perpetrators of crime.

> I'm not knocking the welfare program, because it's a lifesaver—it's there. Because you've got a roof over your head and you're not out in the street. But on the other hand, as far as my own situation is concerned, it's pretty rough living this way. I can't see anybody that would ever settle for something like this just for the mere fact of getting a free ride, because it's not worth it.
>
> —51-year-old divorced mother on welfare, in Randy Albelda and Nancy Folbre, *The War on the Poor*, New York: New Press, page 17.

◆ Put yourself in the place of the three sets of characters from the movie *Grand Canyon*, the driver, the mechanic, and the teenagers.

- What is each character's perspective on poverty in America?
- Are their perspectives different? If so, why?
- How do you think each character views the other characters?

The Myth of the Welfare Queen

Philadelphia newspaper reporter David Zucchino heard people talking about how some women on welfare receive their government checks monthly and lead "the good life" while the rest of us work hard to pay taxes to support them. Being an investigative reporter, Zucchino decided to look into the reality of women on welfare in his home town and write a book about it. Here is part of what he found:

> *If there were any Cadillac-driving, champagne-sipping, penthouse-living welfare queens in North Philadelphia, I didn't find them. What I found instead was a thriving subculture of destitute women, abandoned by their men and left to fend for themselves and their children, with welfare and food stamps their only dependable source of income. Their lives were utterly dominated by subsistence concerns. They spent hours each day foraging for food and clothing and securing safe housing for themselves and their children through punishing heat waves and bitter cold snaps. Out of sight of mainstream America, they survived from one welfare check to the next, making ends meet by picking through trash cans, doing odd jobs, borrowing from relatives, and shopping at thrift stores. They lived at the mercy of the welfare bureaucracy, which demanded documents and economic updates, while sometimes cutting off payments with little warning. Through it all they struggled to stay alive in one of the most dangerous places in America. North Philadelphia is cursed with one of the highest violent crime rates in the nation; its main industry and chief source of employment is the sale of illegal drugs.* ◆

—*Myth of the Welfare Queen*, New York: Scribner, 1997, pages 13–14.

Everyone should be able to draw from work the means of providing for their life and that of their family, and of serving the human community. (*Catechism of the Catholic Church,* #2428)

◆ Imagine that you are a twenty-three-year-old single woman with two pre-school aged children. You had a boyfriend, the father of your children, with whom you previously shared an apartment. When he became abusive, you left with your children and moved in temporarily with a relative. You lack education or training beyond high school, and you have no family members who can assist you financially.

- What would life be like for you?
- What would be your priorities?
- Would you apply for welfare?

- What kind of future would you envision for yourself?
- What steps could you see taking to better your situation?
- What kinds of community support would you like to see?

"Work Is Available for Anyone Who Really Wants It"

The traditional way out of poverty was relatively simple: Get a job. However, at least three factors related to the U.S. economy make this avenue to economic improvement not as effective as it once was. For one thing the number of jobs in this country employing unskilled workers has greatly diminished. To understand why first take a look at where your sneakers, toys, bicycles, sports paraphernalia, and electronic equipment were made. Chances are, as we will note in the chapter on global poverty, most of them were manufactured in one of the Pacific Rim nations where labor costs are much cheaper right now. Also, think about all the tasks that once were done by people that are currently done by machines. ◆

Secondly, employment opportunities for people who are unskilled no longer supply economic security. Ask someone who works at an employment office what kinds of work are now available for unskilled laborers.

1998 Federal Poverty Guidelines

Size of Family Unit	48 Contiguous States and D.C.
1	$ 8,050
2	$10,850
3	$13,650
4	$16,450
5	$19,250
6	$22,050
7	$24,850
8	$27,650

For each additional person, add $2,800.

Federal Register, Vol. 63, No. 36, February 24, 1998, pages 9235–9238

◆ Look into the state of manufacturing jobs in your area. Have there been plant closings in recent years? Are products that once were manufactured in your locale now made elsewhere? Besides ATM banking, list other services now handled more by machines than by people.

Unlike thirty years ago jobs for unskilled workers pay minimum wage or barely above it, offer little hope for advancement, provide no long-term job security, and include minimum fringe benefits. In other words while there are some employment opportunities for the unskilled in today's economy, far fewer unskilled laborers make a decent living wage at the limited job opportunities that are available to them. ◆

Thirdly, many new businesses and industrial complexes are inconveniently located for poorer potential workers. Over the past few decades many U.S. manufacturing plants and other business centers have relocated away from areas where predominantly poor people live to areas where predominantly wealthier people live. Suburban centers of employment often are not accessible by public transportation but are located more conveniently for executives who drive to work. Most workers with higher paying jobs travel by car from one suburb where they live to another suburb where they work. Put these factors together and the result is: few viable opportunities for unskilled workers and a widening gap in wages between more-skilled and less-skilled workers.

Welfare Reform: Exchanging Welfare for Wages

welfare reform

initiated by the federal government in the mid 1990s. These changes in programs aimed at helping people who are poor shifted administration of programs to the state level, limited the amount of time people could receive government assistance, and attempted to move people previously on welfare to being economically self-sufficient.

In the mid 1990s the federal government instituted a program commonly referred to at the time as **welfare reform**. A principal goal of the reform was to assist people receiving welfare to gain a greater degree of self-sufficiency. The administrative board of the United States Catholic Conference has supported the initiative to help people "exchange a welfare check for a paycheck." In 1995 the board voiced concerns and suggested guidelines for welfare reform. They pointed out that:

> *For the Catholic community, the measure of welfare reform is whether it will enhance the lives and dignity of poor children and their families. The target of reform ought to be poverty, not poor families. The goal of reform is reducing poverty and dependency, not cutting resources and programs.*

—*Political Responsibility: Proclaiming the Gospel of Life, Protecting the Least Among Us, and Pursuing the Common Good*, Washington, DC: USCC, 1995, page 30

◆ An unskilled laborer usually begins a job at minimum wage ($5.15 per hour in 1998). Assume that a worker was employed for 40 hours per week for fifty-two weeks per year. What would the worker's annual wages amount to before taxes? Budget this person's annual expenses if he/she were living in your area. Regardless of what is officially designated as the poverty line, how possible do you think it would be to maintain a minimum standard of living with this salary?

Christian Goals for Welfare Reform

- To protect human life and human dignity.

- To strengthen family life.

- To encourage and reward work.

- To preserve a safety net for the vulnerable.

- To build public and private partnerships to overcome poverty.

- To invest in human dignity and poor families.

—Political Responsibility: Proclaiming the Gospel of Life, Protecting the Least Among Us, and Pursuing the Common Good, Washington, DC: USCC, 1995, page 30.

Review

1. What type of poverty was focused on at the beginning of the 1960s war on poverty?
2. What does it mean to say that this type of poverty was *invisible poverty?*
3. List the three reasons given why poverty is still largely invisible in the U.S.
4. Why might non-poor persons prefer to view the poor as "them"?
5. What is the racial background of most poor people?
6. What is the so-called "myth of the welfare queen" that the Philadelphia reporter investigated? What did he discover?
7. Give three reasons why fewer opportunities exist for viable employment for unskilled workers today than existed thirty years ago.
8. What was the primary stated goal of the mid-1990s welfare reform?

Discuss

A. What are your strongest images of poor people in the United States? Why do you think you hold such images?
B. Defining what it means to be poor is an inaccurate science. However, since the 1960s, the U.S. government has used a certain income level as its official poverty line. For the past two decades, the number of Americans *officially* below the poverty line has consistently been around fifteen percent of the population. That is, almost one out of every six people is officially poor.
   - Are poor people still mostly invisible in our society?
   - What does it usually take for poor people to burst onto our national consciousness?
   - Are poor people "invisible" to you, or do you have frequent contact with members of this fifteen percent?
   - What is the nature of your contact? Explain.

Homelessness: A Visible Symptom of the Depth of Poverty

The sight of men sleeping in cardboard boxes over heating vents and women dressed in layers of clothing rummaging through trash cans has become part of the urban landscape of America. Who are these people? Is our society so hardened that it overlooks the irony that homeless and penniless people huddle within a few feet of tall buildings serving as headquarters for multi-million dollar businesses? Besides being uncomfortable with this, what can we (who have a home and plenty of clothes) do for these people? Accurate statistics for the homeless population in the U.S. are hard to come by. People who are homeless are not likely to respond to questionnaires sent through the mail or to show up at voting booths on election day. A 1994 study by the federal government found that in many cases entire families were homeless, often due to economic factors, such as job loss or inadequate income. Many homeless people suffer from mental illness or from drug dependency. A New Jersey rabbi who works with homeless people reports that many homeless people do work but that their wages are insufficient to provide for themselves and their families. The same rabbi adds that:

> *Even more appalling, many homeless children are alone. They may be runaways who left home because there is no money for food, because they are victims of rape, incest, or violence or because one or both of their parents is in emotional turmoil. Some are "throwaways" whose parents tell them to leave home, or won't allow them to return once they leave.*

—Rabbi Charles A. Kroloff, *54 Ways You Can Help the Homeless*, Southport, CT: Hugh Lauter Leven Associates, 1993, page 12.

"One Paycheck, One Rent Payment Away from Homelessness"

One frightening aspect of accounts of homeless people is how much they actually resemble the population at large. Many people fall into the category of being among the **near homeless**—a paycheck, a mortgage or rent payment, or one family crisis away from losing their home. Is the distant cousin who exhibits signs of emotional problems and is no longer able to work on her way to becoming homeless? Is the friend who drinks to excess and has a family history of alcoholism destined to live later life in and out of shelters and treatment centers? Is the fifty-five-year-old neighbor who loses his job and is now too psychologically paralyzed to seek another going to be able to hold himself together until retirement age? Is

near homeless

people with no savings or resources to carry them over during times of financial crisis

the uncle who can't seem to shake his wartime experiences going to survive the strain on his family's finances and his government pension? As these scenarios suggest, the answer to the question, who are the homeless, is: They are our friends, relatives, and neighbors who have come upon hard times. They are children whose families cannot cope with the challenges of our changing economy and who lack the support of a capable extended family or a caring community. They may be the addicted or the mentally ill who cannot find a place in the system. They may be single young men or women whose education and skill levels rule out adequate long-term employment. They may be the person who has lost a job because of corporate downsizing. Who are the homeless? The answer is that any one of us, living in this world where there are no certainties, could become one of the homeless.

Review

9. Give three categories of people who make up the homeless population in the United States.

10. What does it mean to be among the *near homeless*?

Discuss

C. What is most surprising to you about the 1994 report or the rabbi's findings?

D. What types of programs could help the homeless with their immediate needs?

E. What types of programs would address underlying causes of homelessness?

Migrants and Immigrants: A Continuing American Story

All Americans—even those known today as Native Americans—are either descended from immigrants or are immigrants themselves.

—Jim Carnes, "Us and Them," *Teaching Tolerance*, 1995, page 44.

Most communities in the United States now boast a population of people who recently arrived in the country. Often they speak Spanish, sometimes the French dialects of Haiti or parts of Africa, and occasionally one of the Middle Eastern or Asian languages. Their country of origin may be in Latin America, Africa, the Caribbean, Asia, or the former Communist bloc of nations. For instance, a California bishop notes that "the Asian population in the United States today (7.2 million) is equal to the population of Paraguay or Uruguay. . . . The number of Asians in the Archdiocese of Los Angeles alone is greater than the entire population of Guyana or Suriname" (Bishop John Cummins, "Acknowledging the Extent of Asian Immigration," *Origins* 27:25, December 4, 1997, page 421). This same bishop points out that "The prediction for the year 2025 is that the United States will be 25 percent Hispanic, and it will be 12 percent Asian" (page 421). Migration has become a worldwide phenomenon. Not everyone who migrates is poor; but typically people from poorer or politically unstable countries seek refuge in wealthier, more stable environments. Likewise, not every immigrant to the U.S. fits the stereotype of a person living in crowded quarters, working hard at menial jobs to send money home to needy relatives.

Is there a stance that U.S. citizens can take toward immigrants to their country that would combine both justice and sensible immigration policy? In light of the topic of this chapter, the question more specifically is: How do we respond to those people who are poor who feel desperate in their own country and who seek an opportunity for

◆ Answer **yes**, **no**, or **uncertain** to the following statements. Describe the images or information upon which you base your answers.

1. Immigrants take jobs away from U.S. citizens.
2. Unskilled immigrants tend to work harder than unskilled U.S. citizens.
3. The racial background of immigrant groups plays a part in governmental policies and popular attitudes toward them.
4. The United States should restrict legal immigration to a greater degree.
5. The United States should more carefully enforce its laws restricting illegal immigrants.

betterment by migrating to the U.S.? Bishop Cummins observes that the national mood toward immigrants "shifts between hospitality and hostility. The pattern is cyclical, touched by graciousness in good times, by harshness in difficult economic circumstances. When job competition comes to the fore, newcomers are blamed for societal ills" (page 421). In the face of shifting attitudes toward immigrants, Bishop Cummins finds Scripture reminding us, "We are called to be a welcoming Church" (page 421).

> *The more prosperous nations are obliged, to the extent they are able, to welcome the foreigner in search of the security and the means of livelihood which he cannot find in his country of origin. Public authorities should see to it that the natural right is respected that places a guest under the protection of those who receive him.*
>
> —*Catechism of the Catholic Church, #2241.*

Immigrants and the Economy

Have the recent immigration trends helped or hurt the U.S. economy? Wages and unemployment are no more a problem in cities with larger shares of immigrants than in other cities, which suggests that immigrants are not negatively affecting employment in these communities. Some immigrants work at jobs geared directly to members of their own community and so do not displace other workers. Many perform jobs that native-born workers do not want and would not take. On the plus side, immigrant communities help create jobs by requiring goods and services themselves. But for a number of years now, a national debate has been going on about whether or not, and to what degree, immigrants who remain poor should be eligible for government services such as public schooling, healthcare, and public assistance. The trend recently has been toward reducing the amount of government assistance available to immigrants. For their part, illegal immigrants fear deportation and tend to stay away from even those government services available to them. Since they lack power over wages and working conditions, they sometimes receive below minimum wages and work under sub-standard conditions. Since the workers are in the country illegally to begin with, to whom can they complain?

> *While it is difficult to point to any single event as the cause for the upsurge in anti-immigrant sentiment, several factors have played a role. These include the perception that U.S. borders are out of control and that undocumented migrants are flooding the United States to take scarce jobs and to access public benefits. This perception has little basis in reality; the undocumented typically fill jobs unwanted by U.S. workers and are ineligible for most benefits, even though they pay $7 billion annually in taxes and social security contributions. Moreover, 85 percent of immigrants come to the United States through legal means.*
>
> —Wendy Young, "United States Immigration and Refugee Policy: The Legal Framework" in *Who Are My Sisters and Brothers?*, Washington, DC: United States Catholic Conference, 1996, page 45.

Mexican Immigrants and Mexican Americans: Hospitality and Hostility

People migrate to the U.S. for various reasons. One story that illustrates a link between an immigrant experience and issues of poverty and justice is the ongoing story of Mexican immigrants and Mexican Americans. In the decade of the eighties, over 22 percent of legal immigrants to the U.S. were from Mexico. In addition, over the past few decades, Mexicans have made up a large portion of illegal immigrants to the country. History provides some perspective on this phenomenon.

Look at the map of Mexico as Mexico existed a few hundred years ago. It included all of what is now the southwestern United States and much of what is the western United States. The Mexican presence in this part of the United States, then, predates the United States itself. After the United States confiscated this territory in the 1800s, Mexicans and Mexican Americans served primarily as cheap labor for agricultural, ranching, mining, and railroad construction endeavors owned and operated by white Americans. For the most part this pattern of exploitation has continued into our present day and has spread to other parts of the country. For over a century Mexicans have been crossing their northern border in order to find work. Specifically, they want to find jobs that pay better than ones available in their own country. On this side of the border, Mexican workers have either been welcomed or discouraged from coming, depending on how much of a need exists for their labor. For various reasons Mexican Americans generally speaking have not climbed the social and economic ladder to achieve the success that immigrants from Europe have achieved. For one thing, after U.S. expansion to the west took place, Mexicans and Mexican Americans were often assigned the kinds of negative labels that are often placed upon dominated groups: lazy,

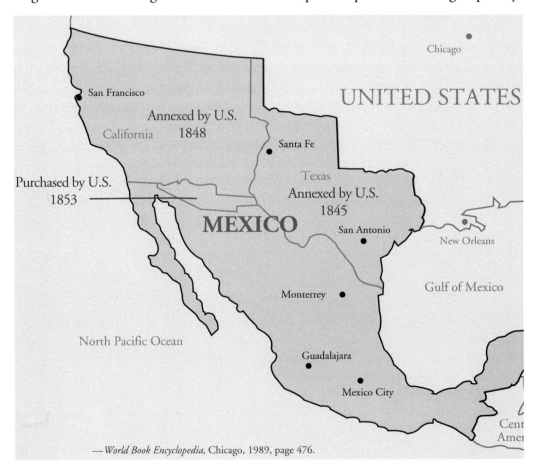

— *World Book Encyclopedia*, Chicago, 1989, page 476.

not very intelligent, carefree, and irresponsible. Secondly, almost all recent arrivals from Mexico and other Latin countries were peasants. The constant flow of new immigrants from Mexico and other Latin countries maintained the image of Mexican Americans as being poor and uneducated and as not blending in as successfully with dominant American culture as their European counterparts. Today, most stereotypes about Mexicans have either changed or become less common. Nonetheless, the economic and educational status, the political power, and the opportunities for advancement of Mexican Americans are well below those of European Americans.

Traditionally, migrant farm workers have numbered among the lowest paid, least secure, and most poorly protected workers. They harvest crops seasonally and are never in one place for long. In parts of the country, such as California, there seems to be an endless pool of workers. If one migrant does not accept wages and conditions offered, another one will. John Steinbeck's novel, *The Grapes of Wrath*, gives a popular depiction of such workers who migrated to California during the era of the Great Depression. It took until the mid-1960s before a serious movement to unionize migrant workers took place. The person who spearheaded the drive to unionize was Cesar Chavez. Like Martin Luther King, Jr., he used nonviolent protest techniques to win support for his cause. When he called for a boycott of California grape products, including wines, vast numbers of Americans refused to purchase these products. Support for the boycott was so great that after five years California growers recognized the United Farm Workers (UFW) union. Formation of the UFW represents a remarkable story of poor and non-poor working together to bring about change. ◆

> *Most immigrants start out poor. As of 1990 approximately one-third, or 32 percent, of recent immigrant households lived below the poverty line, an amount up from the 11 percent counted before 1980. However, after less than a decade living in the United States, the incidence of poverty in those families drops by a third (to approximately 22 percent.)*
>
> —Robert Lavelle, ed., source: Census Bureau, 1990, *America's New War on Poverty*, San Francisco: KQED Books, 1995, page 203.

◆ • Read the book or view the film, *The Grapes of Wrath*. Write a report on the experience.
• Write a report on Cesar Chavez and the United Farm Workers union.

The Church Speaks on Behalf of Immigrants

Surprisingly, in this nation of immigrants, many citizens are now taking a hard stand against immigration. Of course, countries need rules and policies regulating immigration. However, in addition to concern for immigration laws and their enforcement, there should be compassion. Church leaders identify migrants as one group that deserves special attention and compassion. In 1995 the U.S. Bishops Committee on Migration addressed the current crisis of increased migration going on throughout the world. The bishops went back to another historical period filled with people on the move from country to country, the period following World War II. They quote from a post-World War II document, *The Émigré Family*, issued by Pope Pius XII:

The émigré Holy Family of Nazareth, fleeing into Egypt, is the archetype of every refugee family. Jesus, Mary and Joseph, living in exile in Egypt to escape the fury of an evil king, are, for all times and places, the models and protectors of every migrant, alien and refugee of whatever kind who, whether compelled by fear of persecution or by want, is forced to leave his native land, his beloved parents and relatives, his close friends and to seek a foreign soil.

—Statement on IMMIGRATION, *The Flight to Egypt*, December 15, 1995.

refugee

one who flees to a foreign country or power to escape danger or persecution

migrant

a person who moves regularly in order to find work

economic migrants

people who come to a county seeking a better life for themselves and their families

Are conditions in our world today similar to post-war conditions? Traditionally, a distinction was made between *refugees* and *migrants*. **Refugees** are driven out of their homeland under the threat of losing their lives because of warfare or political oppression. On the other hand, **migrants** leave a country voluntarily. Today these distinctions have become blurred. In some cases people (refugees) are leaving their homelands because of the threat of immediate physical violence. Other people (migrants) are leaving their homelands to avoid the threat of poverty and hunger. In both cases people are being uprooted because of real threats to their lives. A bishop whose diocese contains many migrants refers to one group as the **economic migrants**. He places current patterns of migration in the broader context of today's global economy and asks: "Why in this new world is there free movement for goods and capital, but not for persons, especially poor persons? The wealthy seem to move and settle where they will" (Bishop Carlos Sevilla of Yakima, Washington, "The Ethics of Immigration Reform" *Origins* 27:43, April 16, 1998, page 729). Bishop Sevilla concludes that "the Church's teaching holds that there is a right to emigrate for economic reasons" (page 729) and that anti-immigrant feelings that demean people in need are a sign of "a grave spiritual disorder" (page 730). He proposes that "even when people are undocumented immigrants, there is a 'humanitarian zone' in which their human rights must be upheld and their basic needs supplied" (page 731). The U.S. Bishops Committee on Migration admits that an increase in the flow of poor immigrants can lead to conflict with native-born poor. However, it points out that this poor-against-poor conflict is not the main problem. Instead, it calls for changing "wider systemic dysfunctions in this country."

Questions have arisen about the impact of immigrants on the employment prospects of native-born poor, particularly African American poor. There are concerns that where a specific ethnic group dominates an unskilled sector of the local economy, African Americans are not so much displaced as excluded. Scholars generally agree that the effect of immigration in the aggregate is most likely negligible, while at the individual level there are instances of displacement. It is clear, however, that friction exists in some areas between certain immigrant and African American ommunities. This conflict tends to pit the poor against the poor, which deflects attention from the wider systemic dysfunctions in this country. By design or by inertia, these failures of our social system perpetrate the legacy of slavery and racism. The question is not why African Americans are not holding a greater percentage of the jobs in the fast food industry but, rather, why African Americans are not holding a greater percentage of the jobs in Silicon Valley. The real issue is the failure of this nation to offer adequate training, education, and support to minority poor so that they may take their places not at the bottom of the employment ladder, but among the best of the highly skilled and educated workers at the top.

—U. S. Bishops, *One Family Under God*, page 18. ◆

◆ Based on the above passage write a response to the following questions :
- What is the popular misconception about immigrants and jobs?
- Why do the bishops claim that this popular perception is inaccurate?
- What distinction are the bishops making by contrasting *fast food jobs* with *Silicon Valley jobs*?
- What do the bishops believe is the real issue about poverty that the nation should be addressing?
- Do you agree with the bishops' assessment of the impact of immigration?

Immigration and the American Spirit

"Quite close to the shores of New Jersey there rises a universally known landmark which stands as an enduring witness to the American tradition of welcoming the stranger and which tells us something important about the kind of nation America has aspired to be. It is the Statue of Liberty, with its celebrated poem: 'Give me your tired, your poor, your huddled masses yearning to breathe free . . . .Send these, the homeless, tempest-tossed to me.' Is present day America becoming less sensitive, less caring toward the poor, the weak, the stranger, the needy? It must not!" (Excerpt from the homily of Pope John Paul II at Mass October 5, 1995, Giants Stadium, East Rutherford, New Jersey).

When the Holy Father graced New Jersey with his visit in 1995, he remarked that from its beginning, the United States has been a haven for generation after generation of new arrivals and prayed that America will persevere in its own best traditions of openness and opportunity . . .

We recognize that the INS [Immigration and Naturalization Service] has a duty to enforce the laws enacted by the federal government. However, the manner with which the laws are sometimes carried out is deeply disturbing. We believe that every effort must be made by the INS and all law enforcement officials to uphold the basic rights that ensure fairness and respect for the human dignity of all persons in the judicial system. These rights, including the legal rights of undocumented persons, stem from the U.S. constitution and the laws of the United States. We condemn any action which tramples on the individual rights of people simply because of their immigrant status. We urge that the laws be carried out not only with justice but with compassion . . . Today, as before, the United States is called to be a hospitable society, a welcoming culture. If America were to turn in on itself, would this not be the beginning of the end of what constitutes the very essence of the American Experience?

—"Statement of the New Jersey Catholic Bishops on the Treatment of Immigrants in New Jersey," in *Catholic Star Herald*, November 21, 1997, page 13.

Review

11. What reasons does the text give to make the case that illegal immigrants do not hurt the U.S. economy?

12. How does a Mexican presence in the western U.S. pre-date the nation itself?

13. Give one reason why Mexican Americans as a group have not achieved the economic success of their European counterparts.

14. What was the result of the movement headed by Cesar Chavez?

15. How are *refugees* traditionally distinguished from *migrants*? Why has this distinction become blurred?

16. Who are *economic migrants*?

Discuss

F. *The genius of America lies in its capacity to forge a single nation from people of remarkably diverse racial, religious, and ethnic origin.*

—Arthur Schlesinger, "The Disuniting of America" in Nicholas Capaldi, *Immigration: Debating the Issues*, Amherst, NY: Prometheus Books, 1997, page 228.

In 1990 immigrants made up 7.9 percent of the U.S. population, up from 6.2 percent in 1980 but well below the 14 percent of the early decades of the 1900s.

• Do you believe that immigration at its current levels, and in the current form of multicultural emphasis, threatens a spirit of unity among Americans? Explain why or why not.

Christianity and Poverty

In chapter 2 the case was made that not only does the God of Scripture side with the poor, God actually *identifies* with the poor. The popular Christmas season image of the Holy Family searching for shelter reminds us that at its core Christianity knows the hardship of poverty. In his very being Jesus embodies God-become-poor.

Because of its history of involvement with poor people, the Church today claims a special right and responsibility to speak out against poverty. The Church today knows the concrete realities of poverty because of its many programs and institutions aimed at helping poor persons. ◆

> *The Catholic community educates the young, cares for the sick, shelters the homeless, feeds the hungry, assists needy families, welcomes refugees, and serves the elderly. People who are poor and vulnerable, the elderly, and immigrants are not abstract issues for us. They are in our parishes and schools, our shelters and soup kitchens, our hospitals and charitable agencies.*
>
> —Administrative Board of the United States Catholic Conference, *Political Responsibility: Proclaiming the Gospel of Life, Protecting the Least Among Us, and Pursuing the Common Good,* page 8.

What are some of the lessons that contemporary Catholic teaching tells us about poverty and poor people today?

Contemporary Catholic Teaching: To Be Anti-Poverty Means to Be Pro-Child

One common denominator running through the groups of poor people described in this chapter is the fact that the most vulnerable members of society suffer the most from poverty. According to contemporary Catholic social teaching, as the most vulnerable age group, children are to be given priority in anti-poverty programs. In 1991 the U.S. bishops described a crisis of poverty that they saw among America's children:

> *Children are the poorest members of our society—one out of five children grows up poor in the richest nation on earth. Among our youngest children, a fourth are poor. Children are nearly twice as likely to be poor as any other group. Among children, the younger you are, the more likely you are to be poor in America. And poverty means children miss the basics—the food, housing, and health care they need to grow and develop. They are deprived in a way that hurts and distorts their lives.*
>
> —U.S. Catholic Bishops, *Putting Children and Families First,* page 1.

The bishops applaud the work done by groups and individuals who seek to make life better for children. It asks of government that it assist and support these efforts.

◆ Read the following Gospel passages:

- Mark 10:17–25
- Mark 12:38–44
- Mark 14:3–9
- Luke 4:14–19
- Luke 6:20–25

Choose one of the passages and write a paragraph that answers these two questions: What do you believe is the message for you in this passage? How do you feel about the message? Then, create an artistic representation—a painting, collage, song, poem, or short story—of the passage's meaning for you.

Though he was in the form of God,
he did not regard equality with God
as something to be exploited,
but emptied himself,
taking the form of a slave,
being born in human likeness . . . .

—Philippians 2:6–7

The most important work to help our children is done quietly—in our homes and neighborhoods, our parishes and community organizations. No government can love a child and no policy can substitute for a family's care, but clearly families can be helped or hurt in their irreplaceable roles. Government can either support or undermine families as they cope with the moral, social, and economic stresses of caring for children. (page 7)

As a matter of fact, the bishops point out that government programs and policies turned around for the better the economic situation among older people. Now it is time for government to implement such policies that will aid children.

When our nation makes a commitment, it can make a difference. Decades ago poverty haunted large numbers of our elderly citizens. As a society we decided this was intolerable and put in place Social Security, Medicare, and other measures to protect the dignity of the elderly—with an impressive drop in poverty among their population. Now, our children are more likely to be poor, but our government spends less on children's needs. (page 8)

Review

17. Name a Christian image that illustrates why concern for poor people is a core dimension of Christianity.
18. What types of experience lead the Church to claim that it has a special responsibility to speak out on issues related to poverty?
19. Why does Catholic teaching propose that to be anti-poverty today means to be pro-child?
20. What effect did government changes have on the lives of older people?

Discuss

G. What local groups or individuals do you see working to help children in your area?
H. Is there anything your class or school could be doing to help children, especially children with special needs?

Responding to Poverty: Should People Who Are Poor Receive Assistance?

■ After an undistinguished high school career, Steven worked off and on for a janitorial service for six years. He managed to find a place of his own for a few years. Lately, employment has been sporadic, leading him to return home to live with his retired parents. Therapy uncovered that Steven suffers from severe chronic depression. Even with medication he has become increasingly reclusive and unable to work.

■ Yolanda was introduced to crack cocaine at parties she went to with her boyfriend. Her boyfriend has since left her, but Yolanda continues to indulge her habit every chance she gets. Her baby son was born premature and shows signs of his mother's addiction.

■ Since arriving from Ukraine, Peter has worked as a carpenter's assistant. His wife works part time doing nails in a beauty salon. Because of a labor dispute, Peter has not worked now for over a month; and business at the beauty parlor is slow. Peter and his wife have two children but no family or friends upon whom they can depend for help.

■ By saving what money they could from low-paying jobs, Salvador and Maria purchase a van which gives them more flexibility in finding employment. They each take a job cleaning floors at the local hospital for a decent salary. Sometimes their shifts overlap by a few hours. On those evenings their three children sleep in their van in the hospital parking lot until their mother or father is free to take them home. During breaks Salvador and Maria check on the children to make sure they're okay.

■ After being abandoned by his mother, Rasheed grew up in various foster homes. When his latest foster mother forbade him from hanging out with his

friends, Rasheed decided to live on his own—sometimes with a friend's family, sometimes in an abandoned or stolen car. Although he is only fifteen, in the past year Rasheed has attended only ten days of school.

■ When the steel plant closed, Donald's home town began to look more like a ghost town. Eventually he landed a temporary job when the Wal-Mart opened up nearby, but business has been slow and hours sporadic. Now his car needs extensive repairs, but Donald cannot pay for them. The financially strapped garage will not fix the car unless payment is guaranteed. Without his car Donald has no way of getting to work.

All the above scenarios portray people who are poor in some way. If they are to survive or flourish, all of them could use some form of assistance, either short-term or long-term.

- If you were in charge of a public trust fund, would you deny any of these people cash support or money for services? If so, why would you make these choices?
- What restrictions would you place on government help to each of these people? Why?
- What kinds of programs do you think would be most beneficial to each of these people?

The Goal: Eliminating Poverty, Not the Poor

With rare exception every nation on earth provides some assistance to its citizens who are poor. In the United States there are people truly in need, and for many of them the combination of government aid and contributions from private charities remains insufficient to move them out of poverty. Does this country possess the resources to provide for their needs? If so, why does the scandal of poverty, in some cases rivaling that which is found in much poorer countries, continue to exist in the United States? The U.S. bishops consider the degree of poverty that exists in the country to be a scandal. However, as mentioned earlier, they point out that anti-poverty programs must be aimed against poverty and not against people who are poor. Current social and economic realities suggest that large numbers of poor people require help if they are to move out of poverty or even survive. Eliminating poverty requires a delicate balance. First, we clearly and carefully need to provide for those who cannot help themselves. Secondly, we need to assist those who can help themselves to become more self-sufficient. Failure to maintain this balance can lead to people falling between the cracks of the variety of services available to help people in need.

A term for programs aimed at helping poor people become more self-sufficient is **welfare-to-work programs**. Through recent welfare reform initiatives, the U.S. has committed itself to creating and expanding such programs. To be effective, anti-poverty strategies must combine the two approaches to doing social justice described in chapter 4—that is, *involve individuals* on the one hand and on the other, *address social and structural problems* that contribute to poverty. An observation by economist Rebecca Blank is helpful here:

> *The reason poverty is so high in urban ghetto neighborhoods is because a whole host of destructive forces has evolved over time, with institutional problems in the schools, reinforced by lack of nearby employment, reinforced by poorly maintained public housing structures that become centers for drug and gang activities, and so on. The problems in these neighborhoods are deeply structural and environmental at the same time that they are deeply behavioral. It is difficult to know how to break out of the vicious circle.*

—Russell Sage Foundation, *It Takes a Nation*, Princeton, NJ: Princeton University Press, 1997, page 289.

welfare-to-work programs

government assistance programs that provide aid while individuals are trying to learn a new trade or seek employment

Pontius' Puddle

DO YOU HAVE TROUBLE PERSUADING YOUR CHURCH THAT JESUS COULD FEED THE FIVE THOUSAND WITH ONLY FIVE LOAVES?

NOT AT ALL. THEY'RE ALREADY CONVINCED THEY CAN CURE THE SICK, EVANGELIZE THE UNSAVED, AND WIPE OUT WORLD HUNGER BY JUST DROPPING THEIR SPARE CHANGE IN THE OFFERING PLATE!

PONTPUDL@AOL.COM

© Joel Kauffmann

Who Should Pay?

One aspect of the discussion about aid to poor people centers around who should help the poor, the government or private charities such as church groups. Currently, both government and private agencies help poor people, although by far the biggest chunk of monetary aid comes from the government. Actually, many private charities (such as the network of Catholic Charities organizations) already receive most of their funding from the government. In the Catholic social justice tradition, government is not considered evil, something to be avoided at all cost. Catholic tradition holds that programs should be run at the most local level possible and also that various aspects of society should work together to address problems. Given the extent and the nature of poverty in America, centralized government might be the most efficient overseer of key anti-poverty initiatives. In the words of the Administrative Board of the U.S. Bishops:

> *We regret public attitudes that dismiss the legitimate role of government and ridicule public officials in misguided frustration with all politics. We need more, not less public participation—not only in electoral politics, but also in issue advocacy, legislative networks, and community organizations, which give important vitality and substance to public life.*
>
> —*Political Responsibility: Proclaiming the Gospel of Life, Protecting the Least Among Us, and Pursuing the Common Good*, Washington, DC: USCC Publications, page 2.

21. Define *welfare-to-work* programs.
22. Why would relying solely on private charities to help poor people be a difficult course to follow?
23. How does Catholic social teaching view the role of government?

Discuss

I. If an exchange student from another country were staying at your home and asked the following questions, how would you answer him or her: Why does poverty exist in the United States? Why isn't more done to eliminate poverty in this country?

J. Describe attitudes (of poor and non-poor) that need to be addressed if poverty is to be alleviated.

K. Describe behaviors (among poor and non-poor) to be adopted, changed, or discontinued if poverty is to be alleviated.

L. Describe structural problems existing in North American society that would need to be addressed if poor people are to be helped.

In Summary: Poor and Non-Poor Are Sisters and Brothers

The first step toward overcoming poverty in America is accepting the challenge expressed in the refrain running throughout this course: We are sisters and brothers. And because we are sisters and brothers, we ought to care that some of us go to bed hungry. We ought to care that some of us are cold, that some of us are sick with no money for help, that some of us are homeless with no place to go, and that some of us are stranded with no way home. We ought to care. And we ought to do something about it.

Before we conclude . . .

Let us pray . . .

Jesus, God-become-poor, we seek you in children,
just as you called children to come to you. We seek you in immigrants,
just as you welcomed strangers. We seek you in people who need welfare,
just as you extended a caring hand to people in need. We seek you in all
those who find themselves poor, knowing that only with them can we
enter your kingdom.
Amen.

For further study . . .

1. Research the Internet or government documents for statistics on the following questions:

   • What are common characteristics of people who are poor today?
   • Where do the majority of poor people live within a city? Within the U.S.?
   • What percentage of poor people are on welfare?
   • What percentage of poor people work?
   • Give three categories of people who make up the homeless population in the United States.

2. One dimension of recent welfare legislation was to transfer much of the responsibility for administering programs from the federal level to the state level. Find out what types of programs currently exist in your state to help welfare recipients to find work. If sufficient information is available, evaluate your state's welfare program in light of the guidelines outlined in 1995 by the U.S. Catholic Conference and listed on page 93 of this chapter.

3. Contact representatives of local or national organizations for the homeless. Compose a checklist of questions to ask them, questions that would guide you to help homeless people. For instance, if people ask you for spare change, should you give it to them?

4. Describe a welfare-to-work program that is provided by your state. What have been the results of this program on the poor who have participated in it?

5. Follow up on the research of the Philadelphia reporter. Give your own report on "people who currently receive welfare." Does your research support the reporter's conclusion?

6. Find out what organizations exist in your area or state whose goal is helping homeless people. What approach does each organization take to addressing the problem? Are homeless or formerly homeless people involved in the organization? Report on your findings.

7. Find out what you can about various anti-poverty programs, both government run and privately sponsored. Describe the aims of each program and how it seeks to achieve those aims. Explain whether or not you would recommend supporting each program. If possible, get involved in an anti-poverty program and report on its work.

8. Research the following:
   - List groups or individuals who help children, especially children who have special needs.
   - List types of activities or programs that could help children.
   - List examples of government-sponsored policies or programs that could help children.

CHAPTER 6

Global Poverty

Making Interdependence Work

People are poor worldwide for the same basic reasons that people are poor in the United States. However, certain areas of the world are home to large numbers of people whose lives are desperate and cut short because they lack even the minimal resources needed for survival. In this chapter we will look at who these people are and at our relationship to them. Even though they live in distant places, our lives and well-being are more intertwined with theirs than we might think. To care for these people, those who are poor and hungry for reasons that stretch worldwide, is both a Christian duty and common sense.

Major Concepts

A. Examining Global Poverty

Common characteristics among poor countries

- Colonial past
- High rate of population growth
- Single export economy
- Instability
- Gross inequality
- Chronic malnutrition
- Undernourishment

B. Global Poverty in Christian Perspective

- The Scriptures and Church teaching about the poor
- Christian living through sharing bread and feeding the hungry

C. Responding to Poverty

- A triage approach directed toward poor people
- Responding to poverty on a personal level
- Responding to poverty on a societal level

Opening Prayer

Jesus, we worship you as the Bread of Life. As we ponder the extent of poverty and hunger in our world, may we refuse to throw up our hands in despair. Instead, through your Spirit and the reception of Eucharist, may we be energized to seek creative and effective ways to help make the lives of poor people more healthy and hopeful. Amen.

Before we begin . . .

Answer **agree**, **disagree**, or **uncertain** to the following statements. Choose statements that you believe are most significant and explain your answers.

1. Serious hunger and starvation are rare occurrences in the world today.

2. Enough food exists in the world to feed the current population adequately.

3. We should take care of poor people in our own country before helping others.

4. We who live in wealthier countries would have to radically change our lifestyles in order to help people who are poor.

5. People should not purchase products made in sweat shops.

6. Increased aid from wealthy countries is the best way to help poor countries.

7. Poor countries would do well to model their economies and lifestyles after the United States.

8. The experience of being poor in North America is different from the experience of being poor in economically underdeveloped countries.

Maria's Story

My name is Maria Olana. I am a campesina—a peasant girl. I live on a small farm seventeen miles outside of Santa Rosa de Copan, Honduras, with my parents and six brothers and sisters. I once had two other brothers and another sister, but they died. The most recent death was my very young sister Rosa. This past winter, Rosa had diarrhea and weighed only seven pounds when she died. I cried and cried. When Rosa got sick, we went to our friend Cortia, who helps cure us. She told us that there was a cure for Rosa, but it would cost 100 lempira or about fifty U.S. dollars—we just didn't have the money. We also can't afford the medicine to cure the dengue fever, which my father has all the time. Sometimes it's so bad, he can't even work.

Our farm is on a steep hillside. We have one manzana, or about one and one-half acres, of land. We do not own the land—we lease it from Mr. Mendez, who lives in Santa Rosa. When times are good, we have plenty to eat. Our farm grows corn and beans, and we raise some chickens. There are also some banana and orange trees nearby that give us fruit. My father sells some of the corn and some eggs to buy rice, material for clothing, and a few tools. Times are not good now, though. The rains this year were extra heavy, and much of our corn crop was washed down the hillside. Many of our chickens have died, and all we have to eat are a few beans and some bananas. My father put in a new corn crop, but some kind of insect seems to be eating the corn before it gets very big.

We would love to get some of the rich land in the valley so that we could grow more, and our crops wouldn't keep being washed away by the rains. But, of course, all the valley land is owned by the fruit company. My oldest brother, Carlos, used to work for the fruit company in the pineapple fields. He would earn eight lempira a day, which really helped our family through the tough times. Last month, though, Carlos lost his job. The people at the fruit company told him that because of something called a recession, people in North America were not buying as many pineapples, and fewer people were needed to work the fields.

A man from the government came to see us last week. He told us about a new kind of corn that we could plant that did not grow as tall as the corn we are used to. He said that the short plants would be less likely to wash away and that they also produced about three times as much corn. My father was very excited until he found out that in order to use this corn, he would have to buy chemicals to fertilize the plants and protect them from diseases. "The new plants would give us a chance to get ahead," my father said. But we all knew there wasn't any way we could get started with them.

In tough times like this, all that is left is to dream. I have heard that it is possible for young girls to get jobs in the city. I went to school two years ago, and I was told I was very smart. I really liked school, but my father needed me on the farm. He says that girls need only to know how to cook, gather firewood, and make clothes. Someday I will find a way to make life better for my children than it has been for me.

—Adapted from "Maria's Story" in *World Hunger: Learning to Meet the Challenge*, pages 85–86. The story was created by the Impact on Hunger organization to reflect documented family situations in Honduras and other developing countries.

- If Maria came to live with your family as part of an exchange program, what would you want to say to her?
- Could you offer her any words of hope that her dream could come true? What would they be?
- If you went to live with Maria's family as part of an exchange program, what do you think the experience would be like? What effect do you think it would have on you?

Examining Global Poverty

Maria's story contains elements common to many young people's stories who live in the southern hemisphere. If she chooses to remain on her family farm, she will live her life on the edge of starvation or disease caused by poor nutrition and inadequate health care. If she seeks her fortune in the big city, chances are that she will end up serving as some wealthy man's sex object or working for minimal wages making products for consumers in the northern hemisphere. Working conditions in factories in poorer countries typically damage a young person's health and shorten their productive years as well as their life. Even working gruelingly long hours, Maria probably would not earn enough to assist her family or to provide for herself when she is replaced by another young girl with greater stamina and smaller fingers more suited to certain kinds of work.

Where do we begin responding to the Maria stories of our world? First, it is important to acknowledge the extent to which poverty exists. Two ways that international agencies measure poverty are **income levels** and what is called the **physical quality of life index**. The physical quality of life index measures such things as life expectancy, infant mortality rate, and literacy—three concerns important to Maria and her family. Study the following chart below to view statistics about some of these concerns.

income levels

comparative amounts of money earned annually by individuals or families

physical quality of life index

levels on this table are determined by a combination of average length of life, average rate of death for babies, and the number of people who can read

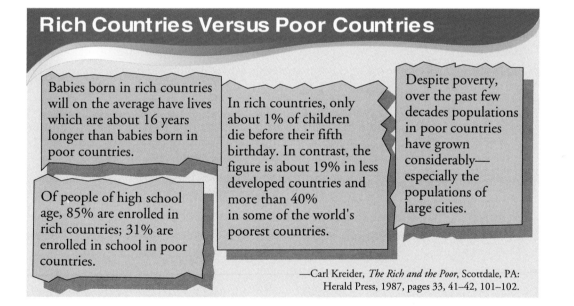

Rich Countries Versus Poor Countries

Babies born in rich countries will on the average have lives which are about 16 years longer than babies born in poor countries.

In rich countries, only about 1% of children die before their fifth birthday. In contrast, the figure is about 19% in less developed countries and more than 40% in some of the world's poorest countries.

Despite poverty, over the past few decades populations in poor countries have grown considerably—especially the populations of large cities.

Of people of high school age, 85% are enrolled in rich countries; 31% are enrolled in school in poor countries.

—Carl Kreider, *The Rich and the Poor*, Scottdale, PA: Herald Press, 1987, pages 33, 41–42, 101–102.

Pontius' Puddle

Whatever measures are used it is clear that the majority of the poor people of the world live in Africa, especially sub-Saharan Africa, and in parts of Asia and Latin America. The extent of poverty is so great in some countries that it is accurate to say that *countries* are poor. That is, in some countries, living without electricity, without running water, and in shacks with dirt floors describes the norm for most people. Professional health care is scarce, so that even minor illnesses are life threatening. Most people attain only minimal levels of education. Governments are so strapped with debts that they can do little on their own to help their suffering citizens. One unfortunate indicator of nationwide poverty is the extent of hunger-related illness and death. ◆

Hunger: When Poverty Threatens Health and Life

When you arrive home from school today, you will probably ask, "What is there to eat?" A trip to the refrigerator or to a kitchen cabinet will, no doubt, provide a quick and satisfactory answer to that question. For about one-fifth of the earth's people, however, trying to answer the question "What is there to eat?" consumes most of their day and a large part of their income.

Sadly, what the poorest fifth of the world's population receives to eat leaves them not only unsatisfied, but also depleted of their health and strength. They end their day with gnawing, empty feelings and with the realization that getting enough food to survive will be their main task again tomorrow. Because hungry people experience many days of poor nourishment, they are more likely to become sick or diseased than well-fed persons. Death is no stranger within the families and neighborhoods of hungry people. They live every day on the edge between life and death.

Of course, *hunger* is a relative term. Just before mealtime we might say, "I'm hungry." Yet, we all know that the hunger we feel is not what people concerned about "world hunger" are referring to. The hunger experienced by the world's poorest people refers to chronic **malnutrition** and **undernourishment**.

Malnutrition: A Lack of Necessary Nutrients

malnutrition

a state resulting from a diet lacking the nutrients vital to good health

undernourishment

amount of food is less than what can sustain life

When we were young we probably tried to read the strange-sounding words on the side panels of cereal boxes. They stated, "Satisfies the minimum daily requirements for the following vitamins and minerals. . . ." We probably took it for granted that we were on our way to meeting our daily nutritional needs with our cereal, milk, and juice. Although the typical American diet consists of too much sugar, salt, processed food, and "junk food," most of us who live in North America receive adequate nutrition.

By contrast one out of five people who are the world's hungry do not receive their minimum daily requirements of proteins, vitamins, and minerals. Because they can afford nothing else, the bulk of their diet consists of one type of food—usually rice, corn, or millet. For six out of ten people in the world, rice is the staple of their diet.

◆ Besides the characteristics listed above, what other characteristics would you look for to determine the wealth or poverty of a country? List theses characteristics, together with the ones listed above, in order of importance in determining the wealth or poverty of a country. Explain your ranking.

Although nutritious in itself rice alone cannot provide complete nourishment. As our grade school health classes taught us, proper nutrition requires a varied diet. Consequently, a poor diet leaves the world's hungry people malnourished. When this condition persists they are said to suffer from **chronic malnutrition**.

Chronic malnutrition leads to protein-deficiency diseases that eventually result in death. Lack of vitamin A causes blindness. Iron deficiency leads to anemia, which results in a feeling of tiredness and sluggishness and reduces energy and motivation. Life expectancy among chronically malnourished people is in the forties, while well-nourished people can expect to live on average into their seventies. Naturally, chronic malnutrition is most damaging to young children and pregnant women. Young children are most likely to die or to become brain damaged from malnutrition.

Undernourishment: A Lack of Sufficient Calories

While malnutrition refers to the quality of a diet, undernutrition refers to the quantity. Undernourishment is a condition in which the quantity of food is inadequate. In recent years we North Americans have become very weight conscious. We fret about eating too many calories. We tend to forget that calories provide needed heat and energy for the human body. The undernourished of the world lack a diet that meets minimum caloric requirements. As a result, their bodies must feed on their own tissues. Here is a description of the physical results of undernutrition:

> When food intake drops below energy expenditure, the body must draw upon its own tissues for energy. When this energy drain continues too long, the person starves. The body burns up its own fats, muscles and tissues; kidneys, liver, and endocrine systems often cease to function properly; blood pressure and pulse fall drastically; edema [swelling from excess fluid] usually happens, skin acquires the consistency of paper; . . . hair grows on the forearms and backs of children; lassitude and confusion set in so that starvation victims often seem unaware of their plight . . . and the body's immunological defenses drop. . . . Once more than 40 percent of the body weight is lost, death is virtually inevitable.

—Medard Gabel, "Ho-Ping: Food for Everyone," *World Hunger: Learning to Meet the Challenge.* New York: Impact on Hunger, pages 15–16.

chronic malnutrition

constant illness caused by lack of proper amount of vitamins and nutrients

Do Natural Disasters Cause Hunger?

All famines are complicated by politics; no famine this century has occurred in a democracy.

—Steven N. Krentel of World Vision

drought

a long period with no rain

famine

a long period with little or no food

When we see images of starving people on television or in newspapers, chances are that there is a backdrop of wasted land where neither crops nor livestock could survive. Once fertile ground has been reduced to a desert. Do **droughts**, **famines**, and floods cause the conditions leading to hunger?

In fact, for most of its history, drought and flooding have plagued humanity. However, these natural occurrences need not lead to large-scale human suffering and death. Social systems can usually meet the challenges of nature. An example of organizing society to work with nature comes from the Bible. When Joseph is in Egypt, he advises the pharaoh to store up grain during the seven years of plenty to meet the needs of the seven years of drought (Genesis 41:28–36). Invariably, where modern famines have occurred, political and social conditions have contributed significantly to the problem. Famine is more often a by-product of war, social upheaval, and other human activity than it is of nature. ◆

◆ Research Ethiopia, Ireland, or another country or part of the world that has experienced famine. Find out what factors led to the famine. To what degree were causes environmental? Did politics play a role in the problem? How did the international community respond to the crisis? Report on your findings.

Why Are So Many People Hungry?

Imagine ten children at a table dividing up food. The three healthiest fill their plates with large portions, including most of the meat, fish, milk and eggs. They eat what they want and discard the leftovers. Five other children get just enough to meet their basic requirements. The remaining two are left wanting. One of them manages to stave off the feeling of hunger by reducing physical and mental output, though she is sickly, nervous and apathetic. The other dies from a virus which he is too weak to ward off.

Well-fed with leftovers–30%

Basic needs are met–50%

Sickly, nervous, and apathetic–10%

Die of hunger–10%

—Arthur Simon, *Bread for the World*, Mahwah, NJ: Paulist Press, 1984, page 18.

This bleak picture leads to the question, "Why are people in our world chronically malnourished and undernourished?" The answer is simple: People are hungry because they are poor. For example, peasants working on lush plantations can be too poor to feed their families what they themselves are helping to harvest. Some countries with severe hunger problems export food to other nations because they need the revenue that these exports bring. And keep in mind that hunger-related problems continue to exist even in rich countries, such as the United States.

Review

1. Name two ways that international agencies measure poverty.
2. Where do the majority of the poor people of the world live?
3. What does it mean to say that some countries are poor?
4. Name the two conditions which are the result of serious hunger and explain the difference between the two.
5. Do natural disasters such as droughts and floods cause hunger? Explain your answer.
6. What is the primary reason why people are hungry?

Discuss

A. If you were in charge of an ad campaign designed to address the problem of world hunger, what slogan would you use? Who would your audience be for this ad campaign? What would be the rationale for using your slogan?

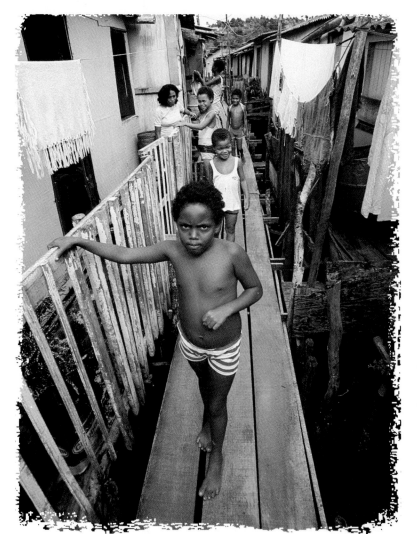

Four Characteristics of Poor Countries

Death, ill health, and being deprived of material things due to poverty are common in poor countries. While each poor country has its own identity and set of problems, most of these countries share a common mix of identifiable characteristics. Knowing common features generally present in poor countries can help us seek solutions to the problem of global poverty.

1. A Colonial Past

Many of today's LDCs [Less Developed Countries] had a long past history as colonies of a major political power. This is especially true of the LDCs in Africa. At the end of World War II, there were only two independent countries in all of Africa, and even in 1957, there were only four . . . In 1957, the former British colony Gold Coast became the nation of Ghana, and in the years since then, 33 other nations in Africa became independent.

—Carl Kreider, *The Rich and the Poor*,
Scottdale, PA: Herald Press, page 37.

A colonial past does not automatically condemn a country to poverty. Hong Kong, Canada, and the United States have fared quite well as former colonies of England—in many ways taking on the characteristics of the empire in the global marketplace. Through colonization many of the cultural refinements and scientific advancements of Europe were brought to the Americas. Nonetheless, to understand poverty as it exists today, it is necessary to step back a few hundred years, and in some cases only a few decades, to note the negative impact colonialism can sometimes have.

Colonialism, as explained in chapter 3, refers to the movement of certain countries, often European, to control other countries by force. One reason to conquer other territories was to benefit the homeland, using colonies to provide natural resources, markets, or in some cases cheap labor. Cities, transportation systems, agriculture, and industry were established to promote commerce with the homeland. Even today, most poor countries trade exclusively with wealthy countries rather than with one another. As a result, they remain **economic colonies.**

economic colonies

poorer countries dependent upon a few wealthy countries to purchase their limited selection of crops or products

High-minded colonialists might claim that colonialism was also good for conquered lands—bringing them the benefits of European civilization, Christianity, and development. However, the bottom line remained how this venture into a foreign land would help the political aims, business interests, and citizens of the controlling country. A side effect of colonialism was that people who were colonized had their language, culture, and identity relegated to secondary status. As you can imagine, the effects of colonialism outlived actual colonial periods.

One Story of a Former Colony's Fall into Poverty

If we . . . tried to imagine what an underdeveloped area looks like, we would probably conjure up a town like Potosí, Bolivia. At an altitude of 15,000 feet above sea level, Potosí is difficult to reach. The roads leading to it are bad. The native Indian people who live there squeeze out a skimpy living from the poor soil. The only other major source of employment is a tin mine in the mountain which overlooks the town. Housing is poor, and running water and electricity are a luxury in the area. . . .

However . . . in the 1600s, in the heyday of Potosí, they say that even the horses were shod with silver. At the height of its boom, the town had a population equal to that of London and larger than that of European centres like Madrid, Rome, or Paris. Potosí attracted silks and fabrics from Canada and Flanders, the latest fashions from Paris and London, diamonds from India, crystal from Venice, and perfumes from Arabia. Something really valuable in the 17th century was referred to commonly as being "worth a Potosi."

. . . The entire economic and social life of Potosí was based on wealth from a single commodity—silver. This silver was mined by the native Indian population and shipped directly to Spain. Potosí silver financed, in large measure, the development of the Spanish empire in the 17th century. . . . The underdevelopment of Potosí, then, began with the abuse of its people and resources through the European colonial system. The Latin American economy was geared by the Europeans to meet their own needs, not those of the local people . . .

—Development Education Centre, "Development and Underdevelopment," in Development Education Viewpoint #1, Toronto: Development Education Centre, 1975.

- Write a journal entry pretending to be a citizen of a nation that is a colony of another country. Describe what you think your life would be like. What feelings might you have? What hopes and fears would you expect to have?

2. Population Growth

Poor countries have higher rates of population growth. Numerous reasons account for this trend. An important point to keep in mind, however, is that as people become wealthier and more economically secure, they tend to have fewer children. When people face poverty conditions, they often depend on many births to help ensure that at least some children survive to adulthood. Children increase possibilities for income, add to a family's support system, and provide for parents when they are old. Therefore, large population growth *results* from poverty rather than *causes* poverty. ◆

Is There Too Little Food, Land, and Water for the World's Population?

Population growth in poor countries raises the question of the earth's ability to feed its population. Most experts agree with the following assessment:

> *If the present world food production were evenly divided among all the world's people, with minimal waste, everyone would have enough. Barely enough, perhaps, but enough.*
>
> —Arthur Simon, *Bread for the World, Mahwah, NJ:* Paulist Press, page 18.

This viewpoint is hopeful but not encouraging. Food cannot be evenly divided, and waste occurs in large proportions. So we can say, "Yes, there is enough food in the world." At the same time it is important to accept that *scarcity of food* is a major problem.

Landowners in both poor and wealthier nations who own large plots of land are more likely to use their land as an investment for cash crops or leave land unplanted and accept a subsidy from the government for doing so than are farmers who own smaller plots of land. Because much of the land in poorer nations is owned by investment landowners, much of the cultivated land in poor countries is now given over to **cash crop** rather than to **food crop** production.

If enough food does exist to feed everyone in the world, then the problem of hunger is one of *distribution* more than production. That makes world hunger a moral problem more than a technological one—that is, a problem of justice. The *material* problem of hunger most strongly affects people in poor countries; the *moral* problem of hunger must be dealt with by people in wealthy nations.

We do possess the ability to feed everyone. However, this would require *a change in priorities* by the world's population. People would have to be considered first over

cash crops

crops grown to be exported in order to raise money

food crops

crops grown to feed the people within a country

◆ Place yourself in the situation of a peasant living in a poor country. What arguments, pro and con, would you consider in deciding whether or not to have another child? Think about factors such as child mortality rates, income level, and availability of government support for people within poor countries. Are there societal changes that could happen that would affect your decision? What would your final decision be?

profits and politics, some change in eating habits would be required, and a definite change in how we view one another would have to take place. On a practical level, food scarcity calls for increased food production, a reduction in waste, and attention to methods of food consumption. It also calls for a settlement of political differences and an end to governmental corruption that stands in the way of distributing food to those who need it most.

Actually, *scarcity of water* may cause more problems worldwide than scarcity of land. Water is used for drinking, cooking, bathing, and crop irrigation—and is essential in holding off hunger and diseases. For many people in poor countries, finding drinkable water is a daily struggle. Sometimes the solution to scarcity of water is as straightforward as digging a well, installing a community water tap, or devising a simple irrigation system. These and more elaborate ventures require planning and community cooperation. They also require money, which poor countries do not have.

> One of the greatest injustices in the contemporary world consists precisely in this: that the ones who possess much are relatively few and those who possess almost nothing are many. It is the injustice of the poor distribution of the goods and services originally intended for all.
>
> —John Paul II, *On Social Concern*, number 50.

3. Multinational Corporations and Single Export Economies

As someone living in a comparatively wealthy country, you know that there exists a great demand for products available only from poorer countries and for products that can be manufactured inexpensively by using poorly paid workers. Therefore, poor countries are under great pressure to rely on one or on a few products as their primary source of income. These products are meant to be exported and not to be used locally.

single export economies

budgets based on one product as the main source of income

Countries which rely heavily on exporting only one product—**single export economies**—or a few products, for example, coffee or bananas, occupy an unstable position within the global economy. If a fruit company does not find a favorable situation in one country or from its workers, then the company can easily threaten to harvest bananas in a neighboring country. When demand for a particular item goes down, a country dependent upon one export has no other resources to help it weather the accompanying financial downfall. Strapped with debt and overrun with citizens desperate for employment of any kind, the country is in no position to hold out for justice for its workers.

multinational corporations

companies that operate in a number of countries

For one, **multinational corporations** benefit from this arrangement. Multinational corporations possess assets in many countries. Sometimes their budgets exceed the whole budgets of the countries in which they are located. The directors of such corporations are expected to make money for company stockholders. Keeping labor costs down is one way of increasing profits. Countries where the standard of living is low to begin with provide a labor pool of workers who have little choice but to work for whatever wages are offered them.

Sometimes both a company and a country and its people benefit from a multinational corporation's business ventures. However, the livelihoods of peasants are often displaced, leaving them to abandon the way of life that had sustained them for centuries. In this case a company and a few well-placed local citizens benefit at the expense of cheap labor provided by poor people whose wages will not raise them and their families out of poverty and hunger. ◆

4. The Social and Political Climate in Poor Countries: Gross Inequality

Not everyone in poor countries is destitute. Poor countries often have a small minority who, along with foreign companies, control practically all of the wealth in the country. They may live in great luxury, with servants and Swiss bank accounts, even though they are surrounded by great poverty. This huge gap between the wealthy few and everyone else leads to a situation such as exists in the town of Cuernavaca, Mexico. Most of the town resembles a typical poor village with one-room dwellings crowded together on dusty streets. But if you travel down one narrow street you come upon a compound surrounded by high and thick walls. Behind these walls is a plush, five-star hotel, complete with an enclosed garden where guests are served cocktails and gourmet snacks by tuxedoed waiters.

The great inequality between rich and poor in such countries raises questions about how best to help those who truly need it. The fact that a country reports an increase in its Gross National Product does not mean that poor people are benefiting.

◆ If you were the head of a company, would you locate its production facility wherever costs were least expensive? Weigh pros and cons involved in this decision and explain your decision to stockholders of your company.

Sometimes it can mean simply that the rich get richer. However, it would be unfortunate if the gross inequality and corruption in poor countries would serve as an excuse not to seek ways to diminish the tremendous suffering that is the common lot there. ◆

Again partially a legacy of a colonial past, poor countries traditionally tended to be **oligarchies.** Political power might shift from one faction to another within this elite, and leadership might at times be more dictatorial or more democratic. However, faced with extensive problems, governments in poor countries seldom have a history of stability and often lack wide or deep-seated popular support. In this situation, a country's military takes on the role of policing its own citizens rather than protecting the country from external threats; and international businesses wield a great deal of power since they hold out the promise of wealth at least for a few.

oligarchies

countries ruled by a few members of an elite group clearly distinct from the masses of people who make up the rest of the population

◆ Rank the following from highest to lowest in terms of their impact on global poverty. Explain your rankings and what role each group listed could play in solving global poverty.

- international businesses
- international agencies (for example, the United Nations and the World Bank)
- wealthy countries
- the governments of poor countries
- societal and structural problems in poor countries
- actions of poor people

Gross National Product

a measure of the overall wealth of a country

A burden of foreign debt plagues most poor countries. International agencies exist that grant loans to countries to aid in their development. Often the welfare of poor citizens is not a primary concern when agricultural or industrial programs are initiated. Rather, the belief prevails that increasing the **Gross National Product** will somehow benefit everyone in the country. Given the governmental instability that exists in many poor countries, sometimes the leaders who actually received the loans are no longer in power. Sometimes the projects for which they received money are never built, and no one can account for what happened to the money. Often, the real groups who profit are international corporations whose primary concern is *not* raising workers' salaries to the level that exists in wealthier countries. Meanwhile, the needs of poor people are often neglected as governments of poor countries try to establish a place in the global marketplace.

In safe and healthy societies, a set of institutions exists to support social well-being—a standard currency, health care facilities, schools, banks, and law enforcement. In poor countries people carve out a support system in families and local communities as best they can since wider institutions are seldom stable enough to be counted on for long-lasting support.

Review

7. Describe a situation where colonialism existed.
8. What are *economic colonies*?
9. Besides political and economic enslavement, what side effects resulted from colonialism?
10. What is the relationship between poverty and population growth?
11. What does it mean to say that hunger is more a problem of distribution than of production?
12. Explain the difference between *cash crops* and *food crops*.
13. What does it mean to say that a country has a *single export economy*?
14. What is a *multinational corporation*?
15. What does it mean to say that poor countries usually exhibit gross inequality?
16. Define *oligarchy*.
17. Why is increasing a country's Gross National Product not necessarily a way to help its citizens who are poor?
18. What do people in poor countries typically use as their support system?

Discuss

B. Would you refuse to work for a company that explicitly exploits cheap labor, such as employing children to work in factories? Why or why not?
C. If you discovered that one of your favorite products was manufactured using exploited labor, would you discontinue buying that product? Why or why not? Explain.
D. If you were on the board of an international agency that oversees loans from wealthier countries to poor countries, would you petition that debts owed by poor countries be canceled? Why or why not?
E. If you were part of an international task force on poverty, what programs, policies, and legislative action would you recommend?

Global Poverty in Christian Perspective

As chapter two points out, Scripture makes it clear that poor people hold a special place in God's heart. Mary, the mother of Jesus, refers to herself as a poor servant girl. Her song of praise at the beginning of Luke's Gospel could be sung by Maria, the Honduran peasant girl whose story begins this chapter:

For he has looked with favor on the lowliness of his servant.
Surely, from now on all generations will call me blessed. . . .
He has brought down the powerful from their thrones,
and lifted up the lowly;
he has filled the hungry with good things,
and sent the rich away empty.

—Luke 1:48, 52–53

Interestingly, throughout Latin America, stories are told of Mary appearing to poor people to offer a message of hope. The most famous of these, the appearance of Our Lady of Guadalupe, occurred in Mexico in 1531. In this story Mary appeared to an Indian peasant named Juan Diego. Mary appeared as an Indian princess on a hill that had been a shrine dedicated to an Aztec goddess. Our Lady of Guadalupe is a symbol of hope to the poor people of Mexico.

Jesus, the Bread of Life

Anyone who has ever visited a Jewish delicatessen or attended a seder meal in a Jewish home knows the importance of food in the Jewish tradition. In that regard Jesus was very much a product of his Jewish culture. Clearly, Jesus appreciated the importance of food and of "breaking bread together" as an essential human experience. The reality of so many starving people in the world is a great sin. Not sharing food with people in need is unchristian to the core. Study the following chart to see a few of the references to food made in the Bible.

A Heavenly Feast

Isaiah 25:6	Heaven itself is described as "a feast of rich food, a feast of well-aged wines."
John 2:1–11	Jesus' first public miracle took place at a wedding feast.
John 6:1–13	Jesus' most famous miracle involved feeding bread and fish to the crowds that had begun to follow him.
Luke 14:7–24	Jesus compared his kingdom to a banquet.
Luke 8:41–42; 49–55	When he brought Jairus' daughter back to life, Jesus immediately told her parents to give her something to eat.
Matthew 26:26	Before his death, Jesus shared a meal with his apostles.
Luke 24:13–35	After Jesus was raised from the dead, he appeared to the disciples on the road to Emmaus where he shared bread with them.
Luke 24:41	Jesus appeared to the eleven apostles, asking them, "Have you anything here to eat?"
John 21:5	Jesus stood on the shore and asked the apostles who had been fishing, "Children, you have no fish, have you?"
John 21:12	Jesus invited the apostles, "Come and have breakfast."

Eucharist: Challenge to Hunger

In the Catholic tradition the Eucharist is celebrated daily. It celebrates Christ's presence in the universal human experience of sharing food and drink. Whenever Catholics want to celebrate something—a birth, a marriage, or the beginning of a school year—the Mass is usually a central part of the celebration. Like every meal the Eucharist is both personal and communal. It is both a physical and a spiritual experience. If entered into properly it reminds us not only of our own need for nourishment and refreshment but also of the common human need for food and drink. In the Eucharist we celebrate our communion with Christ who nourishes us and who cries out for food in the hungry of the world. In other words the Eucharist is both celebration and challenge. Just as in the life of Jesus himself, the two cannot be separated. ◆

Today's Church and Global Poverty

We cannot segregate God's word from the historical reality in which it is proclaimed. That would not be God's word. The Bible would be just a pious history book in our library. It is God's word because it enlightens, contrasts, repudiates, and praises what is going on today in this society.

—Archbishop Oscar Romero

◆ Prepare and give a speech saying what you think Jesus would say to the world today about how we deal with hunger. Decide who your audience would be.

Modern Church documents make it clear that God is a God of the poor. Throughout the world, Church leaders have attempted to apply to their particular setting Jesus' message of Good News to poor people. One area that has been particularly troubled with poverty is northern Brazil. The bishops of that region describe the living conditions that they deplore and a vision of how they would like to see their world:

> We want to see a world in which the fruits of work will belong to all. We want to see a world in which people will work, not in order to get rich, but in order that all should possess the necessities of life: enough to eat for their health, a house, education, clothes, shoes, water, and light. We want to see a world in which money is placed at the service of human beings and not human beings at the service of money. We want to see a world in which all will be able to work for all, not a divided world in which all persons work only for themselves. Therefore, we want to see a world in which there will be only one people with no division between rich and poor.

> —Richard Shaull, "The Marginalization of a People," in *Heralds of a New Reformation*, Maryknoll, NY: Orbis Books, 1984, page 102.

In recent decades Church leaders have often played the prophet's role, affirming that hunger and need should not exist and deploring that everything possible is not being done to eliminate these ills:

> While so many people are going hungry, while so many families are suffering poverty, while so many people live their lives in ignorance, while so many schools, hospitals, homes worthy of the name, are needed, every wasteful spending of money by nations or individuals becomes unbearable and unacceptable. ◆

> —see Pope Paul VI, *On Promoting the Development of Peoples*, number 53.

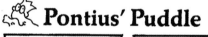

Pontius' Puddle

◆ In the early 1970s the problem of hunger received a great deal of attention. The U.S. bishops at the time recommended three lifestyle changes as ways to help ease hunger. Rate yourself on each of these recommendations.

- responsible consumption (minimizing waste of food and energy, cutting back on buying)
- weekly days of fast and abstinence (cutting back on the amount we eat, especially on the amount of meat eaten)
- involvement in easing hunger locally

Liberation Theology: The Gospel Through the Eyes of the Poor

theologians

scholars of religion

liberation theology

belief that the gospel message addresses today's social concerns, especially those of people who are poor

Latin America is one of those areas of the globe where the great majority of people are extremely poor. Traditionally, it has also been overwhelmingly Catholic. Prior to the late 1960s, the Church sided more with the wealthy few who held power in Latin American countries. For the most part Church leaders believed that if they could help educate and inspire good Christian leaders, then everyone—including poor people—would benefit.

However, when Latin American bishops gathered in 1968, they were challenged by some of their **theologians** to take a different approach to common problems. Namely, the theologians asked: What would it be like to read the Gospels through the eyes of the poor? This simple but challenging question led to the beginning of a movement that has challenged religious thought ever since—**liberation theology**.

Liberation theologians noticed that poor people in their midst were dying before their time, that they spent lives filled with hardship and suffering, and that certain elements within the social order contributed to their problems. In response to this situation, liberation theology proposes that the gospel message should not just offer hope for salvation after death but should also challenge people to make the world we live in a better place for everyone, especially for poor people. The gospel, then, challenges people to work for liberation—for social changes that make the lot of poor people better. Liberation theology suggests a different starting point for doing theology. It seeks to "theologize" *with* poor people, not *for* them. If it is true to Jesus and Scripture, then theology must combine *reflection* on the Gospels with *action* initiated by and on behalf of poor people. As you might have noticed, this message reflects the social action approach to justice described in chapter 4 of this book.

Review

19. Who is Our Lady of Guadalupe?
20. What does it mean to say that Jesus' appreciation of food demonstrates that he was a product of his Jewish culture?
21. In what sense is the Eucharist a challenge to world hunger?
22. How have recent Church leaders played the prophetic role regarding world hunger?
23. How did South American bishops and liberation theology change the approach of the Latin American Church toward solving problems?

Discuss

F. Have you ever experienced a meal that you might call a holy event? If so, explain what made it so special.
G. If you were a bishop, a priest, or someone else concerned about justice, how would you measure out your time with business and government leaders and with poor people? How would you start a justice program in terms of involvement with poor people as well as community leaders?

Responding to Poverty: Has the World Adopted a Policy of *Triage* toward Poor People?

An old movie portrays a lifeboat built for only eight people bearing twelve passengers. If all twelve remain aboard, the lifeboat is in danger of sinking. What should be done?

Some writers suggest that our earth is like that lifeboat. We have to make choices: either some people must be left to die or else the entire boat will capsize. A model called *triage* has been proposed as a way of deciding who will receive food from the earth's limited resources. **Triage**, a system first employed by the French during World War I, places wounded soldiers into three groups: First, those who can survive with little or no attention; second, those who can survive but need immediate attention, and lastly, those who can survive only with intensive treatment. Under triage the third group is left untreated until the first and second groups are cared for. Of course, during the wait they might die.

Applying the triage model to the hungry of the world implies that some people should simply be left to die. Those who

support this model suggest that when we try to help the hungry, all we succeed in doing is creating an even greater strain on the earth's limited resources. So, they reason, people suffering from chronic malnutrition should not be helped because too many people means not enough food for everyone. Of course, the Church condemns and rejects triage and attitudes that support it. All humans are worthy of preservation and love because of their human dignity as images of God redeemed by Christ.

triage

the practice of placing people into one of three groups based on their likelihood of survival and treating first the two groups most likely to survive

Changing Attitudes: Declaring War on Poverty and Hunger

Do you believe in miracles? Chapter 6 of John's Gospel tells of Jesus' feeding five thousand people with the bread and fish carried by one small boy. That is quite a miracle. To feed the hungry of the world requires an equally impressive miracle today.

During much of World War II, certain products were measured out and difficult to obtain in the United States. For the most part citizens did not mind. They knew that the soldiers had to be given first choice of products. So they learned to waste less and to stretch their resources. They also began again the practice of growing their own food in "victory gardens." People saved even small things such as aluminum gum wrappers so that these items could be put to service in the war effort. If sacrifices could quicken the war's end, people at that time were willing to bear them.

Wars cause a great deal of suffering, death, and destruction, but so does hunger. Catholic Relief Services reports that "every year 20 million people suffer hunger-related deaths and millions more experience the irreversible effects of childhood malnutrition: permanently impaired mental and physical development and diminished work performance." This means that on an annual basis, hunger is a greater killer than World War II, in which 17 million soldiers died worldwide. If drastic measures were called for during that war, then equally drastic measures are called for in our current war against hunger. ◆

Overconsumption in Rich Countries and Poverty in Poor Countries Are Related

"Don't waste that food—think of the starving children in China!" In the recent past parents used this stock response to coax their children into finishing their vegetables. The idea is still worth considering: Does our waste help to cause hunger elsewhere? Does overconsumption in wealthier countries contribute to the poverty that is widespread in poorer countries? If the well-fed were to change their eating habits and adjust their lifestyles, would these changes benefit the world's hungry?

Patterns of consumption do have an impact on the world's food supply. For example, grain can be used either to make alcohol, to feed cattle, or to be eaten directly. However, to make a difference, avoiding waste and overconsumption must be combined with societal changes and political action. Here's a simple example of how societal change can benefit poor countries:

> *If high school students throughout the United States decided to fast for a day and contribute money saved to help poor people, they could raise thousands of dollars. However, if they combined their sacrifice with efforts to influence government and business policies to benefit workers in poor countries, their impact would be many times greater. For instance, an increase of only one cent per pound in the price of raw coffee translates into more than sixty-five million dollars a year increased revenue for coffee-exporting countries.*

◆ If you declared a personal "war on hunger," what might you do differently? Make a list of specific changes you might make or specific activities you might undertake. Include possible steps leading to societal change or changes in governmental policies.

Military Spending: Guns or Food?

No discussion of hunger would be complete without mention of military spending. We are discovering more and more that the world is made up of limited resources. Choices must be made. Unfortunately, most countries choose guns over food. For instance, in many poor countries food storage is a major problem. The cost of a modern tank could be used instead to build modern storage facilities for rice, saving over four thousand tons of rice annually. Every minute, thirty children die of starvation or from lack of medications. In the same time the world's governments spend over a million dollars on the military. In fact, one-half of one percent of what the world's militaries spend in one year would pay for all the farm equipment needed for poor countries, so that within ten years the people within these countries could raise enough food to adequately feed their people.

Hunger kills as certainly as war does. Money and energy for weapons production have been bought at the expense of food production and distribution. The ability to overkill the human population has been won at the price of underfeeding millions of people.

International and National Development

International trade and aid agreements are sometimes designed to help wealthy nations either directly or indirectly, often placing profit over people. A famous example occurred in 1972 when a major food crisis hit the world. The United States, which produces over half of the world's grain supply, cut back its grain production to raise the price of wheat and then sold large quantities to the USSR. Meanwhile, great numbers of people in Bangladesh and other places were dying of starvation.

Poor countries require a stronger voice in the international arena if their concerns are to be taken into account by other countries and by important decision-making bodies. Interestingly, leaders in poor countries often call for *trade*, not *aid*, as the best way to help their people. In categories described earlier in this course, trade—greater power on the international marketplace—offers more of a long-term solution to poverty than charity does. Of course, changing rules of international trade to better favor poor countries can lead to loss of control among wealthy countries who now hold "power over" poor countries in trade.

Nationally, development in poor countries must reflect the needs, strengths, and particular characteristics of specific areas involved. In particular, imitating wealthy and highly industrialized countries is not always helpful. For example:

- *Mexico City has an efficient, inexpensive, and greatly used subway system. The United States, in contrast, has made a greater commitment to private transportation than to public transportation. If Mexico City, with its large population, were to imitate the U.S. in its emphasis on private transportation, the results would be disastrous.*

- *In farming, bigger is not always better. Large-scale farming is usually **energy-intensive**. On the other hand, small-scale farming is usually **labor intensive**. The Green Revolution demonstrated the pros and cons of energy-intensive farming. Begun in Mexico, this development project gained worldwide publicity in the 1960s by introducing high-yield strains of wheat and rice. Unfortunately, it also caused unemployment among the rural labor force since their work was no longer needed. Because this energy-intensive method relied heavily on machinery, fertilizer, and other products, the project was best suited to larger farms. As a result, many of the unemployed farmworkers migrated to already overcrowded cities.*

energy-intensive

large-scale farming that depends more on heavy machinery, chemical fertilizers, irrigation systems, and pesticides than on people

labor-intensive

small-scale farming that depends more on people than on machines to do the farm work

Why Help Poor People?

When asked "Why do you help them?", a priest involved in finding housing and work for immigrants who entered the U.S. illegally simply answered: "Because they're here." We face a similar question when we admit the presence of so many people who are poor around the globe: "Why help them?"

On a purely selfish level, the world—our world—becomes a better place when it is populated with people who are not starving, poorly educated, physically deprived, or desperate. The world would be a safer, friendlier, healthier, more beautiful world all around. Only hope-filled people, especially when hope is shared, possess the faith, character, courage, and motivation needed to make a better world for everyone.

On a more idealistic level, the Christian vision offers a view of a world as made up of family—sisters and brothers inseparably bound together as children of one God. As you probably know from your own experience, the family unit hurts whenever any of its members are hurting. Not just Christianity, all the world's great religions call for compassion and caring. Perhaps there's something to their idealistic message.

In the end, the most forceful and also the most profound reason why those who are able should help people who are poor might simply be: "Because they're there." That is, they are our sisters and brothers. They are in need. Do we who are able help them in whatever way we can?

Review

24. Explain the "triage" approach to world hunger.
25. Name two ways that the actions of U.S. citizens during World War II could be applied to a war on hunger.
26. Name three societal changes that could assist poor countries.
27. Give an example of how a societal change can help a poor country.
28. What does it mean to say that the nations of the world must choose between guns or food?
29. How did the U.S. respond to the 1972 world food crisis?
30. Explain the difference between energy-intensive and labor-intensive farming.
31. What was the Green Revolution? What negative side effect accompanied it?

Discuss

H. If your school sponsored a World Food Day event that included the option of skipping lunch and contributing lunch money to an anti-hunger organization, would you participate? Why or why not?
I. Would you support a trade agreement that would benefit workers in poor countries but that would raise the price of consumer items in your country?
J. Discuss the pros and cons of the following statement: "The United States should take the lead in fighting hunger by cutting back military spending even more than we have and contributing the difference to world food programs." Would you sign a petition bearing this statement? Why or why not? Make a case based on Catholic teaching on justice.

In Summary: Poverty and Hunger Can Be Eliminated

The next time that you gather together with your family or with friends to enjoy a meal, recall that many people struggle to provide meals for their families. Let that thought lead you to consider that many people, through their participation in a variety of organizations, are seeking to make a difference, and that you, too, can make a difference. If the Christian message has any meaning, then the suffering of poor people must be recognized as a problem for everyone. Steps taken to eliminate poverty and hunger are essential steps on the Christian's journey.

Before we conclude . . .

Let us pray . . .

Mary's Song of Praise—the *Magnificat*

My soul magnifies the Lord,

and my spirit rejoices in God my Savior,

for he has looked with favor on the lowliness of this servant.

Surely, from now on all generations will call me blessed;

for the Mighty One has done great things for me,

and holy is his name.

His mercy is for those who fear him

from generation to generation.

He has shown strength with his arm;

he has scattered the proud in the thoughts of their hearts.

He has brought down the powerful from their thrones,

and lifted up the lowly;

he has filled the hungry with good things,

and sent the rich away empty.

He has helped his servant Israel,

in remembrance of his mercy,

according to the promise he made to our ancestors,

to Abraham and to his descendants forever.

—Luke 1:46–55

For further study . . .

1. Using the Internet, an almanac, or other reference sources, find out the Gross National Product, life expectancy, and other measures of wealth and health for various countries. Which are the richest countries? The poorest? Besides standard of living, what distinguishes the wealthiest from the poorest countries? In particular, research and compare the countries of Chile and Mexico to find why one is more productive and financially sound than the other.

2. Morality has to do with right and wrong, with what people ought to do. What does the following statement mean: "Hunger is more a moral problem than a technological one"? Give specific examples to illustrate this point. Do you agree with the statement? If so, how do you address the hunger of people in poor countries as a moral problem for you? Explain.

3. Compose a prayer, poem, or work of art that would reflect the struggles, fears, and hopes of a poor person.

4. As a sacrament, the Eucharist stands for hospitality to strangers, sharing of goods, and communion of all people. Write an essay entitled "The Eucharist: Challenge to World Hunger." As preparation, you might attend a Mass when you are particularly hungry or try to view its meaning through the eyes of someone who lives with hunger every day.

5. Find out as many names as possible of people or organizations, either local, national, or international, private, public, or church-related, committed to addressing poverty and hunger. Choose one or two organizations and, by reading their literature or speaking to a representative, report on how they seek to solve problems. As part of your report, indicate whether their approach appears to follow more a charity or social action model. Would you consider becoming involved in one of these organizations? Why or why not?

   - The Campaign for Human Development, sponsored by the U.S. Catholic bishops, sets as its goal supporting projects specifically under the leadership of poor people themselves.
   - Operation Rice Bowl links traditional Lenten fasting with raising funds to help anti-hunger programs.
   - Share Our Strength is an organization based on the belief that people are more likely to donate their personal services than impersonal money in the fight against hunger. Writers contribute stories to collections whose proceeds go to anti-hunger programs. Chefs volunteer their time and talent to fund-raising ventures.
   - For years actor Paul Newman had given homemade salad dressing as Christmas gifts. He decided to market his salad dressing. When it became popular, he began a food company, Newman's Own, all the proceeds of which are donated to anti-poverty projects.
   - A number of musicians donate concert time to raising funds or to alerting their listeners to hunger issues.

6. Write up your own answer to the question: Why help poor people? If you don't believe non-poor people should help those who are poor, explain your reasoning. Analyze whether or not your reasoning parallels the Christian vision of justice.

7. Looking back on the material presented in this chapter, how would you answer the following questions:

   - What are the key factors that lead to global poverty and hunger?
   - What are the most effective ways to ease global poverty and hunger?
   - What are specific steps that you could take to address the problem of global poverty and hunger?

CHAPTER 7

Sexual Identity

Women and Men Created in God's Image

Differences need not result in injustice. However, differences among people, such as differences between the sexes, have led to injustices. Sexism is a term for the oppression experienced by people because of discriminatory attitudes and practices based on their gender. Both women and men have suffered and continue to suffer because of sexism. However, as we will see in this chapter, women have been particularly burdened by this.

Major Concepts

A. Sexual Discrimination: A Matter of Justice

Two signs of sexism
- Feminization of poverty
- Power and wage gaps

B. Sexism and Christianity: A Compassionate Community Is a Community of Equals

- Jesus' attitude toward discrimination against women
- The early Church's vision of women
- Today's Church and treatment of women

C. Responding to Sexism: Changing Attitudes, Changing Social Structures

- Overcoming sexism
- Equal opportunities for both sexes

Opening Prayer

Loving God, in your very being you are a God in relationship, manifested as Father, Son, and Spirit. As we gaze at your people, we pray that we may see them as you do. Therefore, we pray that we may celebrate differences and avoid discrimination, foster freedom, and avoid hurting one another. May the world be transformed into a place where being a man and being a woman are valued equally. Amen.

Before we begin . . .

Answer **agree**, **disagree**, or **uncertain** to the following statements. Choose statements that you believe are most significant and explain your answers.

1. In today's world, girls being sold into prostitution, mutilation of women prior to marriage, and wife burning no longer occur.

2. Men are as likely as women to be poor.

3. In relationships men are as likely as women to suffer psychological or physical abuse.

4. Women and men no longer have different roles.

5. Women and girls are now as free as men and boys to ask someone out for a date or to propose marriage.

6. Typically, schools give priority to boys' sports over girls' sports.

7. In co-ed high schools girls tend to be less assertive than boys in speaking up in class and in taking leadership in school activities.

Six Tales of Gender Dilemmas

■ Stephanie likes Mike. She would enjoy inviting him to go with her to a movie some Saturday night, but she fears this would frighten him off or give the impression that she is "easy." Instead, Stephanie convinces her friends to hang around with her near Mike's friends, hoping that Mike will maybe ask her out.

■ The mother of two young children, Mary has not worked outside the home for six years. Although her husband works regularly, he has always kept tight control of the family's money. For years now, Mary has hidden money from her husband so that she can buy things for the children which he considers unnecessary. Recently, Mary's husband has become abusive toward her. Her main concern is the children. If she leaves her husband, she doesn't see how she could care for them financially. She spends all of her time trying to keep peace in the house so as not to upset her husband.

■ On the morning of career day, Derrick attends the presentation on the nursing profession. He discovers that he is one of two boys along with thirty girls interested in becoming a nurse. Concerned that nursing is not considered appropriate work for a man, in the afternoon he attends the session on becoming a police officer.

■ Like her two brothers forty-year-old Joann has children of her own. Now that her father has died, Joann has taken responsibility for caring for her increasingly dependent mother. Although her older brother has a larger house and a job with more flexible hours, her mother expects Joann rather than one of her sons to arrange doctors' visits and to provide a home for her. Although it is a burden on her own family, Joann concludes that it is her responsibility as a daughter to care for her mother in this way.

■ Seung Ah was the first female regional sales representative for her company. During her first full-scale company meeting, the eight other sales reps went out for a few drinks before dinner. Seung Ah joined them, only to realize that conversation soon sank into telling crude sex jokes. When she complained that the jokes were belittling to women and making her feel uncomfortable, one of the male sales reps replied, "What's the matter? Can't you take a joke!"

■ Twice during the soccer match ten-year-old Ricardo was knocked hard to the ground, and twice Ricardo got up and continued play. Bruised, limping, and in pain, Ricardo played to the end. When the game was over, his coach told him, "You played like a real man today, Ricardo. I'm proud of you."

• Each of the above scenarios represents an example of how people can be hurt because of the way men and women are viewed and treated in our society. Write a story or poem that would illustrate for you how problems occur because of attitudes and practices related to gender differences.

Sexual Discrimination: A Matter of Justice

Men and women possess physical differences. However, what those differences *mean* has been socially constructed. That is, ideas about what it means to be a man and what it means to be a woman have been shaped, molded, and transformed over time and in response to different cultural contexts. These ideas about what it means to be a man and what it means to be a woman also create justice concerns.

In the first scenario on page 140, Stephanie hesitates to ask Mike for a date. Forty years ago, Stephanie probably would not even have *considered* asking Mike for a date. Forty years ago, Joann's decision to be a selfless caregiver for her mother also would not have been questioned; and Seung Ah quite likely would not have been hired as a regional salesperson. Even allowing Ricardo to play hurt so as to instill "manly virtues" can be viewed positively or negatively depending on the social and historical context.

What happened over the past forty years in the United States? Have men and women changed? Or have roles and expectations—what it means to be a man or a woman—changed? Addressing injustices due to sexual identity begins with examining socially constructed roles for women and for men. Here are some popular opinions about male-female differences:

- Men are more logical; women are more intuitive.
- In playing games women are more concerned about everyone getting along; men emphasize fair play and winning.
- Men are more aggressive; women are more passive.
- Men should be the head of a family; women should be the heart.
- Women are more spiritual than men.
- Men are stronger than women.
- Young girls prefer the colors pink and purple; boys are drawn to browns and blues.
- Young boys prefer playing at ball games and with war toys; girls prefer playing with dolls and cooking.
- Women prefer romance movies; men prefer action-adventure movies.
- Women prefer soap operas and hospital shows; men prefer cop shows. ◆

 If a friend of yours voiced one or all of the statements listed on this page about male-female differences, how would you answer her or him?

Sex Versus Gender and Nature Versus Nurture

In 1920 when women achieved the right to vote in the U.S., the Democratic presidential candidate at the time exclaimed, "The civilization of the world is saved. The mothers of America will stay the hand of war." He believed that women view violence differently from how men view violence. If women had their say, warfare would never again occur. Mothers would never allow their sons to march off to war and possibly lose their lives. The candidate was voicing his belief that women are different from men.

Are women and men different? That is, are they different not just physically but psychologically, intellectually, and emotionally as well? For instance, do women typically view an occasion such as a sporting event or a musical differently from how men tend to view it? Do most mothers form a bond with their children unmatched by the bond between fathers and children? If infant boys and girls were left on their own, would they develop differently? Would they end up mirroring notions about male-female differences popularly held in North American culture?

People concerned about justice for women and men generally propose that there is such a thing as "women's experience" different from "men's experience." However, they are cautious about being rigid in identifying these differences and especially in assigning roles to men and women because of these differences.

For one thing it is impossible to separate completely what women and men are by *nature,* compared to what they are by upbringing and cultural conditioning—*nurture.* Some writers on the subject use different terms to distinguish nature from nurture. That is, one's "sex" (nature)—being physically male or female—is a biological fact. On the other hand, "gender" (nurture) refers to what being a man or woman means in a particular society. In actual fact we cannot separate nature from nurture, sex from gender, people's physical make-up from the way that people's physical qualities are viewed by themselves and others.

◆ Look through magazines that depict men and women in ads or articles. Select three pictures that portray a particular view of what it means to be a man or a woman. For each, write a paragraph describing that viewpoint.

Sexism: Discrimination and Oppression Based on Gender Differences

When women's ways and women's roles are viewed as of lesser value than men's, then emphasizing differences between the sexes can lead to **sexism**. Sexist attitudes can become ingrained into the fabric of a society. These attitudes can lead to actions and behaviors that place restrictions on members of one or both sexes. Sexism, then, results when power and privilege are placed mainly in the hands of members of one sex. If viewpoints and characteristics identified with one gender are considered inferior to those of the other gender, then what counts as valuable and important favors members of one gender over the other.

sexism

discrimination or oppression based on gender

In our culture, women more than men are victimized by sexism. For instance, a recent study found that only a small percentage of women lawyers advanced to levels of power in major law firms. The study found that women lawyers were often described differently than men were. Specifically, a female lawyer would be described as having "good people skills"; a male lawyer would be praised for being "good with clients." Both statements describe the same qualities, but the wording of one description, the one applied to the male lawyer, is more likely to imply professionalism and authority than the wording used to describe the female lawyer. Similarly, some business women point out that they are called "pushy" when their male counterparts are called "assertive" for the same behaviors. In every state and in every job, there are professional women who relate stories of being treated less seriously than male co-workers. For instance, women applying for certain types of office work are more likely to be asked "Can you type?" while men are asked, "Can you use a computer?" Even studies of high schools find that it is not unusual for comments by male students to be taken more seriously than comments by female students. ◆

◆ Name generalizations typically applied to women and to men. Survey TV commercials or music videos to determine whether or not women and men are portrayed according to these traditional generalizations. Report on your findings. Then, describe what it would be like if a man played the woman's role and vice versa in the commercials or videos you reported on.

Patriarchy—When Male Power Dominates

Historians point out that in most cultures women's way of thinking and viewing things has been given a secondary status. That is, for most cultures decision-making power and determining what is considered most important rest in the hands of a select group of men. Men's activities and ways of thinking were privileged over women's. A society in which the dominant power resides in the hands of a select group of men is known as a **patriarchy**, a word which literally means "rule by the fathers." Denise Lardner Carmody describes patriarchy in this way:

patriarchy

a society in which most of the power is in the hands of men

> *Historically, most societies have been patriarchies. In most of the societies we know about, fathers have had more say than mothers, official political leaders have been men rather than women, men have predominated in religious rituals and authority. . . . They tend to push women to the margins, making them responsible only for the care of children and the home. In patriarchal societies, men tend to [seize] public affairs—politics, lucrative businesses, higher education, religious authority—to themselves.*
>
> —*Responses to 101 Questions about Feminism*, Mahwah, NJ: Paulist Press, pages 15–16.

The White Male System

> *The White Male System—and it is important to keep in mind that I am referring to a system here and not pointing a finger at specific individuals within it—controls almost every aspect of our culture. It makes our laws, runs our country, sets our salaries, and decides when and if we will go to war or remain at home. It decides what is knowledge and how it is to be taught. Like any other system, it has both positive and negative qualities.*
>
> —Anne Wilson Schaef, *Women's Reality*, New York: Harper and Row, pages 8–9.

This author equates the white male system with air pollution in that we are seldom aware of it unless it shows itself particularly strongly or unless we experience a different type of environment.

Review

1. What does it mean to say that the difference between being a man and being a woman is socially constructed?
2. What distinction do the terms *sex* and *gender* attempt to convey?
3. Define *sexism* and *patriarchy*.

Discuss

A. What does it mean for you to be a man or a woman? To what degree does your understanding of manhood or womanhood result from nature or nurture? Explain.

B. Do you believe that we live in a "White Male System"? Why or why not?

C. Would the cultural system that you would like to live in be more masculine, or more feminine, or would it be a combination? What would a cultural system be like that was built on each of these different viewpoints?

D. Looking back on your school career, do you believe that boys were treated differently from girls? Over time, did the opinions of boys come to be treated differently from those of girls? If you answer yes to either question, give a specific example to support your answer. Explain.

Sexism: A Problem for Women and for Men

We reaffirm the fundamental equality of women and men who, created in the image of God, "are called to participate in the same divine beatitude [and] . . . therefore enjoy an equal dignity" (Catechism of the Catholic Church, 1934).

—U.S. Bishops, *Strengthening the Bonds of Peace*, page 7.

Both women and men can suffer from sexism. Both women and men can be burdened with expectations and restrictions simply because of their sex. Is it "unmanly" for men but acceptable for women to show strong emotions, even to the point of crying? Are home economics classes still filled more with women students because it is assumed that women will be primarily responsible for housekeeping and child care if they marry? (Recent statistics find that currently in seventy-five percent of households wives take primary responsibility for housekeeping chores, even when both partners work outside the home.) Do men feel pressure to be aggressive in relationships with women; do women feel as though they should be more passive? In short both women and men experience pressures that can restrict their development as human persons. ◆

Signs of Sexism: The Feminization of Poverty

It must be noted that the vast majority of poor people in the United States are women and children. In 1993, 14.7 million women ages eighteen and over were officially classified as poor; these women [make up] 37.4 percent of all people living in poverty. In that same year, 15.7 million children under the age of eighteen officially lived below the poverty line; these children [make up] 40 percent of all poor people in the United States. Therefore, women and children in 1993 made up over three-quarters (77.4 percent) of all Americans living in poverty.

—Ruth Sidel, *Keeping Women and Children Last*,
New York: Viking Penguin, page 70.

The statistics above are from 1993. However, they represent what has been a trend for a number of decades now: the **feminization of poverty**. That is, women, and children dependent upon women, make up the largest percentage of people living in poverty. And when poverty increases, women and children are affected the most.

feminization of poverty
trend that results in more women and dependent children living in poverty than men

---

- Suggest ways that men might suffer from sexism and attitudes toward gender in our culture. What are ways that women are more likely to suffer from sexism and gender attitudes in our culture? Do you believe that discrimination against men is more, less, or equally serious a problem today than discrimination against women? Explain.

- Do you believe that men suffer oppression—being denied power and privileges—because they are men? Do you believe that women suffer oppression— being denied power and privileges—because they are women? Explain why there is or is not a difference in your answers to these two questions.

A number of reasons can be cited why women are more likely than men to be poor. For one, statistics indicate that women typically earn less than men for the same type of job. Secondly, types of jobs traditionally labeled "women's work" are usually lower-paying jobs, such as sales clerk, secretarial work, domestics, child care workers, janitorial workers, and non-professional nursing home workers. Thirdly, if a woman is working in a position which could lead to a better paying job, she often hits a "glass ceiling." This is a term which refers to the barriers that women face in moving up to a higher-level job often held by a man. Finally, a rising number of families are now headed by single women (divorced, widowed, separated, and unmarried). In many cases these women have been abandoned by and receive no support from husbands or the fathers of their children. In some cases the women became pregnant during high school and dropped out. These women will never catch up with others income-wise unless they can further their education. The above factors added together result in the feminization of poverty. Both in North America as well as worldwide, many more women than men live in poverty. ◆

Signs of Sexism: The Power Gap

When we look at positions of power in our communities, schools, businesses, churches, and government, we arrive at the overwhelming conclusion that men are still dominant in modern society. For example, no woman has ever been president of the United States, most cabinet members are men, and few women are senators or governors. This imbalance exists despite the fact that women in the U.S. have had the right to vote since 1920 and currently make up a majority of potential voters.

Women constitute half the world's population, perform nearly two-thirds of its work hours, receive one-tenth of the world's income and own less than one-hundredth of the world's property.
—From a 1980 UN report, in Larson and Micheels-Cyrus, *Seeds of Peace*, page 134.

◆ Why do you think traditional "women's work" is comparatively low paying? Why do you think there exists a "glass ceiling," that is, so few women staffing top-level positions in business and other professions? Search for statistics indicating whether a "glass ceiling" exists in contemporary society. If so, to what extent?

Statistics reveal a similar absence of women in key power positions in other areas of life. For instance, in education the majority of less prestigious elementary school teaching positions are held by women while the majority of university professorships are held by men. In medicine most doctors are men; most nurses are women. In business most executives are men; most office workers are women. (This does not mean that certain types of work are less important than others. Rather, it indicates that in our society positions are typically viewed differently. Nurses and elementary school teachers certainly provide services as important as doctors and university professors, but their work is not valued as much and they are not given as much power.)

The *power gap* that exists between women and men affects the way women and men view themselves and each other. If men feel under pressure to "be in charge" and women feel as though they should be weak and dependent, then abuses can result at the level of family relationships and in work situations. Also, as noted earlier, if women overall lack the power that men have, then the rich source of wisdom known as "women's experience" is overlooked or treated less seriously than men's experience in solving social problems.

The opposite of sexism, then, is building a society where there exists equality between the sexes. Given the current state of affairs, that means taking steps to improve the economic status of women. It also means seeking ways to increase the power of women by valuing the contributions they make and also giving them power to run the institutions of society whatever their professional choices. Finally, it means that "women's voices" must be heard much more forcefully to offset the condition of silence that they have been forced to endure in the public arena for so long. In other words, ending sexism requires both a shift in thinking as well as actual improvements in the conditions under which many women and men must live.

Review

4. To what recent development does the *feminization of poverty* refer?
5. List the four reasons given in the text explaining why the feminization of poverty is occurring.
6. To what does the term *glass ceiling* refer?
7. Define and give an example of the power gap between the sexes.
8. Name two ways that society could counteract the power gap between the sexes.
9. Name the four viewpoints typically associated with feminism.

Discuss

E. Although many people associate the word *feminism* with negative stereotypes, the term has come to mean advocating equality for women—economic, intellectual, social, and political. More specifically, feminism refers to the belief that women as a group have long been treated as inferior to men; that women as a group have suffered because of being placed in this inferior position; that women's inferiority is not natural but has been determined socially; that unlike in the past, women as a group should play a stronger role in shaping the present and the future.

• Are you a feminist? Explain why or why not.

Sexism and Christianity: A Compassionate Community Is a Community of Equals

Men and Women in the Bible

All during the time chronicled in the Scriptures, the culture was patriarchal. Therefore, it is not surprising to read a passage such as this one in a letter of Saint Paul:

> *Wives, be subject to your husbands as you are to the Lord. For the husband is the head of the wife just as Christ is the head of the church, the body of which he is the Savior. Just as the church is subject to Christ, so also wives ought to be, in everything, to their husbands.*
>
> —Ephesians 5:22–24

What is surprising is that this same Paul can write the following description of the Christian community:

> *There is no longer Jew or Greek, there is no longer slave or free, there is no longer male and female; for all of you are one in Christ Jesus.*
>
> —Galatians 3:28

Reading such passages in light of the culture of the time, it is expected that wives should be told to be obedient to their husbands. In the ancient Near Eastern culture, women generally had no rights as free persons. They were in fact owned by men, either their fathers or their husbands. When early Christianity declared that no distinction exists between male and female, it was similar to saying that there exists no distinction between slaves and free persons. The passage from Galatians, then, marks a major change from the common thinking of the time.

As the early church communities developed, they adopted the attitudes toward women's and men's roles present in their cultural setting. (The Church also borrowed elements of its organizational structure, many of its ceremonies, and other items from the various cultural settings in which it found itself.) Does Church as a community of equals represent a more valid Christian understanding of Church? True Christianity reflects the teaching and practice of Jesus, whose vision is described most fully in the Gospels.

Jesus and Women

> *The cultural context in which the first Christians lived and wrote tended to devalue women and the feminine. Yet in the early church's portrayal of Jesus, this perspective is never conveyed. Jesus never treats women as inferior to men. His words are filled with positive images of women and he defends their equality and full humanity many times in his ministry. The fact that this impression has been transmitted through the writings of men who shared the assumptions of their culture indicates how strong this feature was in the ministry of Jesus.*
>
> —Barbara J. MacHaffie, *Her Story: Women in Christian Tradition*, Minneapolis: Augsburg Press, pages 14–15.

When we examine Jesus' attitude toward people, an attitude portrayed in the Gospels, one feature stands out most strongly: Jesus lived the message that Paul expressed in his letter to the Galatians. That is, Jesus treated everyone he met—Jews and Gentiles, the righteous and sinners, men and women—with profound respect. For instance, in chapter 4 of John's Gospel, in the story of Jesus meeting and speaking with a Samaritan woman at a community well, Jesus broke three cultural restrictions in place at the time. For one, he spoke in public to a woman who was not his wife. Secondly, she was a Samaritan and they were typically hated by devout Jews. Thirdly, he asked her to spread the news of his message to her townspeople. In effect the Samaritan woman became the first known missionary to non-Jews. Inviting a woman to preach may not sound radical today, but at the time Jesus was proposing a radically uncustomary role for a woman.

Jesus also had both women and men friends, again contrary to common practice of the time. As a matter of fact, after his resurrection Jesus appeared to one of his women friends first. She likewise did not let being a woman stand in the way of her sharing the good news:

> *Now after he rose early on the first day of the week, he appeared first to Mary Magdalene, from whom he had cast out seven demons. She went out and told those who had been with him, while they were mourning and weeping.*

—Mark 16:9–10

Jesus spoke out strongly against those who would "lord it over" others. He envisioned a community instead in which members would serve one another humbly. In Matthew's Gospel, after proclaiming the dual commandments to love God and love neighbor, Jesus criticized those leaders who "love to have the place of honor at banquets and the best seats in the synagogues, and to be greeted with respect in the market places, and to have people call them rabbi" (Matthew 23:6–7). Jesus said to his followers:

> *But you are not to be called rabbi, for you have one teacher, and you are all students. And call no one your father on earth, for you have one Father—the one in heaven. Nor are you to be called instructors, for you have one instructor, the Messiah. The greatest among you will be your servant. All who exalt themselves will be humbled, and all who humble themselves will be exalted.* ◆

—Matthew 23:8–12

◆ Look through the Gospels for passages where Jesus interacts with women or refers to women. Are there indications that he accepts or rejects the patriarchal perspective dominant in his culture? Consider some of the following passages:

- Matthew 15:21–28
- Matthew 28:1–10
- Mark 5:24–43
- Mark 12:41–44
- Mark 15:40–16:8
- Luke 7:36–50
- Luke 10:38–42
- John 4:4–42
- John 11:1–44
- John 20:1–18

Today's Church and Sexism

Since the 1960s the Church has recognized the need to include concern for women as part of its message of justice.

Pope John Paul II sees the gospel message about women to be hopeful and liberating:

> When it comes to setting women free from every kind of exploitation and domination, the Gospel contains an ever-relevant message which goes back to the attitude of Jesus Christ himself. Transcending the established norms of his own culture, Jesus treated women with openness, respect, acceptance and tenderness. In this way he honored the dignity which women have always possessed according to God's plan and in his love. As we look to Christ at the end of this second millennium, it is natural to ask ourselves how much of his message has been heard and acted upon.
>
> Yes, it is time to examine the past with courage, to assign responsibility where it is due in a review of the long history of humanity. Women have contributed to that history as much as men, and more often than not they did so in much more difficult conditions. I think particularly of those women who loved culture and art, devoted their lives to them in spite of the fact that they were frequently at a disadvantage from the start, excluded from equal educational opportunities, underestimated, ignored and not given credit for their intellectual contributions.
>
> —"Letter to Women," *Origins*, vol. 25, no. 9, page 139.

The Church Speaks Out on Women's Rights

1963 | Pope John XXIII stated that one of three distinctive characteristics of our day is that "women are becoming ever more conscious of their human dignity." He affirmed his support for women when they "demand rights befitting a human person both in domestic and public life" (*Peace on Earth*, number 41). Considering that Pope John was speaking before the beginning of the modern women's movement, his recognition that women's rights is one of the key issues of our day was certainly prophetic.

1965 | The Second Vatican Council noted that: "Where they have not yet won it, women claim for themselves an equity with men before the law and in fact." The bishops of the Council recognized that: "Now, for the first time in human history all people are convinced that the benefits of culture ought to be and actually can be extended to everyone" (*Church in the Modern World*, number 9).

1971 | At another international gathering the world's bishops declared that "women should have their own share of responsibility and participation in the community life of society and likewise of the Church" (*Justice in the World*, number 42).

1995 | Pope John Paul II issued an apology to women if in the past the Church itself has not acknowledged women's dignity and has kept them on the margins of society. He called for "equal pay for equal work, protection for working mothers, fairness in career advancements, equality of spouses with regard to family rights and the recognition of everything that is part of the rights and duties of citizens in a democratic state" ("Letter to Women," *Origins*, vol. 25, no. 9, page 140).

Pontius' Puddle

Panel 1: I FINALLY ACKNOWLEDGED A FACT THAT MAKES ME WONDER IF WOMEN REALLY CAN HANDLE AN INCREASED ROLE IN THE CHURCH.

Panel 2: THE FACT THAT WE MEN ARE SUPERIOR?

Panel 3: NO, THE FACT THAT WITH SUNDAY SCHOOL TEACHING, NURSERY CARE, HOSTESS DUTY, COMMUNITY OUTREACH, AND VOLUNTEER WORK, WE WOMEN ARE ALREADY BEARING MOST OF THE LOAD!

© Joel Kauffmann

The Issue of Women Priests

One issue that concerns the role of women in the Church is that of women priests. In 1995 Pope John Paul II reaffirmed the teaching and practice that priestly ordination is restricted to men. The pope insisted that this decision was not to be interpreted as anti-woman. In fact, he made it known that women play a necessary and irreplaceable role in the Church. That same year the U.S. bishops stated that, "we need to look at alternative ways in which women can exercise leadership in the Church. We welcome this leadership, which in some ways is already a reality, and we commit ourselves to enhancing the participation of women in every possible aspect of Church life" (*Strengthening the Bonds of Peace*, page 3). The bishops point out that: "One recent study shows that 85 percent of non-ordained ministerial positions in parishes are now held by women" (page 4). In other words, both the pope and the bishops want women to share power, leadership, and responsibility within the Church, as they have been doing more and more in recent decades.

Review

10. What transition occurred in how women were viewed in the early Church?

11. Describe Jesus' attitude toward women.

12. Summarize the teaching about women as stated by or in the following: Pope John XXIII, Pope John Paul II, the bishops at Vatican II, and the 1971 *Justice in the World* document by the synod of the world's Catholic bishops.

13. What position on ordaining women as priests was expressed by Pope John Paul II in his 1995 pronouncement?

14. What did the U.S. bishops say in 1995 about women in the Church?

Discuss

F. List some specific ways that the Church could improve conditions for women and fight sexism.

Responding to Sexism: Changing Attitudes, Changing Social Structures

Developing Critical Thinking

Sexism is so pervasive that we can easily miss how it affects our lives. While we will never be free from stereotypes in our thinking, we can learn to pause, to reflect, to analyze, to question the way things are, and to imagine how things could be different. In other words, when it comes to examining our own and society's views of men and women, we can develop **critical thinking**.

critical thinking

examining with an open mind what we usually take for granted

Sexism can be so subtle that we can fail to recognize it for what it is. Critical thinking applied to sexism means asking what it means to be a man and what it means to be a woman in our particular family, community, and culture. It means trying honestly to identify problems that typically accompany being a woman or a man. It also means noting possible advantages and disadvantages people face because they are men or women in our society. Critical thinking seeks to recognize who is hurting because of attitudes, beliefs, practices, and social policies related to gender. Finally, it seeks to develop ways that will help people to discontinue hurtful attitudes and practices. ◆

Working for Structural Change

> If someone dreams alone
> then it remains only a dream.
> If many dream together
> then this is the beginning,
> the beginning of a new reality.
> Dream our dream.
>
> —Author unknown, in Elizabeth Schussler Fiorenza, *Discipleship of Equals*,
> New York: Crossroad, page 1.

Domestic Violence

Women, and in a different way men, are hurting when social systems operate on a model of domination and control. One social system where the domination and control model has resulted in harm particularly to women is the family. Women and children are more likely than men to be victims of **domestic violence**. When husbands and fathers know no other way of dealing with problems than with domination and abuse, domestic violence occurs. When women—girlfriends or wives—experience abuse, they need immediate help. Unfortunately, more often than not domestic violence takes place

domestic violence

physical or psychological abuse within a family setting

◆ On the top of one sheet of paper write "being a man." Then make two columns, one labeled "advantages" and the other marked "disadvantages." Fill in as many advantages and disadvantages of being a man that you can think of. On the top of a second sheet of paper write "being a woman." Follow the same procedure as you did for the first sheet. Compare your lists with those of other students; if possible, compare lists created by boys and by girls. Write about what conclusions you draw from these lists.

without even close friends knowing about it. Abused women themselves sometimes don't even recognize abuse for what it is or they make excuses for why it happens.

Moreover, in addition to immediate help for victims, eliminating domestic violence can happen only if a different model of relating and being family emerges. That is, interdependence and equality in relationships must replace domination and control. Changing models in sexual relations once again requires examining what it means to be a man and what it means to be a woman so that more healthy and wholesome images of manhood and womanhood can be found.

Changing Roles for Men and Women

More and more, husbands and fathers are seeking increased participation in child rearing and in doing chores around the home, such as cooking and food shopping; more and more, wives and mothers are working outside the home. Changes in employment practices have been enacted by businesses and government to support these role changes. Policies on **paternity** and **maternity leave**, flexible working hours, and husbands and wives sharing employment time are examples of these supportive changes.

Underlying these policy changes is the recognition that the roles and responsibilities of women and men are changing. For example, women who work full-time outside the home continue to be almost exclusively responsible for child rearing and housekeeping. These dual responsibilities can quickly lead to burn-out. If women in the "sandwich generation," who have parents needing care and young children of their own, take sole responsibility for caring for the older and younger generation while the men of the sandwich generation concentrate on work outside the home, then women are unfairly burdened. ◆

paternity and
maternity leave

paid time off from work for the father and or the mother after the birth or adoption of a baby

◆ • One sociologist refers to women employed outside the home who also take care of housekeeping chores and child care as "working a second shift." Survey two-parent families where both parents work to determine whether home responsibilities are shared or whether the mothers are working a "second shift."

• Interview a number of parents—singles or couples. Or, interview adults in their mid-years who have an older parent. Ask them what mechanisms they find most helpful to balance care for themselves with care for younger and older family members. What difficulties do they find most troublesome?

A Variety of Models

Mutuality as described in chapter one means that we recognize we need each other. This describes the means and the goal of life-giving relationships. Pope John Paul II would like to see Christian families form a *communion of persons in love.* This does not mean that only one model of social organization can attain the goal of mutuality. For instance, if child care and domestic responsibilities were truly valued and not seen as less important work than salaried work, then a family in which only one parent was employed outside the home could be a healthy arrangement of mutuality. If doctors, nurses, and other hospital technicians appreciated their mutual contributions to health care and respected one another as persons, then sexual differences would become less problematic. If high school girls and boys took steps to understand each other's viewpoints, wants, and fears better, then members of both sexes would feel freer to be themselves rather than try to live up to or to combat sexual stereotypes.

The Value of Parenting

Women (and men) who are full-time parents and homemakers pay spiritual as well as economic costs. Because their work is not valued as real work by their peers who enter the paid labor force, they lose self-worth. If a parent chooses to make at-home work and full-time parenting her (or his) vocation, this vocation should be celebrated for the contribution it makes to the community, many of whose institutions, such as schools, religious organizations, libraries, and hospitals, depend upon someone being "at home" to volunteer for support work.

—Carol S. Robb, *Equal Value*, Boston: Beacon Press, page 33.

Identify Who Is Hurting

It is important to realize that real people are hurting because of sexist beliefs and practices at work in our society. Overall, women's work continues to be valued less than men's work. Even late into the decade of the nineties, women were paid on average seventy cents to the dollar earned by men. When families break up, it is women and children who are much more likely to suffer economic disaster. Some people even cast exclusive blame for social problems such as poverty and illegal drug use on "welfare moms" or teenage mothers rather than also on irresponsible or abusive fathers and social systems that provide poor education and low-paying job prospects for poor women. In short, for too many women it is dangerous and harmful being a member of their sex in the world and in our society.

15. Describe critical thinking.
16. What does domestic violence refer to?
17. What description does Pope John Paul II use to define the Christian family?

G. What do you think it would be like to be a different gender? What thoughts, feelings, and images immediately come to mind? What would make you most angry? What joys would you experience? Do you think that young people who are actually members of the other gender would typically answer these questions the same way you do? If you have a chance, try to find out.

H. *One woman theologian makes the following observation: "If men knew what it was like to be women, they wouldn't do the things they do or promote the programs they promote."*

—Carol S. Robb, *Equal Value*, Boston: Beacon Press, page 6.

• Give an example of what you think she has in mind.
• Do you agree with her? Explain.

I. Comedy and drama can either mask or unmask sexism. Name films and TV shows that portray women, men, or the two sexes interacting in ways that you consider sexist. Name films and TV shows that portray men and women in non-sexist ways. Describe the difference. Do you see the sexist portrayals as harmful in any way? Do you see the non-sexist portrayals as positive in any way? Explain. (Some things to look for: Are women portrayed as helpless and men as powerful? Are women or men portrayed as sex objects? Is a woman or a man the focus of the film or TV show? Is there any indication that sexism exists and that many women in particular suffer because of it?)

J. Do you believe that full-time parenting is an economic or social option for many families in your community? Why or why not? Do you find that parenting is viewed as a valued vocation in your community? Explain.

In Summary: Freeing People to Be Images of God

God created humankind in his image,
in the image of God, he created them;
male and female he created them.

—Genesis 1:27

According to the Scriptures, when we look within ourselves or outward toward others, women and men, we are seeing the image of the divine. When we limit the scope of expression, our own or others, to cultural stereotypes, we are limiting God. Likewise, so long as our society is structured in such a way that half of the population is assigned to secondary status due to their sex, we limit full expression of the God who found a home within humanity.

Before we conclude . . .

Let us pray . . .

*Mary, model of courage and compassion
for women and for men,
we pray for gentleness and strength,
patience and perseverance,
so that with you and your Son, Jesus Christ,
we may bring forth justice in our world.
May you who identify with oppressed women,
whose Son died a criminal's death
and who still comforted the grieving,
fill us with hope and peace.
Teach us to celebrate our differences
and never to let them be the cause of
suffering or harm.
Lead us in your way of
concern and care
one for another.
Transform our world
into one
where women's voices are heard,
where women's work is valued,
and where families and workplaces,
schools and communities,
nurture equality and mutuality.
Amen.*

For further study . . .

1. Has the feminization of poverty continued to be a trend today? Using an almanac or the Internet, find recent statistics related to women and poverty. Report on your findings.

2. Seek information about various professions and the sexual makeup of those professions. Is there evidence of a "gender gap" in positions of power in our society today?

3. Write a paper on "women in the Bible," or write a report on one particular woman in Scripture.

4. Write a report on domestic violence. As part of your report, discuss cultural influences that lead some men to be abusive, factors that make it difficult for women to leave abusive relationships, and the way that laws do or do not protect women.

5. Identify one change in your attitude toward what it means to be a woman or a man that would help free you in terms of how you view yourself and others.

6. Name one societal change or one social policy that would help ease problems related to sexism.

7. Think of specific ways that you might work toward bringing about these changes.

CHAPTER 8

Race

Beyond Stereotypes to the American Dream

We live in a rainbow world, rich in endless colors, rich in diverse cultures and races. However, the human rainbow is not always a smooth blending of differences. We need to develop the virtues of tolerance and appreciation of differences. We also need to recognize and counteract racism in our society, and we need to work together to eliminate it.

Major Concepts

A. Countering Prejudice, Cultivating Compassion

Four characteristics of prejudice
- Stereotyping
- Shortsightedness
- Close-mindedness
- Strong feelings

Compassion as the opposite of prejudice.

B. The Question of Race: How Different Are We?

C. Racism

- Prejudice plus power
- Racial inequality within society

D. Prejudice and Racism in the Biblical View

- The story of Jonah, a view of racial prejudice
- Jesus' teachings as counter to prejudice and racism
- The Church's opposition to racial discrimination

E. Responding to Prejudice: Guidelines for Change

Six guidelines to unprejudicial behavior
- Know yourself
- Don't judge others
- Treat others like you want to be treated
- Speak out
- Get involved
- Keep a sense of humor

Opening Prayer

God who loves and delights in all people, we stand in awe gazing at the human family, knowing that the spark of life within each person on earth is the spark of your divine life. Differences among cultures and races are multi-colored manifestations of your light. May our hearts and minds be open to understanding and celebrating similarities and differences among our sisters and brothers. We place our hopes for racial harmony in you, sovereign God. Amen.

Before we begin . . .

Answer **agree**, **disagree**, or **uncertain** to the following statements. Choose statements that you believe are most significant and explain your answers.

1. I treat people and respond to people the same regardless of race.

2. I would not mind if a family of a different race moved in next door.

3. I believe that races should not intermarry.

4. Members of minority races should receive special consideration in educational and employment opportunities.

5. I would show my disapproval if classmates made cutting remarks about the race of another person.

6. Public figures who tell racial or ethnic jokes should be severely criticized.

7. Every racial and ethnic group has had its share of difficulties. No one group or groups should be singled out as being victims of racism.

Stories of Race

■ Julee left her native India ten years ago when she was six. Nonetheless, she continues to wonder how to respond to her classmates who tell her, "We think of you as being just like us. You don't seem Indian."

■ In a mainly white school, Antonio and Glenn, two white males, spend most of their free time with black students. They eat their lunches at the same cafeteria tables and afterward join black students by the soccer field. In the beginning of the year, a few students questioned this arrangement. Within a month, however, it was accepted by black and white students as simply the way things were going to be.

■ Oun Mi, who is Korean, has been dating Patrick, an Irish boy, for a few months now. Oun Mi has not told her parents about this relationship. She knows that they expect her to marry someone who is Korean and would never accept a non-Korean boyfriend for her.

■ Kathy, who is white, sees in a magazine a political cartoon portraying an Arab man as a terrorist. Kathy presumes that this is an accurate portrayal of Arabs. In fact, she has never met anyone of Arab descent.

■ As they approach the mall, Derrick, who is black, jokes with his white friend Bob. "You know when I go into the stores, I'm watched more closely than you are." "No, they're suspicious of all young people, Derrick," Bob insists. "Seriously, Bob, you know it's much worse for a young black person than it is for you. All black people are lumped together as troublemakers by most white and Asian store owners."

■ Nhai struggles to get average grades in school. Her math teacher, who is white, questions her progress in the subject. "You're doing poorly on your tests, Nhai. I expected you to work harder and to do better in math. All of the Asian students are doing great work but you."

■ "Another business operated by Pakistanis," Mike pointed out as he left the convenience store with his friends. "If we're not careful, soon Americans won't own anything anymore."

■ The school has had the Black Cultural Club for many years. Asian and Hispanic students have recently sponsored events to celebrate their heritage. Feeling slighted, a group of white students approach their religion teacher requesting that she serve as moderator of a new "white students club."

■ Raul accepts his company's offer to relocate him. "My one request," says Raul, "is that the company assist me in finding housing. Being Hispanic, I don't have access to certain neighborhoods that a white person would have access to."

• Have you, for any reason, ever felt like an outsider or experienced the sting of prejudice or discrimination? If so, describe the experience. How did you react?

• Recall a negative experience that you have had with a person of another race. What happened? (Where did the incident occur? How old were you at the time? What led up to the incident? How did you feel?)

• Did this experience influence your attitude toward members of that race in general? Where are you today in terms of your view of members of that race? If your view has changed, what led to that change?

Countering Prejudice, Cultivating Compassion

All of us tend to have **prejudices**. Without anything resembling a fair assessment to back them up, we have likes and dislikes about things such as foods, styles of dress, speech patterns, ways of spending summer vacations, and methods of relating to others. Typically, our likes and dislikes are based on limited experiences; usually, they reflect what we have been comfortable with from our earliest years. We can feel so strongly about our beliefs and viewpoints that we hold onto them in the face of solid evidence to the contrary. We might say, "I don't like Chinese food" because we had one tiny bite of an egg roll as a child. We might say, "People who drive Cadillacs are snobs." If we hold prejudices about food and cars, obviously we can have prejudices about racial, religious, and ethnic groups as well.

When directed toward groups of people, prejudice means more than likes and dislikes. Prejudice involves at least four characteristics that, together, harm both those who are objects of prejudice as well as those who hold prejudices.

prejudice

narrow-minded judgment or opinion

Four Characteristics of Prejudice

1. Stereotyping: Overgeneralizing, Applying Characteristics of Individuals to an Entire Group

Making generalizations is both a natural and a helpful use of human intelligence. If we are bitten by a snake and that is our only experience of snakes, naturally we become fearful of snakes generally. Likewise, a near-drowning incident might keep us from going near water for the rest of our lives.

In a similar fashion, we make generalizations about the people we meet. If you attended your first Native American festival and found people selling imported souvenirs, you might falsely generalize that all American Indians have little pride in their heritage. Or, if you had little contact with Polish Americans and were traveling through a mostly Polish section of a large city, you might form an opinion about this ethnic group based merely on the few streets and the few people you saw.

Making swift and sweeping judgments is a normal and healthy human skill. But we must recognize its limitations. We must always be open to new and better information. A true picture of life is always much richer and more complex than **stereotype** thinking suggests. ◆

stereotype

a prejudiced generalization, a way of thinking that is in error

◆ Name three stereotypes held by some people in your school or community. Imagine one of these stereotypes being applied to you. How do you think you would feel if you were the object of stereotyping?

Examples of Mistaking "My Truth" for "The Truth"

- Prior to World War II, Nazi propaganda offered so-called scientific proof that Jews were racially inferior to Germans.

- During the 1800s, British cartoons portrayed Irish people as closely resembling monkeys to support discriminatory practices against the Irish.

- Before the United States Civil War, some supporters of slavery argued that Africans enslaved and brought to America were fortunate to be introduced to Christianity and civilization. Thus slavery was presented as actually being beneficial for them.

- Often during wars enemy soldiers and civilians are considered less than human, thereby justifying taking lives.

2. Shortsightedness: A Narrow View of Truth

Sometimes prejudicial opinions are held without any basis in reality. This is the situation with children who declare that they hate some food even though they have never tasted it. However, prejudiced people are more often shortsighted. That is, they appeal to a narrow, limited view in order to make their positions appear reasonable and correct.

It is important to keep in mind that prejudices can have some basis in fact; prejudiced people often make their claims based on "experience." For instance, some Irish men drink beer to excess; some Italians are involved in organized crime; and some Arabs are terrorists. Prejudicial thinking means jumping to conclusions, making judgments based on limited observations, and generalizing *some* to include *all*. That is, prejudicial thinking considers "my truth" to be the whole truth. ◆

3. Close-mindedness: An Unwillingness to Change

If we were to say "People on welfare are lazy" and hold firmly to that belief in the face of all the studies and statistics that prove otherwise, then we would be close-minded. Other examples of close-mindedness are:

- A man observes a car with left turn signals blinking make a right turn. He immediately says, "Of course! It's a woman driver."
- A white woman watching television for over an hour remarks when a black couple is portrayed in a thirty-second commercial, "All you see on TV any more is black people."

◆
- Describe a time when you experienced labeling someone or being labeled based on a partial judgment.
- Have you ever held a prejudicial opinion and then had it change? For instance, has there ever been a time when you realized that you were mistaken in your judgment of another person? What led to this change? Do you think that this process of change can be applied to other prejudices?

In both cases the observers are closed to all information, such as men driving poorly and the frequency of whites and other ethnic groups portrayed on TV, except that which supports their view of reality.

While we can work only from our own experiences of other people, it is also important to realize that our base of experience is limited. We practice prejudicial thinking when we close ourselves off from new information about other people and groups.

4. Strong Feelings: Hatred of and Fear of Others

When our opinions about other groups are accompanied by anger and fear, then we are likely to think or behave prejudicially. As mentioned earlier, prejudice is not just a matter of likes and dislikes. Prejudice becomes a problem of justice when it includes intense hatred toward persons or groups of people. For example, we may dismiss acts of violence committed by members of our own social group but react strongly to similar acts by members of a different group. The slogan "My country right or wrong" illustrates such prejudicial thinking.

With its intensity of feelings, prejudice divides people into "us" and "them," insiders and outsiders. Prejudiced people hate others simply because of what they look like, where they came from, or what they believe. While all of us find comfort and security through identifying with our particular group, nonetheless identifying with "us" need not result in ill will toward "them." When it does, prejudice results.

In the 1800s in the United States, groups singled out as outsiders by dominant powers were blacks, Indians, and warriors. Classic examples of "us" and "them" thinking earlier in this century were the Nazi era in Germany, the Japanese treatment of Koreans prior to World War II, and the era of racial discrimination in South Africa. In the United States of the early 1950s, during the height of anti-Communist attitudes, fear and hatred of real or imagined communists led to oppression of many and a general atmosphere of suspicion in this country. Numerous international conflicts today are fueled by group hatred. In the U.S. the Ku Klux Klan, neo-Nazis, skinheads, and other hate groups fear and hate people of other ethnic or religious backgrounds. They view them to be a threat to their power and way of life. Indeed, hate groups support violence against anyone who happens to be a member of a group which is disliked. ◆

◆ Read the following scenario. Working in small groups make a case that the man is or is not prejudiced based on the four characteristics of prejudice.

One evening a middle-aged white man is standing at a bus stop alone. A black teenage boy approaches him. The white man stiffens and is fearful of the youth's intentions. The teenager walks up to the man and asks, "Do you know how soon the next bus is supposed to come?"

The Roots of Prejudice

Studies suggest that we tend to treat others the same way we have been treated. That is, children who are loved and cared for usually end up as loving and caring adults. Thus, the roots of prejudice begin in our early childhood experiences. Studies also indicate that people who are prejudiced in one area tend to be prejudiced in other areas as well. In a sense we humans have an instinct for prejudice. That is, we are naturally self-centered; we prefer the familiar over the unfamiliar; and we draw conclusions based on limited experience. On the other hand we are naturally curious and natural truth-seekers. We are drawn to expanding our horizons. That part of us which is open to wonder and surprise represents the human quality that broadens self-centeredness to a more inclusive vision of humanity.

The opposite of prejudice, then, is not simply tolerating differences: "You do your thing, and I'll do mine." Rather, the opposite of prejudice is actively seeking to learn about, feel connected to, and care about those who are different from us. In a word, the opposite of prejudice is compassion.

Review

1. Name and give an example of the four characteristics of prejudice.
2. What is a hate group?
3. What is the root of prejudice?
4. What is the opposite of prejudice?

Discuss

A. Can you think of any prejudices that you have? What do you think are the origins of your prejudices?

B. Answer yes or no to the following statements. Then, discuss whether your answers indicate sound judgment or prejudicial thinking. Do you think people from other ethnic backgrounds would arrive at the same conclusions that you do?

   • If a break-in occurred in your neighborhood, would you tend to assume certain racial, age, and other characteristics about the lawbreaker?

   • Would the report of an act of terrorism call up a certain image of who performed the terrorist act?

   • Would you react as strongly to reports of wrongdoing by someone of your own ethnic background as you would to reports about someone of another ethnic background?

C. *Children who have not yet learned who society's most frequent victims are will pick their own. I had no interest in playing with dolls or dressing up, so I was labeled a "tomboy." My little brother, born brain-damaged, was called "retard." An auburn-haired friend of mine remembers hearing, "I'd rather be dead than red in the head." Indeed, anything that makes a child "different" is justification for slander: glasses, braces, thinness, fatness, tallness, shortness, poverty, or wealth. By the time most children are big enough to ride a bicycle, they know who the outsiders are and they know what to call them.*

   —Sara Bullard, *Teaching Tolerance*, New York: Doubleday, page 8.

   • Why do you think children tend to divide people into "us" and "them"? If you were a parent, how would you seek to help your children move toward greater acceptance of differences? How would you rate yourself on dealing with the outsiders of your school or community?

The Question of Race: How Different Are We?

He prayed — it wasn't my religion.
He ate — it wasn't what I ate.
He spoke — it wasn't my language.
He dressed — it wasn't what I wore.
He took my hand — it wasn't the color of mine.
But when he laughed — it was how I laughed,
and when he cried —it was how I cried.

—Amy Maddox, 16 years old, in Sara Bullard,
"Teaching Tolerance," Tuscaloosa, AL: Southern
Poverty Law Review, page 85.

If you are like most Americans, you feel uncomfortable talking about race. Even when we don't have intense feelings ourselves, public discussion about race issues often brings out anger, pain, disagreements, and frustrations that we would just as soon leave under wraps. Underlying this section is the belief that forthright discussion about race is necessary. Not to talk about race matters in the U.S. is like sitting in a kitchen ignoring a fire smoldering on a stove. Tended to, the fire can be used creatively. Unattended, the fire becomes very destructive.

Many people believe that to not be racist means one must be color blind—that is, not recognize or place significance on a person's racial background and identity. But to ignore the significance of race in a society where racial groups have distinct historical and contemporary experiences is to deny the reality of their group experience. ◆

—Margaret L. Andersen and Patricia Hill Collins,
Race, Class, and Gender, Belmont, CA: Wadsworth Publishing Co., 1992, page 50.

- Do you believe that we should be *color blind* (not seeking to identify or discuss racial differences) or *rainbow conscious* (seeking to learn about and appreciate racial and ethnic differences)? What is the danger of being one or the other?
- Can you envision a future in which being color blind is the normal state of affairs? What would need to happen to bring about such a future? Explain why you would or would not want such a society.
- If you could change the racial landscape of America in any way, how would you change it?

Elizabeth's Story

Elizabeth and her family left their native Czechoslovakia in 1935 and immigrated to the United States when she was twelve. Her family settled in a city in the northeastern part of the country. At first, Elizabeth viewed herself as an outsider, a foreigner who spoke no English and dressed differently from how Americans dressed. She had an olive complexion, darker than that of most people she saw in magazines or at the movies.

As time went by, Elizabeth began to feel more and more at home in her new country. She adopted the ways of her new land much more quickly than her parents did, who themselves started to appear foreign to Elizabeth. By the time she reached adulthood, Elizabeth had learned many of the lessons of America. One important lesson she learned and accepted was that she belonged to a low social class within American society. However, another lesson she learned was that she was white, not colored.

When black families started moving into her neighborhood, Elizabeth was able to purchase a home ten blocks away in an all-white neighborhood. Except for brief periods taken off to bear her children, she worked as a seamstress. She would never think of socializing with the bosses at the company;

nor could she imagine her own children ever achieving such high positions. She was friendly but did not socialize with the few black women who also worked at the factory. Elizabeth's understanding of the American dream was that her children would be able to work hard and live a decent life. She encouraged her sons to consider becoming barbers or auto mechanics. She never questioned whether that same dream was shared by or available in the same way for the children of the black women with whom she worked. Nor did she question that the children of the bosses and owners at the factory had opportunities and privileges not available to her own children. For Elizabeth, America was a land of opportunity. She would encourage her children to do their best and hope for the best.

- A number of decades ago Elizabeth felt that an important American lesson to learn was that she was white, not black. Do you believe that this was an important lesson? If so, in what sense? Do you believe that being black or white makes a difference in America today? Why?

Like Gender, Race Is a Social Construction

One fascinating aspect of Elizabeth's story is that when she came to the United States she did not "know" that she was white, as opposed to black, or African American. She learned this identity by observing *what it means* to be white and to be black in this country. Similarly, some black Americans tell equally fascinating stories of being high school exchange students in Europe or of studying in other parts of the

world. They discover that they are not "black" in the sense that the term means in the United States. Indeed, some African Americans have chosen to live in France or other countries in order to escape the racism that they experienced in their native country. Quite possibly, what it means to be white or black, as well as other so-called races and skin colors, is different today from what it was fifty or one hundred years ago.

Like gender, race is a social construction. It is the thinking of a group of people that attempts to divide humanity according to skin color and body characteristics. Recent U.S. census reports and other surveys that try to identify people by race illustrate how hazy our idea of the term can be. People have identified themselves as "Hispanic" who are either wholly or in part of European, American Indian, or African heritage. The "Asian" class can include—among others—people from Iran, the Indian sub-continent, Vietnam and Cambodia, China, Korea, and Japan. Interestingly, Lebanese, whose country of origin is in Asia, can be designated as "white." Perhaps most telling about the way Americans view race, a person can be seventy-five percent white and only twenty-five percent African American and nonetheless be classified as "black."

Certainly, there are differences among ethnic groups and people from different cultural backgrounds. For example, people from Sweden have lighter skin color and lighter, straighter hair than people of southern Africa; except for the noodles, Chinese food would not be mistaken for Italian food. However, research into the question of race continually arrives at certain conclusions:

- We humans are much more alike than different. That is, we share a common family tree and for most of humanity's existence we were basically much alike in physical characteristics. DNA fingerprinting suggests that we are, in fact, one human family.

- The term *race* is so loaded with culturally imposed views that it is virtually impossible to separate the *meaning we assign* to the word from any *real differences* that actually exist.

For these reasons, the discussion that follows about racism is really about how we view race in our particular culture. For the most part, historically the race question in the United States has been a matter of black and white and, especially in the western part of the country, white and Latino and white and American Indian. Today the United States is obviously multi-cultural; eventually, whites in America will be members of a minority group. Besides expanding as a multi-cultural country, more and more individual Americans themselves are blurring racial and ethnic divisions. For example, when pro-golfer Tiger Woods burst on the scene in 1996, people were confused about how to classify his one-quarter black, one-quarter Thai, one-quarter Chinese, one-eighth Native American, and one-eighth white heritage. Instead of simply being amazed at his athletic abilities, some people felt uncomfortable because he couldn't and wouldn't be labeled according to race.

Review

5. What is the difference between being *color blind* and being *rainbow conscious*?
6. What does it mean to say that race is a social construction?
7. What two conclusions about race does research reveal?
8. What is *dual consciousness*?

Discuss

D. At times people of color in the U.S. talk about constantly living with a "dual consciousness," that is, a consciousness of being themselves and also of being their particular race. Here is one person's experience of dual consciousness:

I love the United States of America, and I love living here. But as an actor and as an individual, I find myself in a dual position. Like others from Latin America, I am part of an alien nation within a larger nation. . . . The fruits of our labor are prized and needed, but we are kept apart due to our language and culture. They like our food and admire our colorful art, but do not accept us as peers.

—Ramon Novarro, in *The Fire in Our Souls: Quotations of Wisdom and Inspiration by Latino Americans.* Edited by Rosie Gonzalez. NY: Penguin Books USA, page 51.

Working in small groups, complete the following activities and then share with the class.

• Name a number of ethnic groups and list characteristics that are popularly associated with each one.
• For each characteristic, identify whether it typically has a positive, negative, or neutral meaning.
• Explain and analyze your lists. (For instance, is a Spanish accent viewed by most people in our society any differently from how an Asian accent, a midwestern white accent, or an African American accent is viewed? Does the word *black* call up certain views or attitudes not connected with the word *white*?)

Racism

So far in this chapter we have discussed prejudice, including prejudices toward racial and ethnic differences. Anyone can have prejudices based on race. However, racism asks an additional question of a society: Are members of certain races hurting more than others simply because of their race? This question of racism, similar to the sexism question, is much more complex than whether or not certain individuals are unfriendly toward members of other races.

Racism = Prejudice + Power

In line with our discussion on prejudice, **racial prejudice** typically involves stereotyping members of another race based on the close-minded or shortsighted views of that group. Racially prejudiced feelings and attitudes can lead to unfriendly or even hateful actions toward members of another racial group. These acts are examples of racism.

racial prejudice

a strong negative feeling that a person holds toward members of another race

Racism points to differences in *power, potential,* and *privilege* within a society. That is, a discussion about racism seeks to determine whether standards in a society (that is, what counts as "the norm") make belonging to one race appear more valuable than belonging to another. Or it might involve elevating some characteristics of one culture over another when it is not appropriate. An investigation into racism searches for possible difficulties that people might face *because of* their race.

Specifically, the racism question asks: Do certain racial groups possess power within a society that other groups do not? For instance, can a black person travel around the country as freely as a white person can? Do white children and Native American children have the same educational opportunities? Can Latino teenagers find jobs the same as non-Latinos? Is one race or ethnic group represented among leading politicians and civic leaders more than others? Is the racial make-up of those who own and manage businesses different from the overall racial make-up of the community? Are members of various races fairly represented among both the wealthiest and poorest segments of society? Can people accused of crime receive a fair and equal trial regardless of their race? Are characteristics popularly connected with one racial or ethnic group held in as high esteem as characteristics connected with other groups? ◆

◆ Look over the questions in this paragraph and respond to the following: Do certain racial groups within our society possess power that other groups do not? Find evidence to support your point of view. Debate this question with your class.

Racism: A Function of a Society More Than of Individuals

As these questions indicate, racism is not simply a matter of some individuals strongly disliking other races. Racism is more a trait of a society than of individuals. Individual racial prejudice does not account for unequal power and privileges between races.

Let's step back in history to illustrate this. During World War II black and white servicemen lived, worked, fought, died—or survived—together. But then African American soldiers returning from the war to southern army bases were not allowed to enter most clubs and restaurants in the area. Certain professions, such as being a professional baseball player, were also denied them. On the other hand, white soldiers could go wherever they wanted to go and pretty much do whatever they chose to do. ◆

Defining Racism: Subordination Based on Race

subordination

being placed in or occupying a lower class, rank, or position

Racism, then, refers to **subordination** based on race. As the following author's definition points out, racial subordination can occur because of the actions and attitudes of individuals. However, it can also result simply because of the way society is structured—the institutions of a society.

> *Racism is any action or attitude, conscious or unconscious, that subordinates an individual or group based on skin color or race. This subordination can be enacted individually or institutionally.*

—Clyde W. Ford, *We Can All Get Along*, NY: Dell Publishing, 1994, page 11.

institutional racism

racist actions and attitudes ingrained and generally accepted by organizations of a society

Racism exists when members of certain races have power and privileges more so than members of other races. As the author suggests, this condition of racial inequality, or racial subordination, results either from the actions of powerful individuals or from the power of society's institutions. Racism that is part of the very fabric of society is known as **institutional racism.**

 Pontius' Puddle

© Joel Kauffmann

◆ Defend or refute the following observation by a former White House official:

> *The root of the problem within black America is not teenage pregnancy, drugs, the decline in family values, anger, rap music, unemployment or even the epidemic of violent crime. These are only symptoms of the deeper problem. The root problem in black communities across America is race and the unjust distribution of our nation's wealth, power and resources.*

—Claude Anderson, *Black Labor, White Wealth*, Edgewood, MD: Duncan & Duncan, Inc., Publishers, 1994, page 10.

Institutional Racism: Racial Inequality Within Society

Institutional racism is a subtle, indirect, often unconscious expression of racism. Institutional racism shows itself when a white police officer pulls over a young black man driving a Datsun Z, presuming that the car is stolen. It shows itself when the police officer holds the man longer and subjects him to more questioning than he would a white or Asian driver, even after the young man produces proof that he owns the car. Institutional racism shows itself when schools and health care facilities in mainly African American, Hispanic, and Native American communities are well below the standards of those in other communities. This results in children receiving poor health care and below average education simply by accident of where they are born. It shows itself when U.S. born Hispanics do not accept Hispanics who come to the U.S. from a another country, or when the U.S. born Hispanics, in turn, are not accepted by other ethnic groups they live among. These examples of institutional racism are not the result of conscious choices on anyone's part to be racist. Rather, they are unconscious, a reflection of the racial landscape in the United States. As racism is racial prejudice at work in situations where power and privilege are unevenly divided, so institutional racism is inequality at work in the very structure of a society.

Review

9. What question is addressed to a society in terms of racism?
10. How is *racism* different from *racial prejudice*?
11. Define *institutional racism*.

Discuss

E. How would you react if you were a soldier returning to your country and certain places of entertainment and employment were closed to you? What would you do if you were a member of a race who was not restricted in these ways but knew such restrictions existed for others?

F. If you were to support the position "Institutional racism exists in the United States," what examples would you use? If you were to support the position "Institutional racism does not exist in the U.S.," what examples would you use? Which position do you believe is stronger? Explain.

G. Determine whether the following situations are examples of institutional racism. Explain your choices.

- A noted heart doctor, an African American woman, is mistaken for a cleaning woman at the hospital where she works.
- A bank has a policy of refusing home loans to people who live within a certain area of a city, an area made up entirely of Hispanic and African American population.
- When the one Native American student at a school walks into the cafeteria, his classmates yell out their version of an Indian battle cry.
- When a non-Italian and an Italian student get into a heated argument, another student chimes in, "Don't fight him, Bill. His uncle is probably in the Mafia."

IN THE LORD SPOKE TO THE FISH:
& THE DRY LAND

AND IT VOMITED OUT JONAS UP OR
JONAS II. 11.

Prejudice and Racism in the Biblical View

The Lesson of Jonah

The Hebrew Scriptures tell the story of a group of people, the Israelites, who came to be known as the Jews. The Hebrew people were originally a mixed crew of wanderers, lacking in power, who were constantly bumping up against more powerful groups. Later, the Israelite people were not only victims of racism but responded to it in kind. One Scripture story that shows the intolerance of some Israelites toward another nation and also offers a lesson about how God expects us to treat "the other" is the legend of Jonah found in the short story called the Book of Jonah. The prophet Jonah is asked by God to go to the city of Nineveh to preach to its citizens. At the time Nineveh was the capital city of the Assyrians, aggressive enemies of Jonah's people. The idea of doing anything nice for Ninevites was so revolting to Jonah that he disobeyed God and set sail in the exact opposite direction. In the section of the story with which we are all familiar, Jonah was tossed overboard and swallowed by a large fish.

Three days later Jonah is spat up onto the shores of Nineveh. Reluctantly, he preaches God's message to its citizens, hoping that they will not heed the message and thus will incur God's wrath. To Jonah's dismay the Ninevites do repent; and God saves them. God then teaches Jonah a lesson by destroying the shade tree under which Jonah has been sitting for shelter. God lets Jonah know that God cares for all people whom he has so carefully created and crafted.

The story of Jonah teaches us some important lessons:
- God does not lovingly create any people for them to be hated, given up on, or destroyed.
- God's vision of people is absolutely inclusive, absolutely compassionate.
- God is not a God only of one group but of everyone.
- All people are sisters and brothers under God. ◆

Write a short story in a modern-day setting whose theme is prejudice or racism. Or draw a cartoon or comic strip depicting the story of Jonah or a modern-day version of the story.

Jesus Teaches Radical Love

A recent document of the U.S. Catholic Bishops Committee on Migration observes that:

> *The New Testament shifts from identifying with strangers based on a common experience to serving strangers because in each face we see Christ.*
>
> *—One Family Under God, page 3.*

The Israelites of old identified with being "the other" and out of that experience they built an ethic of concern for strangers. From the Christian viewpoint "the other" is Christ himself. Therefore, the way we treat those who are different from us—indeed, those whom we would just as soon ignore—indicates precisely our love for or rejection of Christ.

One theologian suggests that in Western society love occurs only within the family and otherwise only at Christmastime. Contrary to such a narrow understanding of love, Jesus has this to say:

> *For if you love those who love you, what reward do you have? Do not even tax collectors do the same? And if you greet only your brothers and sisters, what more are you doing than others? Do not even gentiles do the same?*
>
> *—Matthew 5:46–47*

In his day Jesus confused many of his fellow Jews by treating Jews and non-Jews alike. When he met people in need, Jesus concerned himself with their pain, not their nationality, religion, race, or skin color. One of the most striking characteristics of the early Jesus movement was that it included everyone:

> *The broadening of Christianity to include the gentiles was begun by St. Peter, who said, ". . . in truth, I see that God shows no favors. Rather in every nation, whoever fears him and acts uprightly is acceptable to him" (Acts 10:34–35). The growth of the Christian family marks the shift in the early Church to an emphasis on the universality of Christianity. Through Pentecost, God "gathers into one the dispersed children of God" (John 11:52), focusing the efforts of the Church on building unity among human beings.* ◆
>
> *—One Family Under God, page 3.*

◆ Compose a prayer that you feel reflects the attitude of Jesus toward ethnic and racial harmony.

Jewish Boy Gives Arab Girl Heart, Life

JERUSALEM—At the bedside of an Arab toddler who received the heart of a Jewish child killed by a car, two mothers wept in each other's arms. "Do you know what heart she received? She received an angel's heart—you don't know what a heart this boy had," said Braha Kaveh, whose 8-year-old son Yuval was killed while riding his bike Thursday.

Aani Aljaroushi—whose 3-year-old daughter Rim was listed in good condition yesterday, three days after the transplant—embraced the other woman. "I know that it's very hard, but I thank you," she said through her own tears.

The story struck a powerful chord in a country where Arabs and Jews are often depicted in bitter strife. It was a medical milestone as well. If Rim recovers—and her doctor says the prognosis is excellent—it will be Israel's first successful pediatric heart transplant, the hospital says.

Footage of Sunday night's emotional hospital meeting aired on Israeli television and was front-page news in yesterday's papers. "Heart of Gold" said a banner headline in the *Maariv* newspaper. When the Kavehs were told their son's heart was beating in the chest of an Arab child, "They were really happy," said cardiac surgeon Yakov Lavie, who headed the transplant team. "They thought it might bring the two peoples closer together."

—Laura King, "Jewish Boy's Heart Given to Arab Girl," *Philadelphia Inquirer*, Oct. 14, 1997.

• Discuss how the above story is an example of the radical love with which God loves us.

The Church and Racism

As a product of the cultures in which it found itself, Christianity has not been unaffected by prejudice or racism. Yet, throughout most of its history, Christian enthusiasm for spreading the gospel message has led the Church to seek unity and to recognize the inborn worth of all people. For example, Pope Saint Gregory the Great, who died in 604, lived at a time when to Romans "the other" meant barbarians in particular. One group of barbarians were people from England, the Angles. One day, while walking through Rome, Gregory witnessed a young English boy about to be sold into slavery. He told his companions, "I do not call them Angles, but angels."

The history of the European occupation of America is a ruthless and bloody one, and the Church of the time shares blame because it was so much a part of the culture. Nonetheless, many French and Spanish missionaries risked torture and death to introduce Native Americans to God's love for them. Often these Christian missionaries provided the only voice insisting on respect for and kind treatment of native people in America and elsewhere.

Today's Church and Racism

In their 1979 pastoral letter on racism, the U.S. bishops refer to racism as both a "fact" and a "sin." By calling racism a fact, the bishops are pointing out that racism exists within our nation. The people of the U.S. need to address this issue in an affirmative manner. By calling racism a sin, the bishops are reminding us that we need to respond to the harmfulness of racism with the same zeal with which we would respond to any sinful condition.

The Church today stands as an important voice against racism because of its mission from Jesus to love one another and because of its global makeup. The Good News of Christianity has blended, at times with much struggle, with most cultures and language groups on earth. As a result today's Catholic Church is truly a rainbow community. In the U.S. alone, for centuries there have been both black and white Catholics. From the earliest days of European contact with America, there have been Spanish, French, and English speaking Catholics. The Catholic Church in America has always been an immigrant church. Today many immigrants—Hispanics, Latinos, Haitians, Vietnamese and other Asians, and Africans—add to the mix of cultures in the U.S. Catholic Church.

Review

12. What lessons does the Jonah story reveal?
13. How are Christians to act toward all people?
14. Why must the Church today stand as an important voice against racism?

Discuss

H. Find other scriptural quotes from Jesus that speak of love. What is Jesus saying to us today through these passages?

I. What do you see your local Church doing to become more inclusive and friendly toward those who enter its doors?

Responding to Prejudice: Guidelines for Change

Presuming that we actually would like to be less chained to prejudicial thinking, feeling, and acting, how might we obtain this goal? Refer to the chart on this page for guidelines to consider. Step one acknowledges that eventually hatred destroys us. We hurt ourselves when we hold onto prejudices toward others. Self-awareness, and along with that, self-acceptance, become the first step to any change. To begin overcoming prejudices toward others, first spend time looking in a mirror.

The second step encourages developing a spirit of welcome, creating a space within yourself where strangers can become friends. To do that, learn what you can about other cultural groups and do so with an open-minded and compassionate attitude.

In the third step the wisdom of the Golden Rule holds true for relating with other cultural groups. Develop basic communication skills that help you speak to, learn from, and interact with a number of people.

Resisting prejudice and racism is not accomplished by indifference or inactivity in the face of injustice. We do need to make moral judgments, rejecting offenses without rejecting offenders. Do we have the courage to respond to a prejudiced remark by saying, "I find what you are saying unacceptable and offensive. Please keep such comments to yourself"? We need to speak out to change others' behaviors.

Martin Luther King, Jr. and others who have been at the forefront of social change suggest that the best way to overcome prejudices and racism is for people to work together to achieve common goals. All Americans suffer because of economic and social forces that overwhelm us and seem to control us. If all of us get involved to make the country better, prejudices and racism will disappear.

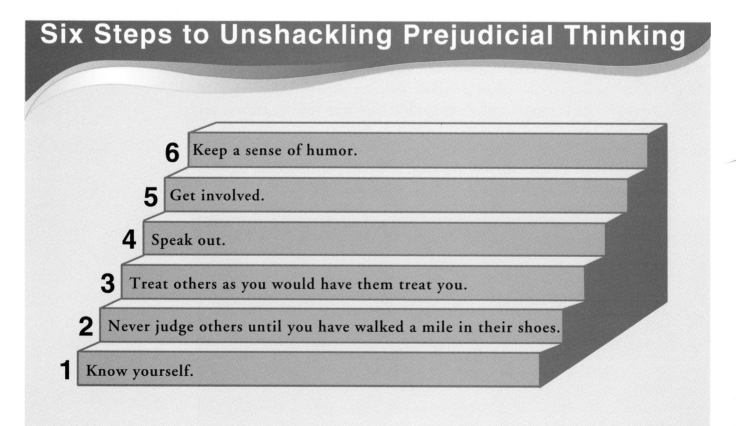

Six Steps to Unshackling Prejudicial Thinking

6 Keep a sense of humor.

5 Get involved.

4 Speak out.

3 Treat others as you would have them treat you.

2 Never judge others until you have walked a mile in their shoes.

1 Know yourself.

The last step may appear strange after the heavy tone of the others. It is not meant to deny the serious nature of prejudice or racism. However, being too quick to take offense can be just as much of a problem as being too patient and accepting of injustice. When it comes to prejudice and racism, some humor can be harmful while other types of humor can be helpful. For instance, humor can be used to belittle others or it can break up tense situations, pointing out the faults of all of us.

Interesting bits of information about various cultures remind us that we have much to learn about ourselves and about others. Racial and ethnic differences can be problems, but they also make our nation and the world a beautiful, exciting place to live.

Did you know:

- African slaves first were brought to America in 1619. At the time there were also many whites who were slaves and subject to the same laws and punishments as African slaves. Both black and white servants could own livestock and work to buy their freedom. As time went by the "servant codes" in the South applied only to black slaves.

- Chinese and other Asian cultures have rich and varied heritages that came before the white Western culture by thousands of years. Every major international religion, including Judaism, Christianity, and Islam, began in Asia.

- While "Native American" or "American Indian" has come to refer to all those people living in America before the arrival of Columbus, in fact Indian cultures varied greatly. Many of the early European settlers would not have survived without the direct help of many Indians.

- Major types of specifically U.S. music—such as, jazz, rhythm and blues, and rock and roll—trace their origins to African American culture. Popular American music and culture are a rich blending of the gifts from a wide variety of ethnic groups. ◆

Responding to Racism: Building the American Dream

I have a dream that one day on the red hills of Georgia, sons of former slaves and sons of former slaveowners will be able to sit down together at the table of brotherhood. . . . I have a dream that my four children will one day live in a nation where they will not be judged by the color of their skin but by the content of their character.

—Martin Luther King, Jr., *I Have a Dream,* 1963.

◆ We probably could come up with jokes that make fun of or belittle members of a particular race or ethnic group. Can you think of examples of humor that can take a stand against prejudice and racism? Examine what makes one type of humor good and another bad or hurtful.

In the 1940s, psychologists Kenneth and Mamie Clark did research with four-year-old children. They gave children white dolls and black dolls to play with. Without fail, both black children and white children said that the white dolls were "nicer." Unfortunately, even with the changes brought on by civil rights and the increase of African Americans in important positions in American society, more often than not young children still select white dolls as better and nicer than black dolls. As one author remarks:

> *Something is clearly wrong when young children, as soon as they get a look at the world we've made, are disappointed with the color of their skin.*
>
> —Sara Bullard, *Teaching Tolerance*, NY: Doubleday, page 11.

One African who learned about this choice for whiteness over blackness in the United States noted that, before Europeans established colonies, in Africa "whiteness"—for example, white skin—meant weak and sickly. These two discoveries reveal that: Our views on race and skin color are deeply ingrained in our society; and perspectives on race are not universal and they can change.

Countering Racism Requires Stopping the Hurt

Racism hurts.

- When unemployment among young people rises, unemployment among *black* youths increases considerably more than the average.
- Studies indicating that women are paid less than men also reveal that on average women of color are paid *even less* than their white sisters.
- When prison overcrowding occurs, when hunger and homelessness reach widespread proportions, or when older people must struggle to keep up with rising inflation—then African American, Native American, and Hispanic populations suffer *more than others*.

Justice, then, includes admitting that members of certain races are commonly denied rights and privileges not denied members of other races. Certainly, wonderful success stories can be told about members of all races in the United States; the American dream has worked for many people of all races. Also, race is not the only factor in determining power, privileges, and opportunities for Americans. Nonetheless, it is important to admit that some people have a greater struggle surviving and getting ahead in society because of their race. In other words racism exists in the United States; thus, overcoming racism is a work of justice.

> *An old rabbi once asked his students how one could recognize the time when night ends and day begins. "Is it when . . . you can tell a dog from a sheep?" one student asked. "No," said the rabbi. "Is it when . . . you can tell a date palm from a fig tree?" another student asked. "No," said the rabbi. ". . . It is when you look into the face of any human creature and see your brother or your sister there. Until then, night is still with us."*
>
> —quoted in Dorothee Soelle, *The Strength of the Weak*, Philadelphia, PA: Westminster Press, 1984, page 41.

In Summary: We Are All One

Astronauts are granted a unique view of our world. In relating their experiences while in space, astronauts often mention that they sense a "oneness" not only of the planet itself but of all the passengers on "spaceship earth." Because of their special point of view, astronauts often realize what important religious figures throughout the ages have proclaimed: We are all one.

Experts who study "peak experiences" suggest that most of us at some time in our lives also experience that the world is one and that we are all members of one family. Perhaps deep down we know that when one person suffers we all suffer and that seeking the good of all people is good for each of us. Prejudices and racism cloud over this bright view of humanity, which is in fact the view that Jesus wished for his followers. Therefore, when we examine our prejudices and participate in overcoming racism, we are doing Christian service—supporting differences, making the world a more plentiful and exciting place for everyone, and creating compassionate community.

Let us pray . . .

*God our Father, who placed a rainbow
in the sky to remind Noah of your constant care,
we thank you for American jazz and Italian opera,
for the earthy drum beat of Native American song,
and the swirling energy of Ukrainian dance,
for the peaceful strains of Zen music,
and the spiritual intensity of Muslim chant.
We pray that we may discover your face
in the many colors and cultures
that live in our world.
Help us to do what we can
so that there will be fewer
experiences of hatred or mistreatment
because of race, creed, or ethnic background.
May your Spirit within us
lead us to build bridges
and break down barriers,
so that your rainbow world will be a holy world.
Amen.*

For further study . . .

1. Write a response to the following statement:

   Most of us are burdened with prejudice and intolerance from our families, friends, and, unfortunately, many of our leaders. There should be no shame in admitting we harbor some prejudice on issues such as race, religion, and sexual orientation. What is shameful is our failure to examine those prejudices.

   —Sara Bullard, "Teaching Tolerance," Tuscaloosa, AL: *Southern Poverty Law Review*, page xix.

2. Write a report on one of the following topics:

   • hate groups or hate crimes in the United States
   • an international conflict in which racial or ethnic hatred plays a role

3. Write an essay describing what you think is the appeal of hate groups.

4. Give at least two examples of each of the following:

   • conscious racism by an individual
   • unconscious racism by an individual
   • conscious institutional racism
   • unconscious institutional racism

5. Do research to find out the current ethnic makeup of the Catholic Church in the United States or the world.

6. Write a report on one ethnic group's experience of being Catholic in the United States, either its current situation or its history.

7. Think back on your own family's history of the last few generations. Draw a family tree as far back as you can go. (If necessary, ask your parents for help.) Do you find that your family's ethnic or racial background played any role in their understanding of the American dream? Do you think that your ethnic or racial background today plays any role in your view of, or in the possibility of your achieving, the American dream?

CHAPTER 9

Groups Seeking Justice

Compassion for the Marginalized

When we ask who is hurting in our society, we know that no one escapes being an answer to the question. When we ask who is hurting because of social injustice, we can identify certain groups who suffer needlessly because of attitudes, practices, and social structures that exist in our culture. Five groups who deserve attention in light of justice will be discussed in this chapter.

Major Concepts

A. Older Persons: A New Look at Old Friends

- Aging versus ageism
- Problems of growing older
- The Christian view of aging
- Responding to the aged

B. Persons with Disabilities: Moving from Exclusion to Inclusion

- The burden of being disabled
- The Christian view of people with disabilities
- Fostering affirming attitudes and social policies for people with disabilities

C. Gay and Lesbian Persons

- Homophobia
- Gay and lesbian struggles

D. Prisoners: Society's Forgotten Ones

- Crimes against people and property
- Responding to prisoners
- The Christian view of capital punishment
- Criminal justice and social justice

E. The Unborn: Cultivating a Culture of Life in a Culture of Death

- The value of the unborn
- Defending the innocent
- Calling things by their proper name

Said the little boy, "Sometimes I drop my spoon."
Said the little old man, "I do that, too."
The little boy whispered, "I wet my pants."
"I do that, too," laughed the little old man.
Said the little boy, "I often cry."
The old man nodded, "So do I."
"But worst of all," said the boy, "it seems
grown-ups don't pay attention to me."
And he felt the warmth of a wrinkled old hand.
"I know what you mean," said the little old man.

Lord, we were young children once and we
remember what it's like to feel like this child
does. Help us to use our own memories of
helplessness and lack of worth to relate better
with those who are old. We pray today for all
the elderly who are forgotten and lonely.
May they come to better know their worth by
our actions toward them. Amen.

Older Persons: A New Look at Old Friends

The insightful humorist points out that "growing old is not so bad
when you consider the alternative." However, as a society we can
make problems faced by older persons more or less troublesome as a
result of our attitudes, values, actions, and policies. In this section we
will identify key issues related to aging, especially society's attitudes
toward aging and toward people who are fifty and older.

Before we begin . . .

Answer **agree**, **disagree**, or **uncertain** to the following statements. Choose statements that you believe are most significant and explain your answers.

1. I treat an older person the same way I treat anyone else.

2. Generally speaking, our society looks upon older people in a positive light.

3. Older people are viewed basically the same way in all cultures.

4. Older people are usually presented in a positive light in movies, in advertisements, and on TV.

5. When I am old, I would like our society's attitude toward and treatment of older people to remain as it is today.

6. Being an older person would be a frightening experience.

7. Older people in my family offer a positive image of what it is like to be old.

8. If at all possible, nursing homes should be avoided for older people.

9. If I were older and in good health, I would choose to live in a community mainly for older people.

10. Our government provides adequate services for older people.

11. Being old has joys not available to younger people.

Snapshots of Old Age

■ Betty never seemed to recover from her husband's death. With some relief, a great deal of fear, and a deep sense of despair, Betty accepted the moves from her own home to her daughter's home and now to the nursing home. She feels continually anxious over the most basic concerns: When will she

eat? Who will help her to the bathroom? Will her medication ease her aches and pains and make her more comfortable? Since she never seems to get beyond thinking about these elementary needs, family members visit her less and less. Whether she suffers from the strokes that damaged her mind and body or simply from a broken heart, Betty is a shell of the vital, energetic person she used to be.

■ Mr. and Mrs. Boyle are preparing for a trip to Italy—their third such vacation since retirement. Both are physically healthy and mentally alert. Although a number of their friends have died in recent years, the Boyles never lack for companions or activities. Their lives are full and rich. They look forward to many active years together.

■ Helen spent three years caring for her husband as he sank further into Alzheimer's disease. Helen would bring her husband to family affairs, even though he spent most of his time asking his children and grandchildren what their names were. Helen finally agreed with her children that a managed-care facility was best for her husband, even though it would deplete the savings they had collected through years of thrifty spending and uninterrupted work. Nonetheless, she spent most of her time by her husband's side, even managing to help other residents on her husband's floor of the nursing home. Helen, whose life was already marked by years of service to her children and her community, continued to serve even into her old age.

• Based on experiences you have had with older people, write a description in story, essay, song, or poetry of what it might be like to be old. Consider the needs and fears of older people, as well as possible joys and pleasures of being old.

The Graying of America

In an earlier chapter one of the characteristics we mentioned about poorer countries is their growing populations. That means that there are large numbers of children and a smaller percentage of older people. By contrast, in the United States, women and men over the age of sixty-five are the fastest-growing age group. One hundred years ago the average person lived to be only forty-seven years old. Today the average is in the mid-seventies. Reaching the age of one hundred, although still noted with fanfare that adds a light touch to morning news programs, is becoming more and more commonplace. According to best estimates, soon one in six U.S. citizens will be what is now considered an older person.

graying of America
the trend toward an increasingly older population in the U.S.

This **graying of America** is a relatively recent event. As a result, not only are problems associated with old age growing ones, they are also comparatively new ones, at least on the scale at which we now must face them.

Biological Versus Societal Aging: Aging Is Different from Ageism

Biological aging refers simply to the amount of time a person lives. Except for occasional movies designed to give older actors a chance to act like children, it is clear that someone who is ninety years old is obviously biologically older than someone turning sixteen. However, in addition to biological aging, we need also to admit that there is such a thing as societal aging or ageism.

ageism
discriminatory attitudes and practices toward people based on their age

Ageism is a term that parallels two concepts addressed earlier in the course—sexism and racism. Biological aging brings on problems associated with health, relationships, and a sense of defenselessness. However, as with sexism and racism, the actual experience of aging cannot be divorced from ageism. As you read through the following problems associated with old age, consider to what extent "societal aging" influences what growing old is like for most people. ◆

Problems of Old Age: The Result of Biology or of Societal Attitudes?

America today faces a great paradox: It is an aging nation which worships the culture, values, and appearance of youth. Instead of viewing old age as an achievement and a natural stage of life with its own merits, wisdom, and beauty, American society all too often ignores, rejects, and isolates the elderly.

—U.S. Catholic Bishops, *Society and the Aged*, number 1.

◆ List as many stereotypes about older people or aging as you can. Do these stereotypes give more of a positive or a negative image of what it means to be old in our society? For each stereotype, try to name an older person, someone you know personally or a public figure, who is an exception to the stereotype.

Physical Health

Physical problems are an important concern for older people. Hearing loss and worsening eyesight, brittle bones, as well as a gradual breakdown of the circulatory and other body systems, occur as people get older, although not at the same rate for everyone. Being sick is frightening. Being old and sick is doubly frightening since every illness or health problem is a reminder of overall physical decline. However, it is important to remember that "being old" and "being sickly" are not the same thing. Ben Franklin helped write the Constitution of the United States while in his seventies. Ronald Reagan was elected president for the first of two terms at age sixty-nine. W.E.B. Du Bois, a civil rights leader for over half a century, continued working on his monumental *Encyclopedia Africana* into his nineties. Mother Teresa of India received the Nobel Peace Prize at age sixty-nine and remained active for many years thereafter.

The list of active, energetic contributors to world culture whom we would label as "old" could go on. Lest we think of such people as the exception, we can also cite studies indicating that older workers, people in their fifties and sixties, often have better records than younger workers: less absenteeism, greater stability, a steadier rate of production, and higher quality work. ◆

Health of the Mind

Have you ever forgotten someone's name whom you had been introduced to several times? Have you ever begun to tell someone a story only to have them say, "You told me that yesterday"? Has someone ever asked you to do something for them, and it totally slips your mind? If so, perhaps you are growing senile!

Actually, when we are younger we can laugh off occasional forgetfulness. But for an older person, forgetfulness can be caused by **senility** or the beginning stages of **Alzheimer's disease**. Senility, which has been called a wastebasket label, refers to a decrease in brain functions which can happen as a person grows older. There is no real physical problem that can be seen. Therefore, senility can be used simply to support the belief that older people are incapable of being productive members of society. Alzheimer's disease is a progressive disease that strikes some people in their sixties or beyond. Its most striking symptom is forgetfulness which causes irritability and the inability to make choices and follow through on actions. It is important to remember that intellectual decline does not have to happen with older people, nor is it a characteristic of aging. When a person is willing to learn, researchers say, the ability to learn may be as high at age eighty as it is at age twelve.

senility

irreversible brain damage that may occur in the aging process

Alzheimer's disease

a progressive disease that may occur in older people, leading to confusion, grouchiness, and impaired judgment

◆ Find other examples of people older than sixty who made or are making strong contributions to their communities. Write a biographical sketch about one of them and share it with your class.

Economic Security

Along with health matters, finances tend to concern older people disproportionately. Actually, in recent years government programs and policies have been designed that have drastically increased the economic security of older people. As mentioned in earlier chapters, older people are now less likely than children to be numbered among the poor. Nonetheless, many older people exist on what is termed a **fixed income**. That is, they depend on Social Security and other pension moneys as their only sources of income. This annual income remains nearly the same in the face of increasing costs for goods and services. ◆

fixed income

income that remains much the same year after year, such as Social Security or pension payments

Safety and Isolation

Rita Ungaro-Schiavone noticed that quite a few older people in her Northeast Philadelphia neighborhood were living alone. She discovered that they were capable of living on their own but that they needed help to get food into the house or to make trips to the doctor or drugstore. She decided to begin in her parish, a program called "Aid for Friends." Some parishioners would cook extra meals for distribution while others would drop off a weekly supply of these meals to a house-bound person, checking

as they did on the physical and emotional well-being of the person. The program proved to be so successful, and the need so great, that Aid for Friends spread to many other parishes and religious organizations in the Philadelphia area.

As a group, U.S. citizens are a people on the move. Older parents can find themselves living in Kansas City while their children are busy with work and their own families in Atlanta or San Diego. When friends their own age die or move to live with children, older people encounter increased loneliness. As their mobility decreases, their need for assistance increases. In some communities, because they are physically more defenseless, older people living alone often fear for their safety. This is especially the case when the older person is homebound. In today's highly mobile and youth-oriented society, some older people are left out of the network of support and social interaction that usually helps people in a community.

◆ The largest organization speaking for older Americans is the American Association of Retired Persons. Find an older person who is a member. (People must be fifty to join.) Ask if you can borrow literature from the organization, or access the organization through the Internet. Review the literature to determine what AARP considers important concerns of older people at this time.

Stereotypes

Would you like to be reduced to the popular image of "teenager" held in our culture? Probably not. A unique individual, you share some things in common with other teens. But you also have your own story—likes and dislikes, personality traits, strengths and interests. Similarly, if we approach older people with openness, respect, and readiness, we are more likely to discover their uniqueness which has been developing for many more years than our own. Contrary to common stereotypes, older people are more likely than teens to be different from one another; and older people are more similar to than different from the rest of us.

Often we forget that our view of older people is heavily conditioned by our culture. Not every culture looks upon old age negatively. In Asian countries, for instance, older people typically are shown great honor. Even during the early years of U.S. history, older people were considered distinguished and worthy of special honor. (Early American men and women actually wore white wigs to make themselves appear older and, thereby, more dignified!) ◆

A Christian View of Old Age

> *Healing the rupture between society and its elderly members requires a major effort to change attitudes as well as social structures. In undertaking this task, we are not simply meeting the demands of charity and justice. We are accepting our own humanity, our link with past and future and, thereby, our link with the Creator.*
>
> —U.S. Catholic Bishops, *Society and the Aged,* number 52.

A casual reading of the early sections of the Bible reveals that the heroes of the Hebrew people are described as living super-human life spans. Scholars suggest that the Hebrew patriarchs did not actually live to such great ages but rather that this was a way to show reverence and respect for them. In the Scriptures, aging is associated with wisdom and understanding; older people are to be cherished and accorded special care. The commandment "Honor your father and your mother" (Deuteronomy 5:16) reflects this belief.

As the above quote states, Catholic leaders today fear that overlooking older people, ignoring their special needs and unique contributions, breaks our link both with the past and with our own future. Both personal attitudes and social structures need examining so that the bond between old and young can be more strongly knit together. If Jesus teaches us anything, it is that life means relatedness. To divorce ourselves from any group lessens our connection to life itself and ultimately to God. ◆

 Are the areas of concern listed here caused entirely by aging itself? Are they in any way also affected by ageism—that is, by personal or societal attitudes, values, practices, and policies? List as many ways as possible how ageism adds to the problems of aging described above.

◆ If you were to design a program for older church members, what would it include? Ask an older person: What would you like from the church? Compare your proposal with what the older person would like.

Sally's Story

Reluctantly, Sally joined the volunteers from her school who would be visiting the nursing home for the next two months. Sally had been to a nursing home only once before, when she had gone along with a friend visiting her grandmother. Sally found that visit completely depressing, and she was anticipating a similar experience this time.

Initially, her expectations were realized. Once in the hall where the residents were gathered, Sally kept trying to hide among the others in her group. She was afraid to go near any of the residents for fear one would touch her. She had been given the name of Mrs. Ruth Lewis who was to be her special friend during her weekly visits. The woman pointed out to her was sitting on a bench where she leaned on a walker and stared absently in front of herself. Mrs. Lewis appeared very frail and wore a sweater even in the warm room. Sally was not looking forward to spending time with this person with the blank eyes and aged skin. What would she do with her? What could she talk about?

Surprisingly, when they got together Mrs. Lewis carried the conversation. She asked Sally about her family and her school and then told Sally about her own family. Perhaps because she felt so nervous, Sally talked away about herself; and Mrs. Lewis actually seemed interested. With a smile on her face, Mrs. Lewis told Sally about an incident from her own school days as if it had happened yesterday.

After her second trip to the nursing home, Sally felt comfortable walking the halls and came to look forward to her visits. She even got the hang of helping Mrs. Lewis up from her chair and steadying her with her walker. When Sally's ten weeks were up, she held Mrs. Lewis' hand for a long time and assured her that she would come back to see her. When she kissed her good-bye, Sally felt as though she had met a beautiful person and had indeed made a special friend.

- Arrange to interview an older person. Prepare a list of items to discuss. Tape the interview. Report to your class on your reactions to your discussion.

Responding to Older Persons: How Can We Make a Difference?

Our Personal Response

Despite the claims of miracle drugs, aging is not going away. However, any shame associated with aging and the difficulties linked to aging can be reduced. A key to young people gaining a more positive and realistic picture of older people is to spend time with them, as Sally did. As anyone who is close to a grandparent knows, a friendship that spans generations is a special friendship. Older people are a storehouse of lived experiences waiting to be tapped.

However, with older people as with people of all ages, it is important to keep in mind that they are precious in themselves, not because they are useful or helpful to us. Therefore, the first step toward justice for older people is fostering a spirit of compassionate care for them.

> *I have learned that a culture which equates material possessions with success, and views the frantic, compulsive consumer as the perfect citizen, can afford little space for the aged human being. They are past competing, they are out of the game. We live in a culture which endorses what has been called "human obsolescence." After adolescence, obsolescence. To the junk heap, the nursing home, the retirement village, the "Last Resort."*
>
> —Sharon R. Curtin, *Nobody Ever Died of Old Age*, Boston: Little, Brown and Co., 1972, pages 195–196.

Societal Changes

In the United States, steps have been taken to put into place a "safety net" for older people. This has eased but not eliminated financial worries for many. Basic health care, although still a major expense, is now viewed as a right for all older people. But surprisingly, a key to meeting the safety and security needs of older people is to improve the lot of children—all children, not just our own. That is, while older people have particular strengths, they also have their needs. In the future the increasing number of Mrs. Lewises will depend more and more on the Sallys of the nation—for physical assistance, for contributing money to Social Security funds supporting retired persons, and in general for weaving the social fabric upon which everyone depends. When one of every five children in a country lives in poverty, it will become harder to provide long-term care for older people. In other words the work of social justice, for old and for young, is all of one piece. ◆

◆ Explain and use examples to defend or refute the following statement: A key to meeting the safety and security needs of older people is to improve the lot of children.

Keys to Making Life Better for Older People

- Improved health and education for children and young people.
- A strengthened spirit of morality and social concern among the young.
- Expanded employment opportunities for young adults.
- Increased support for families.

Review

1. How is the U.S. different from poorer countries in terms of the age of its population?
2. Define *graying of America*.
3. What is the difference between *biological aging* and *societal aging*?
4. Define *ageism*.
5. List the five areas of concern mentioned in the text associated with old age.
6. What is *Alzheimer's disease*?
7. Why is *senility* often a "wastebasket label"?
8. What does it mean to say that many older people live on a fixed income?
9. Why in the Bible are Hebrew patriarchs described as living to such old ages?
10. Why are older persons helped when the lot of children is improved?

Discuss

A. Can you think of examples of ageism in North American culture? Which age group in our society do you believe suffers the most from ageism? Explain.

B. List as many terms as you can think of used to refer to older people, such as, "people in their golden years." If you were older, do you think you would find any of these terms offensive or put-downs? Explain. If you were an old person, what would you prefer to be called? Why?

C. How does your parish or a church near you serve the needs of older people? How does it utilize the services of older people? Are there opportunities for older people and younger people to get together? Describe them.

Opening Prayer

God of Creation, you have made all of us in your image. Help us to see you in the baby who has Down's syndrome, the child who wears leg braces, the teen who will never learn more than at a grade-school level. Let us understand the struggles of persons with disabiltities and offer our support and encouragement to them when they need it. We give thanks to you, tender and compassionate God, that you accept all of us as we are—imperfect earthen vessels that hold the treasure of your love. Let us experience the brokenness of one another and, through your presence in each of us dare to be healers of one another. Amen.

Persons with Disabilities: Moving from Exclusion to Inclusion

Jesus spent much of his time with people whom today we would categorize as disabled. Even so, our society, including our churches, is not known for exceptional care for persons with disabilities. Too often, the response of many people to persons with disabilities parallels what they want from older people— to be out of sight and out of mind. However, in a compassionate community all of us are richer when we care for one another as sisters and brothers.

Before we begin . . .

Answer **agree, disagree**, or **uncertain** to the following statements. Choose statements that you believe are most significant and explain your answers.

1. I know and socialize with a person or persons with disabilities.

2. I treat a person with a disability the same as I do anyone else.

3. I am uncomfortable around people with physical or mental disabilities.

4. Our society has taken adequate steps to provide for persons with disabilities.

5. Children with emotional or mental problems should attend schools separate from other children.

6. Since both disabled and able-bodied persons live in the same communities, they should attend the same schools and share classrooms.

7. If I were a person with a disability, I would feel welcomed in my school.

Snapshots of Persons with Disabilities

Alex is a familiar sight riding his wheelchair through the school halls. His classmates include him in activities, and Alex misses no chance to participate in whatever ways he can. On the sidelines at every game, he proudly wears the school's football jersey and serves as the team's honorary manager. He excels at computer skills, and his classmates don't hesitate to come to him for help running programs. When he encounters a difficulty, such as finding enough space for his wheelchair in the narrow lecture hall, he seeks help without complaint. At his school Alex is not "that boy in a wheelchair." Rather, he is Alex—classmate, computer whiz, football manager, friend.

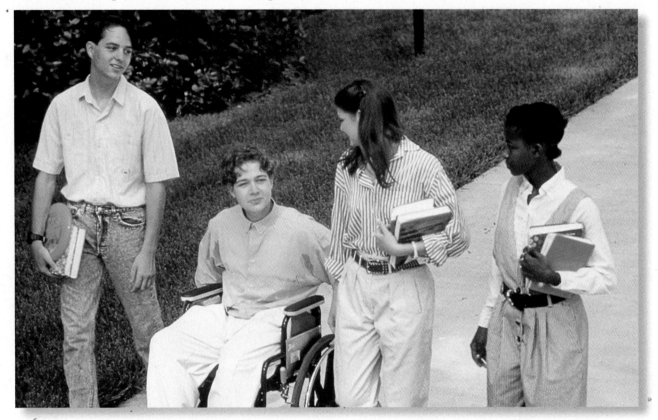

Brad loves his work. Through counselors at his school, a school specifically for students who have mental disabilities, he landed a job cleaning up the theaters at a nearby multiplex. Occasionally, he gets to see the movies, although most of the time he sees only the last few minutes of them. Brad loves being at the center of the excitement. He greets movie-goers warmly, and generally people respond in a friendly manner. Occasionally, regular customers even ask him which movies he recommends. Brad's cheerful personality makes movie-going a more pleasant experience for everyone.

Blind since birth, Mrs. Fielder still managed to graduate from college with a teaching degree.

She impressed the school's administrators so much with her knowledge of history and her teaching ability that she was hired to teach the demanding senior high courses. Students do not dare act out in her classes. Despite her disability she has developed her own system for maintaining classroom order. Mostly students are spellbound by the "behind the scenes" stories she tells about great historical events. In some aspects of her job, Mrs. Fielder works differently from other teachers, and she requires a few special accommodations. Nonetheless, the strongest impression that the school community has about her classes is that she loves her work and her students, and her students love her.

- Think back to your first encounter with a person with a disability. How did you react? What did you feel?
- What types of experiences with persons with disabilities have you had recently? How did you react? How did you feel?

Persons with Disabilities Carry a Double Burden

The previous true stories all paint a rosy picture of the experience of being disabled. They also portray friendly, easy relationships between people who have disabilities and those who don't. However, persons with disabilities often find that other people zero in on their difference and seldom look beyond it. Persons with disabilities can end up feeling set apart from the group, as if to be different in one particular way means to be different in all ways.

People are naturally fearful of the unknown. If we have few opportunities to be with blind or severely hearing-

impaired persons, with someone who has cerebral palsy or Down's syndrome, or with those who use a wheelchair for mobility, then we can easily be cautious and unsure about how to relate to them. As a result, people with disabilities often carry a double burden: coping with a disability while also dealing with rejection or peculiar responses from others. If you think you seldom meet persons who have some disability, the following information may prove helpful.

Who Are the Disabled?

- Although "disability" is not a precise term, many more Americans are disabled than we might think. One estimate suggests that one in seven people in the U.S. can be classified disabled.

- It is important to remember that many people possess *invisible disabilities*. For instance, a child may have mild mental handicaps or any number of learning disabilities. Sometimes people with invisible disabilities encounter more difficulties in life than those who are obviously disabled because others do not recognize their special needs and therefore place unrealistic expectations on them.(They are doing poorly in school because they are "lazy." They get into fights all the time because they are "bad kids.")

- Most importantly, we are all disabled in some way. More accurately, we are all more or less able-bodied and only temporarily so. Some of us just happen to be more noticeably disabled than others.

We Are All Disabled

This third point sets us in the direction of responding positively toward others, whether we are among the noticeably disabled or not. None of us is 100 percent "able"; all of us have shortcomings. Alex in the previous scenario cannot walk, but none of his classmates can master the difficulties of a computer like Alex can. By the same token who is more "disabled"—someone with minimal eyesight or someone blinded by hate? Even though we probably would not label them disabled, people can be emotionally as well as physically or mentally handicapped. ◆

The Needs of Persons with Disabilities and Their Families

The positive tone of the previous stories is not meant to minimize or dismiss the special needs of persons with disabilities or the immense burdens encountered by their families. Depending on the severity of the handicap, caring for a disabled person, child or adult, can be a twenty-four-hour-a-day job. Meanwhile, parents and other caregivers cannot overlook other daily tasks, such as home, employment, relationships, and possibly other children. Children and sometimes even adults can be unintentionally cruel to persons with disabilities and their families. Simple things like shopping become major undertakings. Finances are constantly strained. Siblings of persons with disabilities carry all kinds of added burdens, such as often taking on the role of being "little parents" to a younger or older disabled brother or sister. At the same time, siblings of persons with disabilities often develop into extremely caring persons who are especially sensitive to the needs of others.

The needs of persons with disabilities and their families are great. A just and compassionate community seeks ways to ease their burdens through voicing support, sharing tasks, and planning programs that contribute assistance. In 1990, the U.S. Congress passed the **Americans with Disabilities Act**. You may have noticed in your local community a change aimed at making public space less troublesome for persons with disabilities. This change was initiated by this act. One of the most significant contributions of the act has been the realization that, where possible, the best way to help persons with disabilities is to make it easier for them to help themselves.

Americans with Disabilities Act

act passed by Congress in 1990 initiating changes to ensure that the rights of the disabled are not violated because of a disability

◆ As a class, create a prayer service in which everyone writes down a personal "disability" or a symbol of one. As part of the service, create a ritual by which class members could demonstrate acceptance of one another.

A Christian View: Ability or Disability Does Not Measure Value

Persons with disabilities are often great teachers—modeling courage, patience, joy in the face of hardship, and the resourcefulness of the human spirit. They are gifts from God, an embodiment of Christ's presence, as we all are. Therefore, an important lesson taught to us by people with disabilities is the value of the human person. None of us measures up to perfection, and yet Christians humbly celebrate that we are all created in God's image.

This core Christian teaching applies to a youngster who is mentally or developmentally disabled just as it does to the rest of us. Meditating on that image can provide as much food for prayer as reading the Bible stories about little David slaying the giant Goliath or reading about the child Jesus astounding the priests in the temple with his wisdom.

The U.S. Catholic bishops consider justice for persons with disabilities as a right-to-life issue. Fear of those with disabilities promotes abortion. Killing of the unborn, who may not be perfect, promotes prejudice against those with disabilities. The bishops point out that the right to life implies other rights, in this case the right to full participation in the human community. Therefore, the bishops call for examination of areas such as education, employment, housing, and accessible public buildings to determine whether or not they allow for suitable participation of persons with disabilities. The bishops see justice for persons with disabilities as an outgrowth of Christian love which affirms our common humanity:

> *No act of charity or justice can be of lasting value to persons with disabilities unless it is informed by a sincere and understanding love that penetrates the wall of strangeness and affirms the common humanity underlying all distinction.* ◆

—U.S. Catholic Bishops, *On Persons with Disabilities*, number 3.

◆ Imagine what it might be like to have a particular disability. Use the "special beatitudes" on the next page to write your own set of beatitudes that would reflect the perspective of a person who possesses that disability.

Special Beatitudes

Blessed are you who take time to listen to difficult speech, for you help us to know that if we persevere, we can be understood.

Blessed are you who walk with us in public places and ignore the stares of strangers, for in your companionship we find havens of relaxation.

Blessed are you who never bid us to "hurry up"; and more blessed, you who do not snatch our tasks from our hands to do them for us, for often we need time rather than help.

Blessed are you who stand beside us as we enter new and untried ventures, for our failures will be outweighed by the times when we surprise ourselves and you.

Blessed are you who ask for our help, for our greatest need is to be needed.

Blessed are you who help us with the graciousness of Christ, for oftentimes we need the help we cannot ask for.

Blessed are you, when by all these things you assure us that the thing that makes us individuals is not in our peculiar muscles, nor in our wounded nervous systems, nor in our difficulties in learning, but in the God-given self that no infirmity can confine.

Rejoice and be exceedingly glad, and know that you give us reassurances that could never be spoken in words, for you deal with us as Christ dealt with all his children.

—Stan Carder, *A Committed Mercy*, Grand Rapids, MI: Baker Books, 1995, pages 41–42.

Review

11. What does it mean to say that persons with disabilities carry a double burden?
12. Define *invisible disabilities*.
13. What does it mean to say that we are all disabled in some way?
14. What approach to helping persons with disabilities is advocated in the Americans with Disabilities Act of 1990?
15. What right do the U.S. Catholic bishops claim for persons with disabilities?

Discuss

D. Besides physical handicaps, what are some ways that a person might be "disabled"?
E. List problems that you imagine parents of a severely handicapped child might face. What strains on their lives might they encounter? What types of assistance do you think would be most helpful to them?
F. Name ways that having a severely handicapped sister or brother might affect you.

Opening Prayer

God of the forgotten ones, we pray for all those who find themselves suffering from injustice and misunderstanding in our nation and our world. Help us to examine values in our society that are faulty, or mean-spirited, or hurtful. May we find within ourselves the courage and compassion to stand with the gay and lesbian person. May the loving gaze with which you view them become our gaze. We ask this in the name of your Son, Jesus, who lived his life with the forgotten ones of his day, teaching us that only in their midst will we find you. Amen.

Gay and Lesbian Persons

Even today, when popular TV sitcoms don't hesitate to include gay and lesbian characters as part of their story lines, the topic of homosexuality often brings on a flood of emotions denying it a reasonable hearing. Aside from the many moral issues surrounding homosexuality, insults to the dignity of gay and lesbian persons and lack of acceptance of them by some people in today's society make homosexuality a matter of justice.

Before we begin . . .

Answer **agree**, **disagree**, or **uncertain** to the following statements. Choose statements that you believe are most significant and explain your answers.

1. I am comfortable discussing the topic of homosexuality.

2. I have had serious discussions about homosexuals or homosexuality.

3. I am comfortable in the company of gay and lesbian persons.

4. I view gay and lesbian persons as a threat.

5. If I were gay or lesbian, I would be happy with our society's current attitudes toward homosexuals.

6. Gay and lesbian persons are usually pictured realistically in movies and on television.

7. If a friend of mine admitted to being homosexual, I would be very upset.

8. My parents and close friends would be supportive if I told them I was gay or lesbian.

9. Openly gay and lesbian persons should not be prevented from serving in the military.

10. Openly gay and lesbian persons should not be rejected from holding teaching positions.

11. Gay and lesbian persons suffer from injustice in our society.

12. I would like to see attitudes and societal policies change to make conditions better for gay and lesbian persons.

A Snapshot of a Gay Man

Cindy is sixteen. She feels close to her family. She is especially close to Kevin, her twenty-two-year old brother. Since he went away to college four years ago, Cindy has seen little of her brother. Yet when they have been together on family vacations, she has always shared with Kevin all the important concerns of her life. She would chatter on about school and boyfriends, and he would listen. When she was upset, he always seemed to understand. She would clown around, and he would be the first to join in. All in all, she felt that Kevin was everything that an older brother should be.

On one of Kevin's weekend visits home, he brought along a college friend of his named Bill. Cindy noticed that they seemed to be close friends, but that didn't surprise her. Naturally, Kevin would have close friends, both male and female ones.

On his next visit home, Kevin wanted to talk about himself for a change, and Cindy became the listener. Eventually Kevin told her the shocking news: he believed he was gay.

Cindy was stunned and confused. In quick steps she jumped from denial to anger to confusion. How could this be? She had many images of homosexual men, none of them flattering. She also knew and loved her brother. Her image of Kevin and her image of gay men simply did not belong together.

Kevin asked Cindy not to tell their parents just yet. He also reassured her that he is still her big brother who will always be there for her and that he was not intending to go out and do anything stupid that would upset the family.

Since their conversation Cindy has not changed her life; but her view of life has changed drastically. She still jokes a lot and enjoys watching rented videos with her friends. But now she notices and feels uncomfortable when jokes are about gays. Maybe the same jokes were told before, but she had never paid much attention to them. Now they hold new meaning. Now they touch her deepest self. Now they are about her brother.

- What problems do you think homosexual people encounter? What changes would people who are homosexual want to see in popular images of homosexuals? What laws and policies would protect the rights of people who are homosexual?

What Does It Mean to Be Homosexual?

Homosexuality is a very emotion-charged topic, and perhaps no group suffers more from popular stereotypes and jokes than homosexuals. The jokes may even be considered acceptable because homosexuals are often viewed as distorted versions of humanity or as less than human. Since adolescence marks a time of developing sexual identities, teenagers especially can be particularly nervous about and cruel toward homosexuals or imagined homosexuals. Yet, in truth, within the blanket category *homosexual* exist flesh-and-blood persons who find themselves victimized in many ways. The heterosexual society holds negative attitudes toward them. At the same time they are called to be creative, true-to-themselves, and loving persons, as we all are called to be.

Up front, it is important to note that official Catholic teaching stresses physical-sexual expression as finding its rightful place only in the loving and life-giving context of marriage. Official Catholic Church teaching views physically intimate homosexual activity as falling short of the ideal of married sexual union and therefore as wrong. Also, the U.S. Catholic Conference of Bishops states in their 1997 pastoral message, *Always Our Children*, that those who openly violate Church teachings can be denied public roles of service and leadership by the Church. Nevertheless, because of the negative attitudes toward homosexuals and the harmful actions aimed at them, the American Catholic bishops have stated that homosexuality *is* a justice issue. For instance, the bishops in their 1976 pastoral letter on morality spoke out against prejudice toward people who are homosexual:

> *Homosexuals, like everyone else, should not suffer from prejudice against their basic human rights. They have a right to respect, friendship, and justice. They should have an active role in the Christian community.*
>
> —U.S. Catholic Bishops, *To Live in Christ Jesus*, pg 19.

This condemnation of unjust treatment of homosexual persons is stated again by Church leaders in the 1994 *Catechism of the Catholic Church*:

> *The number of men and women who have deep-seated homosexual tendencies is not negligible. This inclination, which is objectively disordered, constitutes for most of them a trial. They must be accepted with respect, compassion, and sensitivity. Every sign of unjust discrimination in their regard should be avoided.* (2358)

The following information can help us shed light on fostering justice for gay and lesbian persons.

- *Homo* is a Greek prefix meaning "same." (*Hetero* means "different.") A homosexual person has a deep-seated and long-established sexual attraction for members of the same sex. In other words such attraction is not simply shallow or short-lived but rather it truly identifies the person's basic, underlying sexual interests. Only a clear, long-term interest toward same-sex attraction identifies a person as homosexual.

- It is not homosexual behavior that necessarily identifies someone as homosexual. Some homosexual persons marry and have children; others never have any physical-sexual experiences. Similarly, a heterosexual person may never have a physical-sexual experience or may even engage in homosexual activity. (For instance, some heterosexual men, when confined to the all-male environment of a prison, engage in homosexual activity simply because heterosexual activity is not available to them.)

- No studies conclusively identify what causes someone to become either homosexual or heterosexual. Some experts lean toward a biological explanation—that is, genetic make-up or hormones decides sexual

The national Gay Lesbian Straight Educators Network says that 97 percent of gay and lesbian students in public high schools report hearing homophobic remarks from fellow students. The group cites a 1989 federal Health and Human Services study indicating gays and lesbians account for 30 percent of teen suicides.
—*Philadelphia Inquirer*, October 18, 1997, page A6.

preference before a person is born. Other experts believe that early childhood experiences lead a person toward either homosexuality or heterosexuality. In either case sexual preference is usually determined by the age of five or six and generally is not the result of a conscious choice on the part of a homosexual person. Of course, how people respond to their sexual orientation is a matter of choice.

- **Homophobia** is a strong and destructive force at work in our society. Sometimes homophobia leads to acts of discrimination or even violence against people suspected of being homosexual.

- Gay and lesbian persons do not necessarily fit the stereotype painted of them by popular culture. Similarly, not all heterosexual men and women fit a particular stereotype of heterosexual persons. For a variety of reasons, some gay men and lesbian women do mirror social stereotypes. The percentage who do is comparatively small. Unfortunately, all gay and lesbian persons suffer because of society's stereotypes. As with any stereotyping, when we define people solely according to one dimension of their personality, then we lessen their individuality. We run the risk of treating them as objects and of treating them with less than the respect called for in justice.

homophobia
fear of homosexuals or of being homosexual

God does not love someone any less simply because he or she is homosexual. God's love is always and everywhere offered to those who are open to receiving it.

—National Conference of Catholic Bishops Committee on Marriage and Family, "Always Our Children," in *Origins*, Oct. 9, 1997 [27:17], page 289.

Review

16. What is official Catholic teaching on physically intimate homosexual activity?
17. What is the meaning of the Greek prefix *homo? hetero?*
18. What identifies a person as homosexual?
19. Why does engaging in homosexual activity not necessarily identify someone as homosexual?
20. What are the two prevailing theories about why some people are homosexual?
21. Define *homophobia.*

Discuss

G. Are you or is someone you know homophobic? Explain.
H. If a clear case of injustice occurred against a group of gay or lesbian persons in your community, would you sign a petition or participate in a demonstration supporting their concerns? Explain why or why not.

Opening Prayer

Forgiving Lord, you told Peter that forgiveness must be given seventy-times-seven. We search our hearts to question if we are willing to forgive even one time. Have we branded for life those who "have paid their dues"? Help us to see the persons behind the bars as our brothers or sisters and treat them with compassion and kindness worthy of children of God. Make us a source of hope for those who are held or hold themselves captive. Amen.

Prisoners: Society's Forgotten Ones

social justice

focuses on discrimination and unjust social structures

criminal justice

focuses on treatment of people in the judicial system

What is the relationship between social justice and criminal justice, the treatment of people in our judicial system? Aren't prisoners a big part of the problem and therefore not deserving of our consideration under a discussion of justice? In fact, social justice and criminal justice are more closely linked than they might immediately appear. Jesus himself named prisoners as one group to whom his message of justice was directly addressed. "The Lord's Spirit has come to me, because he has chosen me to tell the good news to the poor. The Lord has sent me to announce freedom for prisoners, to give sight to the blind, to free everyone who suffers, and to say, 'This is the year the Lord has chosen'" (Luke 4:18–19, CEV).

Before we begin . . .

Answer **agree**, **disagree**, or **uncertain** to the following statements. Choose statements that you believe to be most significant and explain your answers.

1. People in prison deserve to be there.

2. The threat of prison helps prevent crimes.

3. Generally speaking, the criminal justice system in the U.S. is fair and treats everyone equally.

4. I would vote for a politician who promised to "get tough on crime."

5. My view on criminals is simple: Lock them up and throw away the key.

6. Prisons or capital punishment are the only realistic ways to deal with wrongdoers.

7. If I were an employer, I would not hire someone who had spent time in jail.

8. I know personally someone who is or has been in a prison.

A Visit to a Big City Prison

Although it is in the heart of the city, the prison is a world unto itself. Never having been inside a prison before, you enter cautiously, filled with images and stereotypes gathered from years of watching cop shows and news reports.

Once past the metal detector and the seemingly endless series of locked gates, you enter a room where many prisoners are gathered to see a play to be performed by the prison drama club. Looking around the room you begin picking out the guards from the prisoners. The two groups wear different uniforms, there are many more prisoners than guards, and most of the prisoners are black while a few more of the guards are white. However, the prisoners do not appear more hostile, more angry, more frightening, or more "criminal" than the guards. In fact, the prisoners generally appear more friendly and relaxed than the guards—perhaps because they are not "on duty" and you are a guest in their "home."

One prisoner named Smitty comes over to greet you. A kindly looking man, he appears to be something of a leader and wants to make you feel at ease. Older than most of the prisoners, Smitty serves as a father figure for them, often listening to and settling disputes. He also leads the Tuesday evening Bible study sessions.

Another prisoner, James, is prison librarian and has recently become a Catholic. He longs to talk about Jesus and the meaning of some of the parables. Like most of the inmates, James has been in the prison for a year awaiting trial. (Of the approximately twelve hundred prisoners, only about three hundred of them have been sentenced.)

After the play, a dramatization of several poems by black writers, the warden invites you on a tour of the prison. Entering "F" block, one of eight long corridors with small rooms with metal doors on either side, you receive stares from most of the men. Strangers don't often visit. The warden greets many of the inmates and seems to know their names.

Stepping into one open cell you introduce yourself and chat with a man sitting on his bed, the only furniture in the room. When you return to the corridor and the warden, you mention to him that the man in the cell seems like a good person. The warden responds, "He is a good person. He isn't here because he's not a good person. He's here because of what he did. He's awaiting the death penalty any day."

As you are leaving the prison, you ask the warden: "What are these men doing here?" The warden answers without hesitation: "For you, prison would be a hardship—you have something better to live for. For these men, prison is not an undesirable place to be—the outside world has little to offer them. Many of these men grew up with us; we're the only family they know and the only people who care about them."

As you leave behind the prison walls and enter the "real" world again, you wonder: What kind of society do we have that can offer so many people nothing better than the life within prison?

- Illustrate with a drawing or poem the contrast between how prisoners are viewed in our society and how they are viewed from a Christian perspective.

More than one million Americans— or one every 30 seconds—are injured each year by drunken drivers. Two in every five Americans will be involved in an alcohol-related crash at some time in their lives, according to federal statistics. Traffic crashes remain the leading cause of death for teenagers and adults in their 20s. And alcohol is involved in about 40 percent of those fatalities.

—Robin Estrin, Associated Press, "MADD Becoming Victim of Its Own Success," *Philadelphia Inquirer*, August 6, 1997.

White and Blue Collar Crimes

crimes against persons

killing or physically hurting someone

crimes against property

stealing or damaging property

Crime has to do with harming others. There are **crimes against persons** (killing or physically hurting another) and **crimes against property** (stealing or vandalizing property). (There are some laws that outline crimes for the sake of good order; for example, in the United States failing to drive on the right side of the road.) You may be surprised to know that the most commonly occurring harmful crimes are not committed by people who fit most people's image of a criminal. Also, those who commit them spend a proportionately small amount of time in prison. Of all crimes against persons, one kills far more people than all others combined—drunken driving. Drunken driving is a middle class crime, one that even "respectable citizens" commit.

Of all crimes against property, fraud and embezzlement rate the highest. Fraud and embezzlement are white collar crimes, committed by persons in business or government in the course of their occupational activity. These types of crime tend to be treated less harshly. People who commit them often can afford bail money and quality legal services—keeping them out of jail until their trial and providing them opportunities to make as strong a case as possible. In effect, those who commit crimes and go free and those who commit crimes and are in prison have not always been treated equally. A great difference exists between criminal justice for poor people compared to that for wealthier people.

Crime traditionally escalates most where social injustice prevails.

—New Zealand Catholic Bishops Conference, *Creating New Hearts*,
August 30, 1995.

The answers to the questions "Who is in prison?" and "Why are they in prison?" may seem obvious: People who commit crimes are in prison, and people who commit crimes deserve to be in prison. These apparently obvious answers mask many mistaken ideas about prisoners and the entire criminal justice system. Such an answer can lead us to sit back comfortably and ignore our country's prisons, to view them as necessary inconveniences, while the human reality of prisoners and their problems is lost.

A case can be made that our country's prisons serve as *human warehouses*. The vast majority of people in prisons are poor, uneducated, and members of a minority group. Most adult prisoners had their first taste of imprisonment in a youth detention center. Those who end up in prison usually have a long history of failure in their lives. Typically, they possess one or more of the "invisible disabilities" mentioned earlier. (A great need in most prisons is for volunteers to teach basic reading skills. Finding legitimate work is difficult when a person can't read street signs or fill out employment forms.) More often than not, they come from unstable family backgrounds, have had repeated failures in school, and lack job skills or a record of long-term employment. Along with family, the school system, and the job market, prison becomes one more institution of a society that has not provided enough support to help them move anywhere but where they end up. In prison, a person's sense of self-worth and human dignity comes under constant attack. Again, this description of prisoners is not meant to excuse crime or simply to "blame the system" for society's ills. Prisoners who make it to a better life take responsibility for their lives and work hard to overcome the odds. ◆

Plea Bargaining and the Bail System

Even though jailed offenders come mainly from a poor and disjointed socio-economic background, it may be argued nonetheless that those in prison have been found guilty by the best that our society has to offer—trial by a jury of their peers with adequate legal counsel. To the contrary, most inmates plead guilty, and spend time in jail as a result of plea bargaining. **Plea bargaining** is a process whereby someone accused of a crime pleads guilty to the charge or to a lesser crime in exchange for a recommendation of a lighter sentence than the one usually given for the offense. In our overworked court system, plea bargaining speeds up decision making. For individual defendants, guilty or not, it becomes the best "deal" they feel capable of getting from a system that has given them few breaks in the past.

plea bargaining

pleading guilty in exchange for a lighter sentence

In our current system of justice, then, the following scenario is possible. A man unable to raise bail is accused of a crime and sent to jail. He is later told that a court date will not be forthcoming for at least a year; but if he pleads guilty, he can get off with a sentence of six months, part of which he has already served. The accused person, guilty or not, might reasonably choose plea bargaining for the shorter sentence than spend an additional six months or so awaiting trial. Such a scenario may sound outlandish, but in fact it represents the norm in many local prisons. Nationwide, over 50 percent of county jail inmates are awaiting trial, presumably "innocent" but unable to raise bail or hasten a court date.

◆ One rationale for prisons is that they serve as a way to decrease crime. For what types of crime and potential wrongdoers do you believe prison would serve as an effective hindrance? For what types of crime and potential wrongdoers would prison not serve as a very effective hindrance? If there is a difference in your two lists, explain why.

Develop Critical Awareness of Prisons and the Prison System

Remember those who are in prison, as though you were in prison with them.

—Hebrews 13:3

Prison officials represent us. So do police, judges, and lawmakers. We want to believe that our criminal justice system is fair and just, that all people are treated equally under the law, and that the punished deserve what they receive. Few of us know the criminal justice system or life behind bars. Even when a newspaper exposé describes inhumane conditions in prisons, we shrug it off with, "What do these prisoners expect, a country club?" It is as if, because of one mistake or one incident of mistaken identity, convicted persons become free game for any degree of inhumane treatment because "they deserve it."

Casting blame on people who work in the criminal justice system is unfair. While mistreatment can occur any time one group holds absolute power over others, those involved in criminal justice work have a difficult and thankless job and operate under countless adverse conditions. Some taxpayers want no money spent on prisons but want the system to be "tough on crime." Some don't want a prison facility in their neighborhood. In fact, people want to be shielded from the unpleasant reality that prisons exist at all. While no one wants to think about prisons, frustration at crime rates runs high. Those who end up in prison serve as scapegoats for all of our anger at the ugliness of crime. We want nothing to do with them. We want professionals to handle them, preferably harshly, and most especially to keep them out of sight.

In recent years crime has escalated. Murders, street violence, sexual assault, burglary, theft, domestic violence, car conversion, and white collar crime have become more widespread. Yet the traditional means of dealing with such crime seem unable to bring about reconciliation and healing. Re-offending rates remain high. The prison industry is expanding. Fear of crime dominates too many lives. It is time to re-evaluate what it is we need for true justice to flow throughout this land.

—New Zealand Catholic Bishops Conference, *Creating New Hearts*, August 30, 1995.

A first step toward making prisons work better is simply to become informed about prisons and the criminal justice system. Secondly, similar to our attitude toward other groups mentioned during this course, we need to realize that prisoners are not all alike and that they are more like us than different. The difference is that circumstances surrounding their lives or their particular response to needs or wants brought them into conflict with civil authorities and the criminal justice system. This does not mean that people who commit crimes are harmless or that prisoners are innocent. (Well-intentioned persons wanting to help a prisoner may quickly discover that he or she doesn't want their help or tries to "con" them.) What it does mean is that we look upon prisoners as human beings still worthy of respect and not as inhuman "others."

On this point an interesting experiment took place at Stanford University in 1972. Researchers created a mock prison to test how various people would respond when placed in the roles of prisoners and guards. After six days the experiment had to be called off. Even though conditions did not come close to duplicating the horrors of real prison life, the people involved started suffering severe psychological side-effects.

We might think the system works in the following simple manner: A person commits a crime, pays his or her debt to society, and then goes free. Such is far from the truth. A person who has been imprisoned has been affected for life, both by the experience itself and by society's attitudes and policies toward "ex-convicts."

The U.S. Catholic bishops make the following points about the country's prison system:

- The prison system as it now exists is inhumane and inadequate. Prisoners must not be overlooked while political leaders address other issues.

- The crime problem must be addressed by the entire community.

- Underlying causes of crime must be attacked.

- The gospel message of forgiveness, compassion, and mercy must be applied to our treatment of and attitude toward prisoners. (See U.S. Catholic Bishops, *Community and Crime*, 1978.) ◆

Capital Punishment: Deterrent or Revenge?

If the threat of life in prison isn't enough to decrease crime, some people argue that we need an even harsher punishment. The answer for these people is **capital punishment** or "an eye for an eye" as stated in Exodus 21:24. As a result of a series of decisions by the U.S. Supreme Court, capital punishment was restricted for a number of years in the U.S., but was reinstated in 1977.

Once again the numbers show that justice is not always handled equally. The legal system does provide lawyers for people accused of a crime who can not afford to hire their own. However, those who are wealthy can obtain better resources and more talented and skilled lawyers who can present the evidence in a better light and obtain better results. Thus, those who are condemned to die are nearly always poor, have had minimal education, and are in higher proportion Black Americans.

The arguments for and against capital punishment are numerous. Those in favor of it say it decreases the crime rates, is less costly than life imprisonment, and permanently removes from society people who are a threat to others.

capital punishment
the authorized killing by a nation's legal system of a person convicted of a particular crime

◆ Describe one concrete way of putting into practice each of the points made by the U.S. Catholic bishops.

In reality, there is no hard evidence that the crime rate has dropped in states which have capital punishment. Because of numerous appeals and other legalities, it can cost more to keep a criminal on death row than imprison him or her for life. Aiming for prudent firmness in ensuring the safety of innocent citizens, forty-eight states have reworked their laws dealing with first-degree murders. When someone has taken the life of one or more people, capital punishment might satisfy those who feel a need for revenge. However, revenge cannot be the objective of a humane and Christian approach to punishment.

A Christian View of Capital Punishment

Capital punishment is an act of total despair. It is in essence saying that there is no hope for this person for they will not change. *The Catechism of the Catholic Church* proposes that when possible (and it is almost always possible), punishment should incorporate the possibility of "contributing to the correction of the guilty party." (2266)

Catholic belief maintains that modern society has ways of effectively suppressing crime by rendering criminals harmless without resorting to state-sanctioned killing. The problem must be viewed in the context of a criminal justice system that strives to maintain human dignity and the worth of a person while offering hope for rehabilitation. Also, Church teaching fears that taking the life even of a person convicted of committing a horrible crime cheapens the value of all human life and contributes to an atmosphere of violence.

Christianity and Prisoners: God of the Forgotten Ones

In chapter 2, we stated that the God of the Bible is in a special way God of the forgotten ones. The lowly Hebrews, imprisoned in their slavery in Egypt, would be forgotten to history were it not for the God who would not stand by until they were set free. The first saint whom Jesus invited to share in paradise with him was a prisoner—Dismas, the good thief, patron saint of prisoners. We might forget that Jesus himself (and Saints Peter and Paul and, to the best of our knowledge, most of the other apostles) served time as a prisoner and died a criminal's death. We have softened the meaning of the cross, symbol of slow torture and capital punishment. Perhaps replacing crucifixes with images of electric chairs and scenes of lethal injections would conjure up for us more starkly the original impact of the cross.

The practice of the death penalty is the practice of torture. By the time the people I have been with climb into the chair to be killed, they have died a thousand times already because of their anticipation of the final horror.

—from a speech by Sr. Helen Prejean, C.S.J., author of *Dead Man Walking*, January 24, 1995.

Criminal Justice and Social Justice

Criminal justice emphasizes the individual's responsibility to society. Social justice emphasizes society's responsibility to individuals. People who commit crimes live within a social context. Without denying personal responsibility for actions, isn't it true that a person's environment plays a significant role in prescribing values, attitudes toward others, ways of solving conflicts, and other factors that may or may not lead to crime? For instance, our society overwhelms people with materialistic values but condemns individuals who pursue these values in the only way they believe is available to them—crime. Television and movies overwhelm us with scenes of violence, and yet we are shocked when people resort to violence in their own lives. We allow cheap handguns to be readily available, and yet we expect them not to be used in family quarrels or during a robbery. Community leaders provide few programs for teenagers to come together in creative ways and then stand back and point a finger at young people when they engage in vandalism and petty offenses.

In short, one way to cut down on crime is to avoid doing it oneself. Another way is to help build a society in which crime is less likely to occur. That is, improving criminal justice must go hand in hand with addressing concerns of social justice.

Review

22. What does it mean to say that prisons serve as *human warehouses*?
23. What are the two major categories of crime?
24. What are the three most prevalent crimes in the U.S.?
25. What are the typical characteristics of most people in prisons?
26. Define *plea bargaining*.
27. How does the bail system favor wealthier criminals?
28. What did the 1972 study at Stanford University discover?
29. Define *capital punishment?*
30. What are the three common characteristics of people who are sentenced to die?
31. What is the Catholic view on capital punishment?
32. What does it mean to say that criminal justice and social justice are linked?

Discuss

I. If you were arrested for a crime that you did not commit, were sent to jail, and were unable to raise the required bail, would you plead guilty to a lesser crime in order to shorten your stay in prison? What are the possible consequences of deciding either to plea bargain or to await trial?

J. Give an example that illustrates what the author means in the final sentence above: "improving criminal justice must go hand in hand with addressing concerns of social justice."

K. Give three reasons why you think teenagers engage in more crime than people in other age brackets.

L. In Taiwan many people leave helmets and backpacks unlocked on their scooters. Rarely are such items taken. Besides those listed above, name other societal values and practices that might influence people in the United States to commit crimes. Explain why and how they might do this.

Opening Prayer

God our Father, you called a young unwed girl to be the mother of your Son. Mary knew the anxieties of being a mother, but she also recognized the priceless gift of being able to bring a child into this world. Help us to recognize that every life has the right to be lived. Let our voice ring out loud and long for the many unheard voices of the children who were never given a chance to be born. Amen.

The Unborn: Cultivating a Culture of Life in a Culture of Death

A characteristic of all the groups highlighted in this chapter is their vulnerability. In our society one group stands out as being particularly defenseless—children taking shape in their mother's womb, making their way toward birth. Church leaders have been strong in trying to give a voice to these voiceless ones, many of whom are discarded or experimented upon as if they were a property to be dealt with as we wish. Our culture's attitude toward the unborn reveals a lack of concern for human life itself.

Before we begin . . .

Answer **agree**, **disagree**, or **uncertain** to the following statements. Choose statements that you believe are most significant and explain your answers.

1. The decision concerning what to do about pregnancy is a private matter between a woman and her doctor.

2. Church leaders should refrain from speaking about personal matters such as pregnancy decisions.

3. It is wrong to try to "legislate morality," making laws denying the option of abortion to those who believe it is acceptable.

4. Laws permitting abortion should be done away with.

5. I would participate in organizations or programs aimed at overturning laws permitting abortion.

6. Experimentation on fetuses is acceptable since it can help bring about important medical breakthroughs.

7. I have a clear sense of where I stand regarding abortion and concern for the unborn.

Two Fates

The baby girl was born three months prematurely in a hospital in Minneapolis. She weighed only three pounds. The doctors told her parents that she was not expected to live, but promised to do everything possible to save her life. As scores of people around the country prayed for this little girl, the most sophisticated medical technology available was employed to aid her fight for survival.

During the first six weeks of her life, which she spent enclosed in an incubator, she began to develop serious complications. Her weight began to drop. Her lungs had not had time to fully develop within the safety of her mother's womb, so she continually struggled with hyaline membrane disease and other pulmonary infections. Each day was a life-and-death battle.

She was kept on oxygen and monitored by machines and nurses twenty-four hours a day. Later, she was placed on a respirator and administered a powerful drug that temporarily paralyzed her entire body. At this point, one of the doctors took the father aside and told him, "You should begin to prepare your wife for the worst. We think your baby probably won't live much longer."

But the baby did live, and within a few more weeks the battle appeared to be won. She began to gain weight and strength, and was finally released to go home with her parents. . . .Today, she is a completely normal, happy, healthy young girl, full of life. The pediatric radiologist who cared for her . . . has shown the X rays of her lungs at medical conferences around the country, demonstrating to other physicians that it is indeed possible for a baby so premature and critically ill to survive. . . .

Less than two years earlier, in a Boston hospital in late 1973, another baby, a boy, snuggled in the womb of his mother . . . growing within his mother for about six months. But this little boy would never be born. He was scheduled to be aborted.

The doctor prepared to inject a saline solution into the amniotic fluid that surrounded the baby. Normally this is a simple procedure. The concentrated salt solution causes the baby to convulse and die within the womb, after which the mother goes into labor and expels the dead baby. . . .

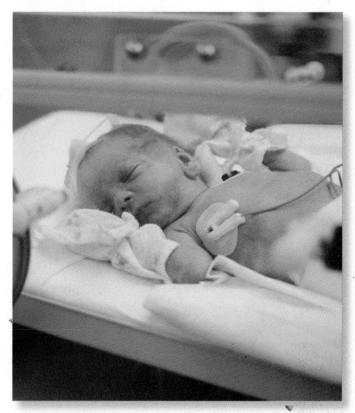

After repeatedly attempting to make the injection . . . he proceeded to perform a hysterotomy, that is he surgically opened the mother's womb through an incision in her abdomen. . . . If the objective is a live birth, this procedure is called a cesarean section; if the objective is abortion, it is called a hysterotomy.

The doctor completed the incision . . . then waited several minutes. . . . The baby's struggles ceased.

The doctor then removed the seemingly lifeless baby and placed his hand on the baby's chest for a mere three to five seconds to check for life signs. Since the doctor clearly did not want to find any life signs (the object of this procedure, after all, is a dead baby), he failed to make even a minimal effort—such as taking just one minute to listen for heartbeat and breathing with a stethoscope—to determine whether or not the baby was truly alive or dead. He then placed the baby in a steel basin held by a nurse and instructed her to dispose of it.

—Dr. Ron Lee Davis with James D. Denney,
A Time for Compassion, Tappen, NJ: Fleming
H. Revell Company, 1986, pages 11–14.

• What justification might each doctor use for doing what he did? What would be the Catholic response to each doctor's reply?

The Value of Unborn Life: Pope John Paul II and The Gospel of Life

culture of death

culture which values having over human beings

culture of life

culture which values life over all else

The preceding two stories are a study in contrasts. In both cases a human person six months along in development encountered modern technology and medical science, doctors, nurses, and early separation from the life-sustaining environment of a mother's womb. One journey led to life, the other to death. How can some of the best that the modern world has to offer serve such drastically different purposes? How can one life be so cherished and receive such care and attention while the other is discarded?

Pope John Paul II has also pondered this dilemma. He observes that all of us today find ourselves in the midst of a clash of cultures—one a **culture of death** and the other a **culture of life**. His insights, presented most forcefully in his 1995 encyclical *The Gospel of Life*, are worth pondering.

A Manifestation of a Culture of Death

euthanasia

killing or permitting the death of hopelessly sick or disabled individuals

Pope John Paul II links dismissal of the value of unborn life with other signs of a culture of death: reliance on warfare to solve international conflicts, the use of capital punishment as a means of addressing crime and social ills, overlooking the problems of starving children in the world, and supporting **euthanasia** as a solution to problems associated with sickness and old age.

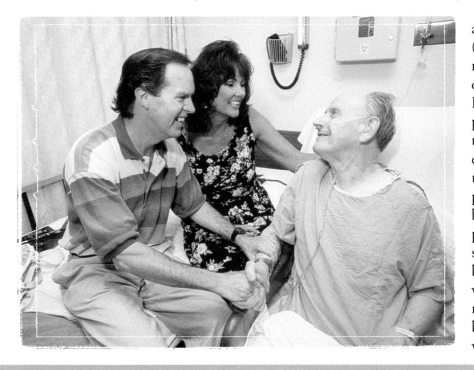

In this culture the "values of being are replaced by those of having" (number 23). This distortion of values represents a whole different viewpoint on both persons and things. Emphasizing being means treating people and things as precious in themselves. On the other hand an emphasis on having leads to the belief that the "only goal which counts is the pursuit of one's own material well-being" (number 23). No doubt, in the previous story the parents and medical staff intent on seeing the prematurely born girl through to a full and wholesome life did not see her as a means to their own material well-being but as a person of inner beauty and worth, precious in herself. ◆

◆ Bring to class an example of a culture of life and an example of a culture of death, either in contemporary music, advertising, movies, or some other product. Explain your examples.

God Is "Defender of the Innocent"

Reading through Scripture reveals a God who is a defender of the innocent. The God of Scripture cares for human beings at every stage of existence and in every form. Pope John Paul II paraphrases Psalm 139 to describe this attitude of God toward human life:

> Human life is sacred and inviolable at every moment of existence, including the initial phase which precedes birth. All human beings, from their mother's womb, belong to God who searches them and knows them, who forms them and knits them together with his own hands, who gazes on them when they are tiny shapeless embryos and already sees in them the adults of tomorrow whose days are numbered and whose vocation is even now written in the "book of life" (number 61). ◆

Call Things by their Proper Name

Pontius' Puddle

POST-BIRTH ABORTIONS SHOULD BE DONE ONLY UNTIL A CHILD LEARNS TO TALK!

--UNTIL HE'S FINANCIALLY INDEPENDENT.

I SAY UNTIL HE STARTS SCHOOL!

HELP!

ETHICS DEBATE OF THE FUTURE

On this point, the pope is describing how we can attempt to mask the culture of death in deliberately deceptive language. During warfare, language used to report on the effects of military operations and their casualties have often shrouded the real horrors of war. (For example, a civilian hospital hit by a stray missile is referred to as "collateral damage.") Pope John Paul II notes a similar tendency toward a widespread use of deliberately unclear wording—for instance, referring to abortion as "an interruption of pregnancy"—to deceive people about its true nature. To counteract this temptation of self-deception, he calls for courage "to look the truth in the eye and to call things by their proper name." (number 58)

A Contemplative Outlook

To counteract the culture of death and the deception that accompanies it, the pope urges developing "a contemplative outlook." **Contemplation** is being attentive to life and approaching life filled with a sense of wonder. Essential to living life filled with wonder is accepting the gift of life itself. The pope describes a contemplative outlook in this way:

contemplation
being filled with a sense of wonder; seeing all life as a gift and acting responsibly toward that gift

> It is the outlook of those who see life in its deeper meaning, who grasp its utter gratuitousness, its beauty and its invitation to freedom and responsibility. It is the outlook of those who do not presume to take possession of reality but instead accept it as a gift, discovering in all things the reflection of the Creator and seeing in every person his living image (number 83).

◆ Read Psalm 139. Use it as a model to write your own psalm in praise of human life, or compose and set it to music, or fashion an illustration of the psalm.

God Has Made Us Responsible

Initially, contemplation appears to be a passive gesture—sitting back basking in the wonder of life. However, the pope connects contemplation with action. Specifically, if we truly see others as gift, then "we must care for the other as a person for whom God has made us responsible" (number 87).

The pope's words on responsibility once again link care for the unborn with care for all those groups crying out for justice in our world.

As disciples of Jesus, we are called to become neighbors to everyone, and to show special favour to those who are poorest, most alone and most in need. In helping the hungry, the thirsty, the foreigner, the naked, the sick, the imprisoned—as well as the child in the womb and the old person who is suffering or near death—we have the opportunity to serve Jesus (number 87).

33. In what context does Pope John Paul II place dismissal of the value of unborn life?

34. What title does Pope John Paul II associate with God in Scripture?

35. What tendency is Pope John Paul II seeking to eliminate by insisting that we "call things by their proper name"?

36. Define *contemplation*.

37. With what does Pope John Paul II associate contemplation in order to insure that it is not simply a passive gesture?

Discuss

M. Identify and discuss ways that modern society seems to be a culture of death. Identify and discuss ways that modern society seems to be a culture of life.

N. Give examples of how the use of language can deceive or soften what is really happening in life and death situations, especially situations related to abortion and unborn life.

O. Are there specific ways that you might practice responsibility toward unborn life? Describe possibilities.

In Summary: Compassion for Our Own and One Another's Weaknesses

In this chapter we looked at five categories of people crying out for justice. Other groups could be mentioned. In fact, all of us have our areas of weaknesses—our weight, our school grades, our poor communication skills, our body shape, the force of our emotions, our secret invisible disabilities. In a compassionate community we seek to not let our own vulnerabilities prevent us from helping others but to see our vulnerabilities as stepping stones toward concern for and involvement with others in creating a more just world.

Before we conclude . . .

Let us pray . . .

Lord, you have searched me and you know me;
you understand everything I do;
you are closer to me than my thoughts.
You see through my selfishness and weakness,
into my inmost self.
There is not one corner of my mind
that you do not know completely.
You are present before me, behind me,
and you hold me in the palm of your hand.
Such knowledge is too awesome to grasp,
so deep that I cannot fathom it.
Where can I go from your spirit?
Where can I flee from your presence?
If I take the wings of the morning
and fly to the ends of the sea,
even there your hand will guide me
and your spirit will give me strength.
If I rise to heaven, I meet you;
if I lie down in hell, you are there;
if I plunge through the fear of the terrorist
or pierce through the rapist's rage,
you are there, in your infinite compassion,
and my heart rejoices in your joy.

You fashioned my inward parts;
you knit me in my mother's womb.
My soul was not hidden from you
when I was being formed in secret,
woven in the depths of the world.
How can I keep from praising you?
I am fearfully and wonderfully made,
and all your works are marvelous.
Your eyes saw all my actions;
they were written down in your book;
all my days were created
before even one of them was.
How measureless your mind is, Lord;
it contains inconceivable worlds
and is vaster than space, than time.
If ever I tried to fathom it,
I would be like a child counting
the grains of sand on a beach.

Search me, Lord; test me
to the depths of my inmost heart.
Root out all selfishness from me
and lead me in eternal life.

—Psalm 139, *A Book of Psalms,* by Stephen Mitchell,
New York: Harper Collins Publishers, pages 76–78.

For further study . . .

1. Contact an Alzheimer's support group in your area. What does the group do to help people understand the effects of this disease? Ask for flyers or brochures the group distributes. Write a report either on senility or Alzheimer's disease. Share the report with your class.

2. Survey fellow students about the following and write a report on your findings.

    • How many have moved during their lifetime? To a new neighborhood? A new town?

    • How many have parents who live in neighborhoods different from the one where they grew up? A different town? A different state?

    • How many have a grandparent or another older relative living with them?

    • How many have a grandparent or other relative living in another state or country?

    • How many have a grandparent whom they have not seen in the past month? The past six months? The past year?

3. Imagine that you are an older person. Describe in writing how you would like younger people to relate to you and to treat you. Do you believe that the older people you currently know would like to be treated this way?

4. Compose a prayer that could be included in a church service celebrating aging and older people.

5. Visit a residential facility for persons with mental or physical disabilities. Report on your experience.

6. Find out what changes have been made in your community to help persons with physical disabilities. What additional changes would you recommend to make your community more "handicap accessible"?

7. Imagine what it might be like to have a particular disability. Use the *Special Beatitudes* found on page 198 to write your own set of beatitudes that would reflect the view of a person who has that disability.

8. Use two or three movies you have recently seen to compare and contrast the images of prisoners that were given. State your reasons for believing that the images presented are realistic or unrealistic.

9. Make a case that capital punishment does or does not reflect a Christian attitude toward prisoners. (In making your case, find out what recent Church leaders have said about capital punishment.)

10. Write an essay describing how "a contemplative outlook" might help us in our appreciation of the unborn.

11. If you were assigned to write a chapter on concerns of justice other than the ones discussed in this chapter, what issues would you address? To make a case for including these issues, consider the characteristics of a just world listed in chapter 1.

12. In a book about justice, would you have not included any of the five groups discussed in this chapter? If not, why not? Would you have treated any of the five topics differently? If so, how?

CHAPTER 10

Earth Justice
Nurturing Nature, Our Home

Recently, the human assault on the rest of nature has raised the question: How far do we extend the hand of compassion and justice? Do we stop with the human community or do we include the non-human as well? Applying the principles of justice to the earth does not mean caring for nature simply so that it can better meet our needs. Rather, in a spirit of justice and compassion, we proclaim that dogs and butterflies, rivers and rainforests, are one with us, reflections of God's grandeur, and deserving of being treated as members of an intricately interconnected living family.

Opening Prayer

God of all creation, we walk the earth as holy ground and gaze at the sky as a sacred canopy. Flowering plants, towering trees, earthworms, land animals, and the birds of the air are the works of your fingers and sing of your glory. Planets and moons, stars and galaxies praise you. The water we drink and the food we eat are gifts of your goodness. We pray that we may stretch our minds to see all creation as one, brothers and sisters to us, manifestations of your glory. Amen.

Before we begin . . .

Answer **agree**, **disagree**, or **uncertain** to the following statements. Choose statements that you believe are most significant and explain your answers.

1. My school takes seriously concern for nature.

2. Concern for the environment influences my buying habits.

3. If we are to survive as a species, drastic changes must occur in the way we treat nature.

4. I believe that science will provide solutions to handle whatever environmental problems arise.

5. I have noticed a worsening of our natural environment during my lifetime.

6. The U.S. is more environmentally friendly than most other nations.

7. Taking care of the earth should be a main concern for everyone in our world.

8. I feel true kinship with the rest of nature.

9. Concern for less farm land should not be part of a discussion about turning a farm into a shopping mall.

Major Concepts

A. Ecology: Making Our House a Home

Ethical treatment of the environment

- Land
- Air
- Water
- Animal and plants
- Waste

B. A Christian View of the Earth

- Sacramental vision of nature as God's creation
- Scripture and Catholic documents' call to stewardship

C. Working with the Earth

- Changing personal practices

Two Visions of the Garden of Eden

In the day that the Lord God made the earth and the heavens, when no plant of the field was yet in the earth and no herb of the field had yet sprung up—for the Lord God had not caused it to rain upon the earth, and there was no one to till the ground; but a stream would rise from the earth, and water the whole face of the ground—then the Lord God formed man from the dust of the ground, and breathed into his nostrils the breath of life; and the man became a living being. And the Lord God planted a garden in Eden, in the east; and there he put the man whom he had formed. Out of the ground the Lord God made to grow every tree that is pleasant to the sight and good for food, the tree of life also stood in the midst of the garden, and the tree of the knowledge of good and evil . . . . The Lord God took the man and put him in the garden of Eden to till it and keep it.

—Genesis 2:4–9, 15

The effects of environmental destruction surround us: the smog in our cities, chemicals in our water and on our food, eroded topsoil blowing in the wind, the loss of valuable wetlands, radioactive and toxic waste lacking adequate disposal sites, and threats to the health of industrial and farm workers. The problems, however, reach far beyond our own neighborhoods and workplaces. Our problems are the world's problems and burdens for generations to come. Poisoned water crosses borders freely. Acid rain pours on countries that do not produce it. Greenhouse gases and chlorofluorocarbons affect the earth's atmosphere for many decades, regardless of where they are produced or used.

Opinions vary about the causes and the seriousness of environmental problems. Still, we can experience their effects in polluted air and water; in oil and wastes on our beaches; in the loss of farmland, wetlands, and forests; and in the decline of rivers and lakes.

—United States Catholic Conference, "Renewing the Earth," in
And God Saw That It Was Good, Washington, DC:
USCC, 1996, pages 223–224.

- Describe the contrasting vision of creation portrayed in each of the above passages.
- What is the vision of humanity's role in creation that is shared by each passage?
- What emotions do these two passages evoke in you?

Ecology: Making Our House a Home

According to the Bible, God created the earth to be a garden. In the quoted passage the U.S. bishops catalog ways that this garden has become depleted and endangered. The biblical vision of the earth as a garden and the bishops' concerns about the environment echo the message we have been getting recently from the science of **ecology**. The Greek word *oikos* from which ecology is derived means "house." In fact, nature is our house, the dwelling place that we share with other creatures. In this chapter we will follow the lead of the U.S. bishops and "explore the links between concern for the person and for the earth, between natural ecology and social ecology" (*Renewing the Earth*, page 224).

ecology
study of the environment and the relationships among the elements of creation

Justice and Nature

We read stories about poisons seeping up from the ground near chemical waste dumps. Every summer, people living near beaches wonder whether ocean water will be safe for swimming. Numerous species of animals are in danger of extinction. Because of pollution in the air, the healing rays of the sun are now also more likely to be cancer producing. Water we depend on for drinking must undergo greater and greater treatment for it to be safe. As human waste piles up, communities struggle to figure out what to do with all the garbage we produce. Automobiles continue to pollute the air while alternatives to the internal combustion engine receive little industry or public support.

The problems we face reflect the choices we make. For a long time, at least in Western culture, the main belief was that nature and the earth offered unlimited resources. Harnessing the earth's resources to benefit humanity was the goal. Pollution was a necessary side-effect. Long-term depletion of resources was not a particular concern.

More recently, at least the language of environmental concern has become an important part of public discussion. Nowadays, from an early age, school children hear the message about taking care of the earth. Grade schools celebrate "Earth Day" and sponsor tree plantings. Fifth graders are assigned to do reports on endangered species. One way to measure the degree to which positive attitudes, behaviors, and policies have actually taken root in our society is to look at nature in terms of the four elements of a just world listed in chapter 1. ◆

◆ Have you ever participated in an organization or an activity whose goal was improving the environment? Describe the experience.

Ethical Treatment of the Environment

Faced with the widespread destruction of the environment, people everywhere are coming to understand that we cannot continue to use the goods of the earth as we have in the past.

—Pope John Paul II, *The Ecological Crisis: A Common Responsibility*, Introduction.

anthropocentric

emphasizing the rights of humans at the expense of all else

Western culture has tended to be very **anthropocentric**. That is, it has centered on the human (in Greek, *anthropos*). From an anthropocentric view, non-human things such as redwoods and cheetahs are important only insofar as they serve human beings. In other words, redwoods and cheetahs are creatures beautiful for us to look at, interesting for us to study, valuable for us to learn from, and profitable for our use.

Certainly, we humans occupy a unique role in the natural order. No other creature can either destroy the earth and everything on it or nurture the earth for the benefit of all.

Along with our power and our unique self-awareness comes a unique responsibility. We set standards for ethical treatment not only of human beings but of non-human creatures as well. For instance, in our court system we are subject to punishment if we mistreat a dog or a cat. The environmental movement has alerted us that we need to examine our treatment of all of God's creation, if we are to maintain a healthy environment for everyone. ◆

◆ Debate the issues involved in the following scenarios:

- The owner of a large parcel of rich farmland is offered a great price by a developer who wants to build a mall on it. Should the owner be free to do whatever he or she wants to do with the land? Who should be involved in making the decision? Should the land itself be taken into consideration in the decision?

- A strip of land serves as a nesting ground for the endangered California condor. Should the federal government restrict development around the area in order to preserve the condor's nesting ground? Upon what basis could you make a case for or against this action?

- A company, the major employer in its area, has been dumping chemicals into a nearby stream for decades—a practice it claims is necessary for it to stay in business. Recently, citizens in a community downstream have petitioned the state government to require the company to stop this practice. Make a case on behalf of the company; on behalf of the citizens. Then, make a case on behalf of the stream and the wildlife who live in or near it.

- The spotted owl uses only the forests of the northwestern U.S. as its habitat. The forests are also a rich source of lumber. Should the lumber industry be denied access to forests in order to protect the spotted owl? Make a case both for and against this position. Where do you stand on the issue? Why?

- A complaint is lodged against a group of teenagers for abusing a stray cat in a neighborhood park. They tell police officials that the cat belongs to no one and, therefore, no crime was committed. Should the teens be punished for their actions? If so, decide on an appropriate punishment. If not, explain why.

- A hotel chain wants to build a lodge in the middle of a national park. The hotel chain would put in paved walking trails in order to make the park and lodge accessible to more people. Another group wants to keep the national park as primitive and natural as possible, even though this means only hardy travelers can enjoy it. Make a case both for and against each position. Where do you stand? Why?

Love all of God's creation, the whole and every grain of sand in it. Love every leaf, every ray of God's light. Love the animals, love the plants, love everything. If you love everything, you will perceive the divine mystery in things.

—Fyodor Dostoyevsky, *The Brothers Karamazov*, quoted in Thomas Berry, CP, with Thomas Clarke, S.J., *Befriending the Earth*, Twenty-Third Publications, page 1.

Respect for Nature

Think back on all the groups already discussed in this course. In all cases respect for their inborn dignity underlies justice for them. In their analysis of justice and the environment, the U.S. Catholic bishops point out that respect for human life "extends to respect for all creation" (*Renewing the Earth*, page 230). When the dignity of people is overlooked, exploitation often results. Similarly, exploitation occurs when we do not display the respect for the rest of creation that it deserves.

The opposite of treating others with respect is exploitation. Exploitation means using people or things for our own ends without respecting their inborn dignity. Applied to nature it views the natural world as a commodity to be bought and sold, used and used up: "I own it; therefore, I can do with it whatever I want." Exploitation dismisses the divine mystery manifest through creation and is concerned solely with what can be gained from it. Exploitation of created things flows from humanity's arrogance and acquisitiveness that the Bible says has led to alienation from nature (See *Renewing the Earth*, page 229). By way of contrast, the U.S. bishops remind us that "Every creature shares a bit of the divine beauty" (page 232), and that we are not free "to use created things capriciously" (page 229).

If exploitation seeks to exert *power over* nature in an unjustified way, then respect means *working with* nature. Exploitation represents a care-less approach to nature. On the other hand respect is a care-filled treatment of nature. It flows from a spirit of nurturing rather than of abusing or carelessly using nature. Note that respect for nature does not rule out the use of nature but its *abuse*. That is, care and respect for nature are not the same as **pantheism**. Treating cows or monkeys or rats as divine can harm humans, who are actually more important. It can also prevent the scientific advances that help humans and even other creatures. Science, technology, experimentation, and human inventiveness can be respectful and non-exploitive in the interplay between the human and the non-human world. The goodness and beauty of creation do not cease when transformed by human hands in an appropriate way.

pantheism

regarding nature or the elements of nature as divine

The Web of Life

The web of life is one. Our mistreatment of the natural world diminishes our own dignity and sacredness, not only because we are destroying resources that future generations of humans need, but because we are engaging in actions that contradict what it means to be human. Our tradition calls us to protect the life and dignity of the human person, and it is increasingly clear that this task cannot be separated from the care and defense of all of creation.

—U.S. Catholic bishops, *Renewing the Earth*, page 224.

Describing the relationship between human beings and the rest of creation, the U.S. bishops speak about "our kinship with all that God has made" and "the harmony between humanity and the natural world" (page 229). Pope John Paul II speaks of a "profound sense that the earth is 'suffering'" (*The Ecological Crisis*, number 5). The pope and bishops are pointing out that during our earthly existence we share our lives with the soil, the air, the water, the animals, the trees, the flowers and plants, and the insects. Yesterday's soil, water, and plants are today's human tissue. In turn, our bodies replenish the soil and nourish plant life. From the air we take oxygen produced by plants and in exchange give off carbon dioxide for their use. When one part of the earth suffers—the air, the oceans, or forests—the entire earth suffers.

Our relationship to the rest of creation builds rather than lessens our responsibility toward it. We are sisters and brothers with other creatures who live in God's garden. Because of today's environmental crisis, we are called to come to their defense.

Review

1. Define *ecology*. What does the Greek root of the term mean?
2. What has been the prevailing view in Western culture toward nature?
3. Define *anthropocentric*.
4. What would be an exploitive approach to nature?

Discuss

A. Make a case for or against each of the following statements:
   - Today's young people are more aware than earlier generations of the need to preserve the environment.
   - Today's young people treat the environment more carefully than earlier generations did.

B. Answer **yes** or **no** to each of these statements. Explain your answer.
   - Does overemphasizing respect for the rest of creation lessen respect for humanity?
   - Has the progress achieved by Western culture resulted from a lack of respect for nature? Has it led to a lack of respect for nature?

Concern for Social Structures

Public policies and practices, expressions of social structures, are an important sign as to what degree the earth matters in a society. We can identify policies and practices that relate to five different aspects of nature.

Land

If we travel through the western part of the United States, land seems plentiful enough. However, land that is best for farming is also best for development. In most cases, selling land for housing developments, shopping malls, and rural business centers can make more money for the landowner than farming the land would. Maintaining land for farming is a primary land issue facing the U.S.

A second issue related to land is the way farming is done. One important difference is between **inorganic farming** and **organic farming**. Inorganic farming produces immediate high crop-yields but in the long-term depletes valuable topsoil. On the other hand organic farming can actually create topsoil. For a number of years, larger farms relied more heavily on inorganic farming. More recently other farming methods, such as **low-tillage farming**, have been developed. With low-tillage farming, narrow slits are cut in the sod, and seed and fertilizer are placed in the slits. With this method the sod remains relatively undisturbed and erosion problems are reduced. This method seeks to avoid the deficiencies of both organic and inorganic farming.

Making choices about how crops are planted, which crops are planted, and how often they are planted can make the difference between protecting and enriching the land or destroying its productivity for future generations. Agricultural experts and farmers dedicated to efficient land use are making life-sustaining contributions through their efforts. Government policies can help ease financial risks that farmers take and can also support healthy land use.

A third issue related to land is preservation of wilderness areas. Anyone who has visited one of the great national parks, especially in the western states, knows the precious resource that a Grand Canyon or a Yosemite National Park can be. Conflicts related to wilderness lands are between public versus private ownership and between development versus maintaining areas as close to a natural state as possible. Development makes wilderness areas easier to reach and more helpful to a greater number of people but also affects the animal and plant life in the area. ◆

inorganic farming

farming dependent on chemical fertilizers and pesticides; produces immediate high-crop yields but depletes topsoil

organic farming

farming without the use of toxic chemicals; can create topsoil

low-tillage farming

farming that disturbs topsoil as little as possible, leaving some ground cover to prevent erosion, but still allowing some use of fertilizer and pesticides

◆ Interview someone over forty. Ask them how they have seen land use change in your area over the past few decades. Has there been a vast decrease in the amount of farmland or wilderness area? If so, what has taken its place? Has there been a decrease in the number of small farms and vegetable gardens? What effect have these changes had on the life of the earth? What effect have these changes had on human life in the area? Report on your findings.

Air

If people were stuck in an elevator, it wouldn't be long before all the passengers would have exchanged at least once the air they breathe. In fact, we are still breathing in air molecules breathed at the time of Jesus. What we add to the air today will stay with us long into the future. Already there are indications of **global warming** caused in part by the **greenhouse effect**.

Cars account for the greatest amount of air pollution in the world today. The haze covering major cities comes mostly from car exhaust fumes. There are basically two schools of thought about how best to cut down on automobile pollution. One group wants manufacturers to create more fuel-efficient cars. Another group fears that this is merely a stop-gap measure. The real solution lies in alternatives to the gasoline engine, such as electric cars and improved public transportation. Most consumers consider gas mileage and fuel efficiency only in terms of their pocketbook—better fuel economy saves money. As a society we have not yet faced the fact that cutting down on fuel use also saves clean air and thus our health and that of the environment.

In addition to automobiles, factories, power plants, and waste-disposal units pollute the air. In the past few decades, the public outcry for cleaner air has led to stricter anti-pollution regulations, and many communities and companies have developed creative ways to cut down on pollution and to use waste products effectively. Nonetheless, the environment still often loses out to the economy. ◆

global warming

an increase in the temperature worldwide

greenhouse effect

a warming of the earth's surface and lower atmosphere that tends to intensify with an increase in atmospheric carbon dioxide

Water

We all know about endangered animal species. However, clean water could be classified as an *endangered resource*. Water exists in such large quantities on our planet that we find it difficult to imagine a shortage of it. Yet experts agree that the lack of clean, drinkable water creates more problems worldwide than the lack of farmable land. Those of us used to having water available at the turn of a faucet overlook the importance of this endangered resource. Even in some communities of the United States, the demand for fresh water is beginning to go beyond its availability.

◆ Look through automobile magazines or books about cars. Look for evidence that air pollution is a major health concern related to cars. How much space is given to this issue? If air pollution is mentioned at all, how is it treated? Report on your findings.

When we think of water pollution, we probably imagine the streams, rivers, and lakes that chemical pollutants have made unsafe for drinking, swimming, or fishing. Due to the spreading problem of acid rain, when air pollution and moisture in the air mix, even turning our faces skyward to drink falling snow or rain is a questionable practice. Considering that problems related to pollution were not seriously faced until after World War II, much has been done to curb water pollution. However, the threat to all forms of water supplies remains, despite the scant attention it receives in the media and in political discussions. Even more importantly, as a society we have not seriously faced the fact that all of our resources need much more careful handling if they and we are to remain lively and healthy.

Animals, Plants, and the Natural Habitat

Our world is becoming increasingly inhabited by humans. If we tame much more of the earth, we may lose the unique beauty of wilderness places and the creatures who live in them.

Inhumane treatment of animals occurs in the name of real or imagined human benefit. Two areas of concern here are **animal experimentation** and **corporate farming**. Few people demand ending all animal experimentation. Nonetheless many questionable practices are performed in laboratories in the name of scientific research. For instance, animal rights groups call for ending or stricter regulation of *vivisection*, the practice of operating on live animals.

animal experimentation
scientific research on animals, including some questionable practices

Today's farms are typically very different from the image of farm life shown in our first grade readers. More and more, small family farms are being purchased by large corporations. These corporations buy the land then hire others to plant, cultivate, and harvest it. The corporate office's main purpose in buying the land is to make a profit. Since the corporate offices do not have the personal interest in the land that the family farmer had, they are less concerned with care for and future use of the land.

corporate farming
ownership of a large number of acres and animals by persons or organizations that oversee production but do not actually work with the land or the animals

Sometimes these corporate farms become "farm factories" where cattle, pigs, chickens, and other animals are raised in large number and treated like mere products. Most egg-laying chickens spend their lives confined to small cages and never see the light of day. Their eggs are carried away on conveyor belts, and food and water are given through the use of automatic machinery. The production of veal, pork, and beef requires similar confinement for calves, pigs, and cattle. In addition to the "farm factory" treatment of the animals and land, the disposal of the huge amount of waste from such confinement-lot operations causes yet another danger to the environment. ◆

◆ Write a conversation that might take place between a farmer of fifty years ago and a farmer today. What questions and concerns might be raised in such a conversation?

Waste

recycling

converting waste products and other goods we throw away into usable products instead of putting them into a landfill

Concern for the environment requires being attentive to resources we are using up. However, it also requires being attentive to what we put back into the environment. Just because the trash that we wrap in a plastic bag and place on the curb disappears on trash day does not mean that it no longer concerns us. We are surrounding ourselves with our own garbage, and the earth is choking from an overdose of human waste. Certain items that we may use for only a few seconds will remain with us for centuries. They are easy and inexpensive to produce but ultimately difficult to dispose of.

Hazardous waste and waste from nuclear power plants are particularly disturbing problems. Plutonium waste from nuclear power plants will remain radioactive for half a million years. Every community wants easy access to unlimited electrical power, but no community wants nuclear waste stored in its backyard.

Essentially, we diminish our waste problem in three ways:

• Cut back on the amount of waste that we produce, including waste from using electrical energy.

• Use products that are reusable, recyclable, or otherwise environmentally friendly.

• Come up with environmentally sound ways to dispose of or use the waste that we produce.

Of course, a major aspect of the solution is **recycling.** ◆

◆ Do research to find out which products are healthy or harmful for the environment. What products could you substitute for products that are harmful?

Environmental Misuse: Who Suffers?

Clearly, since all of us are of the earth, we all suffer from its misuse. Two groups are particularly hard hit by enviromental problems—poor people and people yet to be born. Poor people suffer the most from nature's misuse. When crop production decreases because of a reduction in available farmland, poor people are the ones who go hungry. While those who can afford it walk around with bottled water, poor people in the poorer countries of the world scramble to find drinkable water. Very often poor people live in areas most subject to poor air quality or work where toxic chemicals or pesticides are a hazard. Migrant farm workers, for instance, work in fields where harmful pesticides may have been used.

Secondly, future generations must contend with the effects of current environmental misuse. The way we treat the environment today is borrowing from the future. When we weigh the costs and benefits of our use of resources and of the waste we produce, we seldom think about the impact such use will have on coming generations. That is, the cost of gasoline is not just the price we pay at the pump. Gasoline use may also cost our children environmental problems that they will need to address both in terms of depleted resources and of the effects of air pollution. The Styrofoam cup we use today is being left for future generations to deal with. Therefore, the *true cost* of items we make and of resources we use is not just the expense of current production. Plastic toys and trinkets may be inexpensive to buy, but their *true cost* includes the effect they have on the environment now and in the future. ◆

Nature and War: The Ultimate Environmental Crisis

Clearly, war represents a serious threat to the environment, as the darkened skies and oil soaked beaches of Kuwait clearly remind us. The pursuit of peace—lasting peace based on justice—ought to be an environmental priority because the earth itself bears the wounds and scars of war.

—U.S. Catholic bishops, *Renewing the Earth*, pages 236–237.

◆ Choose a natural resource or manufactured product. Using the above definition, calculate the *true cost* of the item. Include in your calculation: depletion of resources, pollution that occurs in manufacture or use, and problems related to disposal of the item after its use.

War scars every natural setting that it encounters. In Vietnam, sections of otherwise lush tropical forest lie barren due to the destruction heaped upon the country thirty years ago. Land mines used during warfare are a hazard to civilian travelers and local farmers, now and into the future, as much as they were to enemy soldiers. Use of nuclear weapons, of course, represents the ultimate environmental crisis. What we have seen of nuclear weapons already warns us that their use can wipe out the delicate eco-system that sustains life on our planet.

Review

5. Describe differences among inorganic, organic, and low-tillage farming.

6. What conflicts typically occur related to wilderness areas?

7. Define the terms *global warming* and *greenhouse effect*.

8. What accounts for most of the air pollution in North America?

9. What does it mean to say that, in much of the world, water is an endangered resource?

10. Define *acid rain*.

11. Define *vivisection*.

12. What is the difference between a family farm and a corporate farm?

13. Why is nuclear waste a particular problem?

14. Name three ways to diminish the waste problem.

15. Which two groups suffer most from environmental misuse?

16. What needs to be included when calculating the *true cost* of items?

17. What is the ultimate environmental crisis?

Discuss

C. After housing, North Americans typically spend the largest single chunk of their income on cars. North Americans are known for having a love affair with cars. Is this true for you? If public transportation were improved in your area, would you forego buying a car? Why or why not?

D. How would you respond to the following statement of a government official in a poor country: "Your country is already wealthy, but we are poor. It is more important for us to increase industrial production cheaply than it is to be concerned about whether we are harming the environment." How might a government official from a wealthy country respond to this statement?

E. Name possible pro and con arguments to the following proposals. If you were a member of the U.S. Congress, would you vote for these proposals? Explain why or why not.

- The U.S. agrees never to use biological or chemical weapons.
- The U.S. agrees to ban production and sale of land mines as well as their use during military operations.
- The U.S. agrees never to use nuclear weapons, even to counterstrike nuclear weapons used against it.

A Christian View of the Earth

In 1967 a controversial article appeared suggesting that the Judeo-Christian tradition has contributed to our environmental crisis because it places human beings over and above the rest of nature. Is it true that the Judeo-Christian tradition is anti-nature?

In the first place, Scripture begins by describing creation as good. Certainly, human beings play a special role in creation. Sometimes Scripture has been interpreted to imply that nature exists for human use and that people can do whatever they wish with it. The actual passage from Genesis (2:15) says that human beings should "cultivate and care for" the earth. It means literally that human beings are to be servants to nature, not masters who lord it over nature. The term for this human role in the order of creation is **stewardship**.

> *Just as the owner of an estate places a servant, a steward, in charge of caring for her or his property, so God assigns human beings to be caretakers of the earth. To read Genesis as an invitation for human beings to do whatever they wish with the rest of creation is to miss what stewardship really means. As one biblical scholar puts it, "the commission given by God to humankind, to those creatures who are made in God's image, is to protect the balance of life that God's ordering word has built into the earth and to promote the continuation of all species having a place in that delicate balance."*
>
> —Anne M. Clifford, CSJ, "Foundations for a Catholic Ecological Theology of God," in *And God Saw That It Was Good*, Washington, DC: USCC, 1996, page 28.

stewardship

humanity's role, designated by God, to protect, care for, and sustain the rest of creation

The earth is the Lord's
and all that is in it,
the world, and those who live in it.

—Psalm 24:1

In the Bible humans are warned that if they misuse the earth, the earth will rebel against them. Jesus himself certainly demonstrates an appreciation for nature. People in need in his community are clearly the focus of his concern. Nevertheless, in his sayings and stories, he constantly includes references to animals, plants, and other creatures of the earth. The U.S. Catholic bishops describe Jesus' sensitivity to his natural environment in these words:

> *God's grace was like wheat growing in the night (see Mark 4:26–29); divine love like a shepherd seeking a lost sheep (see Luke 15:4–7). In the birds of the air and the lilies of the field, Jesus found reason for his disciples to give up the ceaseless quest for material security and advantage and to trust in God (see Matthew 6:25–33). Jesus himself is the Good Shepherd, who gives his life for his flock (see John 10). His Father is a vineyard worker, who trims vines so that they may bear more abundant fruit (see John 15:1–8). These familiar images, though they speak directly to humanity's encounter with God, at the same time reveal that the fundamental relation between humanity and nature is one of caring for creation.*
>
> —*Renewing the Earth,* page 230.

A Sacramental Vision

While respect for the earth has not always been a hallmark of Christian teaching and practice, nonetheless Christianity and in particular Catholicism has a theology that supports an appreciation for nature. The sacramental life of the Church uses earthy things such as water, oil, bread, and wine to help us encounter God. A sacramental vision recognizes that nature points to God, that created things can be viewed as signs of God's glory and presence. In fact, a sacramental vision affirms that: "The whole universe is God's dwelling" (*Renewing the Earth,* page 231). In other words, by its rich tradition of sacramentality, Catholicism keeps us in touch with God not through isolating us from the rest of nature but through holding up the things of nature as signs of God's presence.

Two saints who modeled the sacramental vision of Christianity are Saint Francis of Assisi and Saint Benedict. Statues of Francis frequently found in gardens and on birdbaths attest to his association with nature. He had a strong sense of his own creatureliness and of God's presence in the world. He listened intently to birds and crickets and at one point befriended a troublesome wolf. Saint Benedict established monasteries throughout Europe employing sensible farming practices so that communities could live self-sufficiently and in tune with the land. Francis, then, models the person who loves God's creatures and who sees in them God's goodness and grace. Benedict models being a good steward of creation. ◆

◆ Write a response to the following statement: Christian tradition does not demonstrate a positive attitude toward nature and the material world. Christianity has not inspired humanity to take adequate care of the earth. In fact, it has contributed to our current environmental crisis.

The Church Today: Pope John Paul II and the Natural Order

Well-traveled Pope John Paul II begins his many pilgrimages to the countries of the world by descending a plane and kneeling down to kiss the ground. This symbolic gesture can be interpreted to fittingly demonstrate his plea to Christians to reverence the earth. In his 1987 encyclical *On Social Concern*, the pope points out that misuse of nature violates the dignity of creation and the mutual connection that exists in the world. Secondly, he alerts us that certain resources are not renewable, which is a danger in particular for future generations. Finally, he warns that pollution injures the quality of life and health of industrialized countries (number 34).

Review

18. What controversial position regarding Christianity and nature surfaced in 1967?
19. In Scripture, what is the relationship between humans and the rest of nature?
20. Describe a *sacramental vision*.
21. Name two saints who modeled a sacramental perspective on nature. Describe the unique approach to nature taken by each one.
22. What three points regarding nature does Pope John Paul II make?

Discuss

F. Argue for or against the following statement: Young people today demonstrate great reverence for the earth. I personally feel great reverence for the earth.

Working with the Earth

To cherish nature does not mean to avoid changing it. In the spirit of stewardship, we are called upon to be co-creators, technicians, artists, and lovers in our work with nature. We might think that technology is necessarily hostile to nature. In fact, although technology has at times been harmful to nature, it need not be destructive. To be effective, technology must work with nature now and in the future. Solar energy and windmills are good examples of nature-friendly technology. However, all products and appliances can be more or less nature-friendly.

Changing Personal Practices: Refuse, Reuse, Recycle

Perhaps more than any other justice-related issue, our society says in regard to nature, "We'll worry about that tomorrow." We feel secure that lush forests and bountiful farmlands will continue to exist, even though we see them more frequently on television than in real life. We breathe the air freely, and only occasionally do the fumes remind us of potential danger. We drink water and swim in lakes and oceans, hoping that the latest pollution scare proves to be exaggerated. We continue to dispose of waste without thinking where it is all going.

To change the direction of environmental decay, we need to remember:

- The foods we eat have an impact on nature.

- What we build and where we build affect land, water, air, plant and animal life.

- Use of the automobile affects the quality of our surroundings.

- Easily accessible driving and parking facilities, labor-saving devices, fast foods, packages wrapped in layers of plastic, disposable diapers and containers, and other modern conveniences leave their mark on the environment.

- Every time we throw a bottle or can into the trash we are adding to the garbage that the earth must absorb.

A listing such as this can overwhelm us. However, rather than having the vastness of the problem sap our energy, it can be energizing to know that we can make a difference. On environmental issues, we need not wait for government policies to change. We can make conscientious changes in our lifestyle—especially conscientious usage of resources—that are environmentally friendly rather than environmentally faulty.

A quick guideline for conscientious consumption is *refuse*. Our primary focus should be on refusing—resisting the pressures of our consumer society to accumulate things. When possible, resist buying or using materials which cause damage to the environment. Secondly *reuse*—for example, using grocery store bags more than once saves paper and plastic. We help the environment more when we reuse items rather than recycle them. The third dimension to conscientious consumption is recycling. *Recycle* newspaper, cardboard, wrapping paper, aluminum and tin cans, glass, grass and leaves, and plastic containers. ◆

Review

23. How can technology contribute to nature?
24. What three practices make up the guideline for conscientious consumption?

Discuss

G. Respond to the following statement: As a society, we have not seriously faced the fact that all of our resources need much more careful handling.

In Summary: Turning Around Our Environmental Crisis

We face an environmental crisis. Only recently have we come to be aware of this. Church leaders admonish us to take seriously our God-given responsibility to care for the earth. Inspired by the biblical refrain, "and God saw that it was good," by our gratitude for life, our care for all beings, and our sacramental vision, we can take steps, as individuals and as a society, to cultivate God's garden.

◆ For a week, try to cut back on purchases you make, the amount of resources you use (for example, food, water, electricity), and the waste that you produce. Be attentive to the guideline *refuse, reuse, recycle*. Keep a diary of all the ways you conserved things during the week. When the week is over, write about how it felt to be a more conscientious consumer. Compare notes with other students to share experiences and to discover other possible ways to restrict using and wasting resources.

Before we conclude . . .

Let us pray . . .

Bless the LORD, O my soul.
O LORD my God, you are very great.
You are clothed with honor and majesty,
wrapped in light as with a garment.
You stretch out the heavens like a tent,
you set the beams of your chambers on the waters,
you make the clouds your chariot,
you ride on the wings of the wind,
you make the winds your messengers,
fire and flame your ministers.
You make springs gush forth in the valleys;
they flow between the hills,
giving drink to every wild animal;
the wild asses quench their thirst.
By the streams the birds of the air have their habitation;
they sing among the branches.
From your lofty abode you water the mountains;
the earth is satisfied with the fruit of your work.
You cause the grass to grow for the cattle,
and plants for people to use,
to bring forth food from the earth,
and wine to gladden the human heart,
oil to make the face shine,
and bread to strengthen the human heart.
May the glory of the LORD endure forever;
may the LORD rejoice in his works—
who looks on the earth and it trembles,
who touches the mountains and they smoke.
I will sing to the LORD as long as I live;
I will sing praise to my God while I have being.
May my meditation be pleasing to him,
for I rejoice in the LORD.

—Psalm 104:1–4, 10–15, 31–34

For further study . . .

1. Compose a story or poem or create a poster or art work that illustrates respect for nature. You might try composing from the perspective of a non-human creature.

2. Research one of these categories: land, air, water, plant life, animal life, human waste.

   - Describe environmental concerns associated with the topic.
   - Describe specific steps that people can take to preserve and protect the environment related to that topic.

3. Research and write a report on one of the following topics: wilderness preservation, animal experimentation, vivisection, corporate farming.

4. Interview someone from your local government. (Sometimes townships have web pages so that you can communicate with officials via the Internet. Also, some local governments publish annual calendars that provide information about trash collection and recycling.) Find out what you can about the following questions:

   - How much trash tonnage has been collected annually in your community for the past few years?
   - Where does your community's trash go? Is finding available landfills a problem now? Will it be a problem in the foreseeable future?
   - What percent of the people in your community recycle?
   - What recycling programs does the community offer?
   - How much in tax dollars does recycling save?

5. Environmental problems can overwhelm us. One way to simplify and clarify our response to such problems is to list specific things that we can do to help the environment. Look back over this chapter and make such a list. Mark with an **A** those steps that you already take. Mark with a **B** those steps that you sometimes do. Mark with a **C** those steps that you could do without great effort. Mark with a **D** those steps that would be particularly challenging.

6. Write an action plan that would demonstrate your concern for the earth. Use ideas from these action plans to write, as a class, an action plan for your school. Present it to the student council for school approval and for putting it into action.

7. Calculate rough estimates to answer the following statements. Then use the information to write about the effect that your time spent with nature has had on you.

   - The amount of my day that I usually spend in a natural setting is . . .
   - The percentage of my diet that consists of foods in their natural state is . . .
   - The amount of time I spend in interaction with animals is . . .
   - The number of experiences I have had growing or caring for plants is . . .

CHAPTER 11

The Challenge of Peace

The Christian Resolution of Conflict

True peace cannot exist without justice. That is, only a world where justice prevails is a peaceful world. Therefore, the entire course so far has been a discussion about peace. In this chapter we will zero in specifically on conflict and on Christian approaches to dealing with it. Is the use of violence ever acceptable as the means to an end? Are there rules governing the use of violence in international conflicts? What alternatives to violence exist for resolving conflicts? Finally, are violence and warfare compatible with the Christian message of peace?

Major Concepts

A. The Continuum of Conflict Resolution

- Militarism
- Just-war theory
- Pacifism

B. Christianity and Peacemaking

- War and peace in the Bible
- Jesus and pacifism
- The Church and pacifism

Opening Prayer

God of peace, may we ponder with heartfelt sincerity the words of your Son, Jesus: "Put down the sword" — the sword we carry either in our hands or in our hearts. Through your spirit of peace, and with honest efforts at truth-seeking and reconciliation may we face the conflicts that come our way. Amen.

Before we begin . . .

Answer **agree**, **disagree**, or **uncertain** to the following statements. Choose statements that you believe are most significant and explain your answers.

1. Violence is always an immature means of trying to resolve conflicts.

2. During wartime, an army can do whatever quickens victory and cuts down on its own loss of lives.

3. As part of my schooling, I have been taught ways to resolve conflicts nonviolently.

4. Jesus rejected all violence.

5. Jesus' teaching about "turning the other cheek" instead of using violence is unrealistic.

6. If my country's leaders called upon me to engage in a war they considered just, I'd serve.

7. I am conscientiously opposed to war.

8. People who refuse military service during wartime should be punished.

9. Citizens should not publicly protest a military action that government leaders decide is necessary.

A World in Conflict

■ In the years from 1949 to 1961, about 2.5 million skilled workers, professionals, and intellectuals fled from East Germany to West Germany. The loss threatened the economic viability of East Germany. To counteract this flow of people, a barrier was built. This barrier came to be known as the Berlin Wall. By the 1980s the concrete Berlin Wall extended 28 miles through Berlin and extended another 75 miles to separate East and West Germany. In 1989, in the face of huge but peaceful demonstrations for democratic reform, the Communist leadership granted travel freedom for East Germans and most of the wall was removed over the next two years.

A Communist party conference was also held after about 5,000 disgruntled lower-ranking party members protested outside party headquarters. The conference and the fall of the Berlin Wall were seen as the beginning of the end to the Cold War between the U.S. and the Soviet Union.

■ Two police officers sitting in their patrol car observe a driver passing by at an excessive speed. They pursue the car with sirens blaring and lights flashing. But instead of pulling over, the driver speeds up. The police follow the car and call for backup. Soon two other police cruisers join the chase. When the driver finally stops, he is quickly surrounded by five police officers. The driver gets out of the car, he stumbles slightly, apparently drunk. Two police officers drag him to the ground and a third begins hitting him with a club on the side of his legs and then his head.

■ After World War II, most political leaders of the United States felt that the country had something special to offer the rest of the world—an emphasis on individual freedoms, a democratic form of government, and an economy based on free enterprise. For most of the decades in the latter half of the twentieth century, these leaders viewed Communism as the greatest threat to what the U.S. had to offer. When Communism appeared to be gaining a foothold in Korea, Vietnam, and some Latin American countries, the U.S. government often responded by using violence against people in those countries whom they considered sympathetic to Communism.

- Would violence have been as effective as the nonviolent tactics employed by the East Germans? Could similar nonviolent tactics be used in other national or international conflicts? What are possible nonviolent tactics that people might use in conflict situations?

- Was the violence used by the police justified? Should police be taught nonviolent techniques along with training in the use of weapons? What underlying social factors might have contributed to the police responding in such a violent manner?

- When intentions are honorable, is violence ever acceptable? Was the use of violence appropriate during the Korean War of the 1950s or the Vietnam Conflict of the 1960s? Should the U.S. supply weapons to other countries who are engaged in internal struggles, such as it did in the civil wars of El Salvador and Nicaragua during the 1970s and '80s? Should one country ever send troops to participate in an international conflict in which it is not directly involved, such as in Bosnia and the Middle East?

The Continuum of Conflict Resolution: Approaches to Resolving Conflict

In our private lives and in our imperfect world, conflicts abound. Sometimes the dimensions of a conflict appear to be clear. There is a right side and a wrong side. Sometimes only one possible solution to a conflict appears workable. Ordinarily, however, simple and clear-cut scenarios—"good guys" versus "bad guys"—exist only in childhood games and Hollywood movies. Similarly, relying on only one method of conflict resolution—violence—is short-sighted and unimaginative. More frequently, lasting resolutions involve a process of negotiating and bargaining between two parties who feel as though they have valid concerns to be met.

A helpful way to view nonviolence and violence is to imagine them at opposite ends of a conflict-resolution line. At one end violent tactics are not only acceptable as means to resolving a conflict but are actually admirable. On the other end of the spectrum, violence is considered evil in itself and is always rejected. Only nonviolent techniques for resolving conflicts are acceptable. In between these two extremes, there is a range of attitudes toward the use of violence. The line from absolute acceptance of violence to total rejection of violence can be termed the **continuum of conflict resolution**. Three prominent standpoints on this line have emerged in Christian tradition. ◆

continuum of conflict resolution

refers to the degree someone will accept violence as a means for resolving conflicts, ranging from absolute acceptance of violence to absolute rejection of violence

Militarism: The Glorification of Violence

In themselves, violence and war are not evil. In fact, they are often good. They can bring about positive results—righting wrongs, restoring order, and protecting the weak. Killing for wrong reasons is evil; but killing for a good cause is honorable, a noble act. Human beings are violent and war-like by nature. Realistically, good people should not shy away from violence. Rather, they should strive to outgun the "bad guys." Wrongdoers deserve to be dealt with violently at the hands of righteous people. "Good violence" is courageous; rejecting violence is cowardice.

This position holds that violence is natural, acceptable, and at times good. Of course, unjustified violence is unacceptable. However, when wrongs occur, then use of violence to overcome evil is both proper and honorable. This position describes what so many people whom we consider heroes of history have done. Used to put down evil, warfare is viewed as "holy war."

◆ Draw a horizontal line across a sheet of paper near the top. On the left side write *glorification of violence*; on the right side write *rejection of all violence*. Place an X on the line where you see yourself in terms of the use of violence in resolving conflicts. Under the line, write a description of why you placed the X where you did.

militarism

enthusiastically advocating the use of righteous violence; glorifying the use of violence to resolve conflicts

A term for this position on the continuum of conflict resolution is **militarism**. Beyond allowing violence, militarism glorifies it. The crusading spirit of militarism regards as noble any violence for the sake of one's country or violence for one's cause. Teaching children the use of weapons and the ways of war prepares them to come at conflicts from a position of strength. Countries and individuals should not hesitate to use violence. Those who take up arms to resolve conflicts with another person, group, or country deserve the glorification given to our heroes. Since in our world "might makes right," then to the best of their ability those who believe themselves to be right should use their might. In other words militarism encourages righteous violence—not hesitantly or unwillingly but enthusiastically. ◆

The Just-War Theory: Limited Violence Used Only as a Last Resort

In itself, violence is evil. However, when all other means of resolving a conflict have been exhausted and injustices remain, then violence may be employed. Resorting to violence is regrettable and certainly should never be glorified, but in certain limited circumstances it may prove to be a lesser evil than not using it. When and how violence is used must be strictly regulated, always with an eye toward restricting to the barest minimum the harm that it produces.

◆ Write a letter responding to the following inquiry:

Dear _____ ,

My name is Mutombo. All the people in my village are very poor. Nonetheless, each year government officials take a portion of our crops and livestock. The soldiers are cruel. People suspected of questioning the authorities are carried off and never seen again. I have heard stories of children being killed with a machete while their parents were forced to watch. I am young like you. I wish to be a student. However, some of my friends from the village have formed a group of revolutionaries who have taken up arms against the government. They have encouraged me to join them. What do you think I should do?

On the continuum of conflict resolution, a middle position toward use of violence and warfare is the just-war theory. For a long time, this theory has represented the standard Catholic position toward violence. Therefore, the theory deserves an extensive explanation.

Examining Just-War Principles

The just-war theory includes seven principles regulating *when* violence is acceptable and also *how* violence is to be restricted during warfare. The following example will provide a more visual image with which to examine the questions that need to be asked with each principle and to examine the difficulties involved.

> **A plane carrying ten citizens of country A is hijacked by a group from country B. The plane is taken to country B where the travelers are held hostage in a military compound near its capital city. In exchange for the ten passengers, officials from country B demand release of ten of its citizens imprisoned in country A for earlier acts of terrorism.**

Considering each principle of the just-war theory individually, the question will be repeated: Would country A be justified in using violence?

Just cause: Does a real and certain injustice exist?

When the U.S. Catholic bishops addressed the issue of war and peace in the 1980s, they stated: "War is permissible only to confront a 'real and certain danger,' i.e., to protect innocent life, to preserve conditions necessary for decent human existence, and to secure basic human rights" (*The Challenge of Peace*, no. 86). By itself, this principle greatly limits situations when violence is acceptable. According to this principle, violence is permitted only when life or justice is clearly and immediately endangered. Question: Does the taking of hostages meet the standard for just cause, allowing the use of violence in our example?

Basic Principles of the Just-War Theory

1. Just cause
2. Right intention
3. Legitimate authority
4. Proportionality
5. Reasonable hope of success
6. Noncombatant immunity
7. Last resort

Right intention: Is justice the intended outcome of the action?

Even if a just cause exists, actual intentions for using violence must also be in order. As you can imagine, when a conflict builds warring parties can lose sight of original intentions that led to using to violence in the first place. For instance, as a war progresses and emotions flare an initial intention to "free hostages" can become "overthrow their government" or "kill the enemy." The principle of right intention, then, requires that throughout a conflict, violence is meant only to serve the concerns of justice and life. For instance, in the hijacking scenario described above, country A's intentions to free hostages could also lead to access to country B's rich oil resources. Question: Does the freeing of the hostages meet the standard for *right intention*, allowing the use of violence?

Legitimate authority: Are recognized leaders following accepted unwritten rules in declaring war and in overseeing how it is carried out?

This third principle asks the question *who is responsible* for addressing a conflict? In the case of the hijacking, the government of country A has responsibility for the welfare of its citizens. The issue of legitimate authority is not always as clear-cut as this. For instance, over the past century many revolutions have occurred. Can revolutionaries ever claim "legitimate authority" for resorting to violence? As you recall from your history books, the leaders of the American revolution wrote the Declaration of Independence stating why the government of England no longer deserved to be the legitimate ruler of the American colonies. Also, today neither the boundaries nor the rightful rulers of nation-states are necessarily clearly defined. Sometimes members of a minority group within a particular country believe that their rights are not being adequately represented by the government in power. Therefore, they feel justified in using violence to overthrow the government or to gain control over a portion of the country. Question: Who would the recognized leaders be in country A?

Proportionality: Will the foreseeable good of the military action outweigh the possible damage caused?

Another way to state the question that the principle of proportionality asks is: Does the good likely to result from using violence outweigh the probable damage caused? According to the just-war theory, violence and warfare cause great harm. Weighing the cost of warfare in human life and suffering is difficult but crucial in determining whether or not war is justified. Proportionality attempts to judge the merits of the various options open to those who find themselves faced with a conflict. Question: In the plane hijacking scenario, what factors might influence the principle of proportionality? For instance, would country A be justified in causing the deaths of hundreds of people from country B in order to save the ten hostages? Is "giving in to terrorists" a greater evil than the deaths of the ten hostages? Would endangering the lives of dozens of its own soldiers be worth the risk to country A's saving the lives of the hostages?

Reasonable hope of success: With a fair degree of certainty, are intended results likely to be achieved?

According to this principle, certain uses of violence might be acceptable while others would not be. Question: Can country A provide military actions that would probably succeed in carrying out the objective of freeing hostages?

Noncombatant immunity: Will people not directly involved in fighting be spared becoming victims?

Noncombatants are those persons not directly involved in the manufacture, direction, or use of weapons. In an earlier era when the just-war theory was taking shape, the distinction between combatants and noncombatants was much clearer. Modern weaponry makes it possible to pinpoint targets with some degree of accuracy but it can also cause great amounts of destruction. Destroying a country's water supply system, filling hospitals with wounded persons, causing loss of limbs or eyesight to a large number of civilians, and leveling cities can demoralize a country and hasten conclusion to a war; but they also involve violence against noncombatants. The traditional just-war theory states that *no military action may be aimed directly at noncombatants*. Question: In the actions undertaken to free the hostages, will there be any chance that innocent people will be killed or harmed?

Last resort: Have all other means of resolving the conflict been tried?

Finally, the just-war theory maintains that *violence must be the last resort*. All other means of resolving the conflict must be tried before resorting to violence. Of course, it is impossible to determine whether or not all other avenues of conflict resolution have been tried. Sometimes the heat of the moment or a lack of knowledge and imagination leads a person to believe that all other options have been tried and have failed. Because the just-war theory argues for violence only as a last resort, it follows that a just-war approach to violence supports use of the vast assortment of nonviolent techniques that have been developed over the past century or so. Question: What other ways of solving the hijacking incident could be used before using violence?

Just-war theory has always played a part in official arguments about war. No political leader can send soldiers into battle, asking them to risk their lives and to kill other people, without assuring them that their cause is just—and that of their enemies is unjust. And if the theory is used, it is also, inevitably, misused. Sometimes it serves only to determine what lies our leaders tell. . . .It is important not to give up the theory just because of its misuse—no more than we would give up our ideas about friendship just because they are exploited by false friends. ◆

—Michael Walzer, *Just and Unjust Wars,* New York:
Harper Collins, Basic Books, pages xi–xii.

When the Shooting Stops: The Just-War Theory Applied After a Conflict

In 1994 theologian Michael J. Schuck wrote an article about a dimension of the just-war theory that has been overlooked. He notes that the theory offers principles to help us determine when war is permitted and how war is to be conducted. Schuck suggests that we should also think about how the concept of a just war can be applied after a conflict. He proposes three principles that the just-war theory promotes following a war.

Repentance

Typically, celebrations follow victory after a war. However, a victory celebration need not be an angry or humiliating display toward the former enemy. In the spirit of a just war, accompanying any celebration should be a spirit of repentance for all the pain suffered by both sides in the conflict. In a sense any war is a defeat for all humanity. Along with celebration that peace is restored, there should be repentance that war occurred.

Honorable surrender

History affords us examples when victors used the occasion to humiliate and degrade the defeated and also of examples when victors saluted and honored the vanquished. The aim of a just war is justice, not shaming enemies. Therefore, an appropriate just-war principle following a war is attempting to preserve the honor of those who are surrendering.

◆ Make a case for or against the following action as a just use of violence: After the French government surrendered to Germany during World War II, some French people, calling themselves the Resistance, continued to fight the German occupying forces by using guerrilla warfare tactics. In one incident Resistance troops posed as farm workers working in a field as a contingent of German soldiers marched by. Since the location was far from the front, the soldiers were not battle-ready. The Resistance fighters picked up guns hidden in the field and fired on the soldiers, killing a number of them.

Restoration

A defeated country is a ravaged country. The land itself cries out for restoration, and many innocent victims will continue to suffer well after guns are silent. Perhaps the thought of working as hard to restore a defeated country as armies had worked to destroy it sounds unrealistic. If so, then the just-war theory itself is unrealistic. According to the theory the only rightful intention for entering into warfare in the first place is restoration of justice. The goal of restoration cannot end when the shooting stops.

Review

1. What is the *continuum of conflict resolution*?
2. What attitude toward violence is expressed through the term *militarism*?
3. What attitude toward violence is expressed through the term *just-war theory*?
4. List the seven principles of a just war.
5. What just-war principle is especially problematic for revolutionaries?
6. Define *proportionality* as it applies to just war.
7. How has the principle of *noncombatant immunity* been clouded by modern warfare?
8. Name and explain the three principles of the just-war theory for after a conflict.

Discuss

A. Think about a conflict you have had with someone in your family or group of friends. How did you feel? What was the conflict about? Was it resolved, and if so how? Was violence involved to any degree? Apply each of the just-war principles to the conflict. Based on your application, state whether or not and in what specific ways the just-war theory might help in resolving interpersonal conflicts in positive ways.

B. Name three characters from films who you believe represent the attitude of militarism. What is the attitude toward violence and conflict resolution held by each character? Can you name three characters from films who reject militarism? If you can, what is the attitude toward violence and conflict resolution held by each of these characters?

C. Referring to specific just-war principles, use examples to argue for or against the following statement: Given the scope and complexity of modern warfare, the just-war theory is no longer helpful in evaluating when the use of violence is justified.

D. The three principles of a just war after a conflict are *repentance*, *honorable surrender*, and *restoration*. If you were to attach additional principles to the ones mentioned here, what would they be?

Pacifism: Rejection of All Violence

Using violence to right wrongs is like eating to lose weight. Violence itself is wrong. It is an attack on people's lives and well-being. Believing that violence solves problems is shortsighted and unrealistic. True peace comes only through peaceful means, not through violence. If absolute pacifism—rejection of all violence—appears unrealistic, it is only because pacifism has so seldom been tried. A maturing world community must reject violence and adopt pacifism as the only hope for its continued survival.

At the opposite end from militarism on the continuum of conflict resolution is pacifism. Pacifism might at first appear to be off the scale of conflict resolution altogether. Isn't pacifism the same as passivity, not doing anything to resolve conflicts? Actually, throughout history many of the great voices for peaceful resolution of conflicts have not led quiet, passive lives. Jesus appears to have rejected violence and yet died in mid-life at the hands of others. In the twentieth century the two leading advocates of pacifism—Mohandas K. Gandhi of India and Martin Luther King, Jr., of the United States—both upset others so much that they were assassinated. During the Middle Ages Saint Francis of Assisi rejected violence and yet was involved in the major conflicts of his day—rich versus poor, healthy versus sick, and Christians versus Muslims. He lived life with such zeal that he died, physically worn out, in his early forties.

Pacifism, then, is not the same as passivity. **Passivity** means not getting involved, not attempting to resolve conflicts, being detached. On the other hand, **pacifism** literally means making peace, doing peace, creating peace. It is important to keep these distinctions in mind.

Pacifism is at the opposite end of the line from militarism because it rules out violence in resolving conflicts, not because it overlooks them. Actually, the Indian pacifist Gandhi once remarked that: "Where there is only a choice between cowardice and violence, I would choose violence." In Gandhi's mind, pacifism meant fighting—nonviolent fighting—fighting for peace and justice through nonviolent means. Pacifism is *nonviolent* conflict resolution.

(Nonviolence) is an attitude of refusing either to meet violence with violence or to bow down in the face of it. It is an attitude of engagement, of respect for opponents and enemies, of searching for peaceful means of resolving conflicts.

—Gerard A. Vanderhaar, *Beyond Violence*, Mystic, CT: Twenty-Third Publications, 1998, page 39.

passivity

making no attempt to resolve conflict; not getting involved; detached

pacifism

conflict resolution through nonviolent means

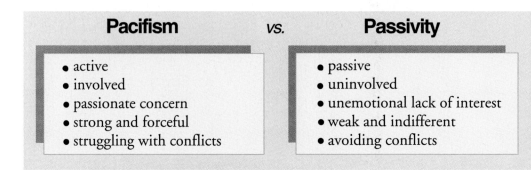

Pacifism	vs.	Passivity
• active • involved • passionate concern • strong and forceful • struggling with conflicts		• passive • uninvolved • unemotional lack of interest • weak and indifferent • avoiding conflicts

Absolute Versus Practical Pacifism

Two categories of pacifists exist. **Absolute pacifists** believe that violence is *always* wrong. In their view any use of violence would violate their religious or humanitarian principles. On the other hand **practical pacifists** believe that nonviolence is a better way to resolve conflicts than violence. Practical pacifists would point to the wars and bloodshed of the past few centuries to make the case that violence has proved to be much more destructive than constructive. It is now time for all nations and all people to practice a more creative and life-affirming way of resolving conflicts—nonviolence.

Both absolute and practical pacifists believe that other choices than violence must be explored and encouraged if the human race is to survive and thrive. Because of the commitment of a number of people to nonviolent conflict resolution, pacifism has grown from being an idealistic dream to being an agenda for action. ◆

absolute pacifists

persons who believe that all violence is wrong and violates their religious or humanitarian principles

practical pacifists

persons who believe that nonviolence is a better way than violence to resolve conflicts

◆ Write an essay addressing the following questions:

How would you respond to a pacifist? How would you feel about the person's position? What would you want to say to or hear from the person? Would you vote for the person for national political office? Why or why not?

Pacifism *Before* Conflict

Creating a Climate of Peace

As the just-war theory has principles that apply both before and during a conflict, so does pacifism. A first principle that supports the goals of pacifism and can help prevent violence is: Create a climate of peace.

A climate of peace does not exist when leaders, media, or even private citizens blame people in another country for the world's problems. When people constantly find fault with others, insulting and belittling them, and generally view them as evil, then clearly a climate of peace is wanting. Creating a climate of peace requires first of all *examining attitudes toward others*, especially toward potential enemies.

When countries are in conflict, their citizens can view enemies as either subhuman and therefore not worthy of respect or as possessing *super*human prowess or determination. In either case the enemy is to be feared and not reasoned with. Small groups within countries, such as politicians and talk-show hosts, and even groups within small communities, such as schools, can stir up violence by voicing attitudes toward the "enemy." ◆

Secondly, creating a climate of peace implies *examining ourselves*. We can have as distorted an image of our own goodness and right-mindedness as we do of the faults and evil intentions of people in a country with whom we are in conflict.

Finally, creating a climate of peace means *placing a higher priority on peacemaking than on war-making*. In other words the resources of a nation—financial, educational, governmental, and economic—can be used for peaceful efforts or they can be used for preparing for war. A climate of peace supports efforts aimed at creating and maintaining peace, such as student exchanges between nations, rather than war-mongering.

Rooting Out the Causes of Conflict

> *Actually, we who engage in nonviolent direct action are not the creators of tension. We merely bring to the surface the hidden tension that is already alive. We bring it out in the open where it can be seen and dealt with. Like a boil that can never be cured as long as it is covered up but must be opened with all its pus-flowing ugliness to the natural medicines of air and light, injustice must likewise be exposed, with all of the tension its exposing creates, to the light of human conscience and the air of national opinion before it can be cured.*
>
> —Martin Luther King, Jr., *Letter from a Birmingham Jail*, April 16, 1963.

◆ Review the words of a politician, a talk-show commentator, or a newspaper editorial. Do they speak about others in a way that promotes peace or violence? Explain.

A second principle of pacifism before violence is rooting out the causes of conflict. As Dr. King describes in his letter, the sores of conflict often fester when untended. He is really drawing attention to what pacifists call **the spiral of violence**. ◆

The Spiral of Violence

* Injustice itself is a first level of violence.

* If victims of injustice respond violently under the weight of their oppression, then second-level violence occurs.

* Authorities who forcefully crack down on second-level violence are engaging in a third level of violence, and the spiral continues.

In other words injustices described earlier in this book (such as poverty or racism) are in fact forms of violence—specifically, first-level violence. When certain poor people or members of a particular ethnic group feel as though other ways are unavailable to them, they may respond to what they consider to be an injustice with either organized or spontaneous violence. This second level of violence is more likely to make the headlines of newspapers than the daily grind of poverty or oppression that victims of injustice experience. Attempts to "restore peace," putting down second-level violence without addressing injustices that helped lead up to it, do not end the spiral of violence. When we are truly concerned about peacemaking, then we seek to uproot unjust conditions boiling below the surface of potential conflicts that might explode into visible violence. The spiral of violence reminds us that *the pain and frustration of injustice are violence even before they reach the boiling point.* Pacifism tries to end violence at each level of its spiral.

◆ Look through recent newspapers or news magazines for stories about conflict. Look for evidence that the spiral of violence was or was not at work in these conflict situations. Write a report on your findings.

Pacifism *During* Conflict

Pacifism before conflict seeks to prevent violence. When serious conflicts occur, however, as they always will, then pacifism demands at least as much energy, creativity, strength, wisdom, and courage as violence does. What exactly does nonviolent conflict resolution look like? Gandhi is the modern era's greatest apostle of nonviolence. He applied his strategies of nonviolent conflict resolution to a situation that has frequently led to violence—a colony (India) seeking independence from a colonial power (England). Therefore, Gandhi serves as a valuable model for pacifism in action.

Gandhi called his approach to nonviolence **satyagraha**. With this term Gandhi was proposing that "right makes might" rather than the other way around. Gandhi and his followers practiced a wide variety of techniques to achieve his goals, sometimes altering plans in highly imaginative and unexpected ways. (For instance, during World War II Gandhi called off protests against England because he felt that England was rightfully preoccupied with fighting Germany. He didn't want to take advantage of its moment of weakness.) Throughout, Gandhi held to two principles that guided his approach to resolving conflicts. First, both sides in a conflict possess some truth. Secondly, a conflict is not resolved until both parties agree to a common solution.

Seeking Truth on Both Sides

Gandhi believed that both sides in a conflict always possess some truth, even though not always equally so. He regarded *satyagraha* as an attempt to discover the truth of each position in a conflict and then to act according to that truth. He felt that violent ways of resolving a conflict did not lead to true but to false resolutions.

Simply put, domination by one party reveals only which side of the conflict is physically stronger. Domination does not reveal where truth lies. Since truth is not served by domination, the underlying problem remains for future generations to resolve. In addition the use of violence creates new conflicts between the two groups.

Interestingly, Gandhi held the same reservations about compromise as he did about domination. He saw compromise as each side winning a little, but each side losing a little as well. Likewise, when a judge or court of law decides which side is right, Gandhi believed that the losing side would feel that the truth in their position has been overlooked. The losing party might also feel humiliated and thus cooperate only reluctantly. For Gandhi neither compromise nor appeal to law truly resolves a conflict.

satyagraha

truth force; soul force; belief that right makes might, not that might makes right

Seeking Truth in Common

An opponent is not always bad simply because he opposes.

—Mohandas Gandhi

Gandhi rejected the word *enemy* because its use gets in the way of the search for truth. For Gandhi, an opponent in a conflict is not an enemy. The pacifist's first task is to see the conflict from the points of view of each of the combatants. One side may have the greater weight of truth, but that does not mean that the other side has no legal claims and concerns. Gandhi taught that combatants are not enemies. In a conflict the real enemy is falsehood.

Gandhi believed that a conflict is not resolved until opponents agree to a solution. In other words true resolution of conflict occurs only when two parties formerly on opposite sides of an issue occupy the same side. Seeking to resolve differences calls for constant bargaining. When one party refuses to bargain in good faith or dismisses the concerns of the other party, then the opponent may need to engage in some form of nonviolent campaign. A nonviolent campaign might include activities such as we have come to associate with nonviolent protests: demonstrations, boycotts, strikes, sit-ins, fasting, and civil disobedience.

For Gandhi these activities do not involve using force—either physical or psychological. Instead of attacking an opponent, Gandhi taught noncooperation. That is, Gandhian fighters would not cooperate with falsehood but would act according to their understanding of the truth. For instance, when the British issued a tax on salt in India which he considered unjust, in open defiance of British law Gandhi organized a great march to the sea where salt was available. In an example from the early days of the civil rights movement in the United States, some black and white students went to lunch counters in southern states marked "whites only" and sat down together. The moral force of their actions eventually led to laws making such discrimination illegal. In the 1970s, when gasoline prices suddenly skyrocketed, a large group of truckers drove their trucks to Washington, DC. There they obstructed traffic by driving slowly around the capitol building, thus drawing national attention to their problem. ◆

Civil Disobedience: Is It Nonviolent?

If you believed strongly that abortions should not be performed, would you join a group of protesters who try to disrupt the practice by chaining themselves to the doors of a local abortion clinic? If you believed that airplanes equipped to carry weapons used against civilian targets are immoral, would you break into an air force base and pound one of these planes with a hammer while pouring blood on it in a gesture meant to symbolize its destructiveness? Would you find it acceptable to attempt to disrupt whaling ships from killing whales, even if people had to break a law to do so? If your government decided that everyone who reaches age eighteen must register for a military draft, would you publicly burn your draft card in an act of defiance against the law?

◆ Name three conflict situations, either interpersonal, communal, or international. Identify as many truthful claims as possible that each side is making. Then, for each conflict describe a resolution that would represent truth rather than selfish interests. Based on this exercise do you agree with Gandhi that each side in a conflict possesses truth, although not equally so, and that it is possible to find common truth? Explain.

Practices such as these have come to be associated with nonviolent protests. Clearly such tactics stretch the limits of nonviolence. For instance, it would be legal for a group of residents in a graffiti-filled neighborhood to carry signs in front of a store protesting the sale of spray paint to children. It would be another matter if this same group chained themselves to the front doors of the store or spray painted its outside walls. Different people might or might not label such actions nonviolent.

Civil disobedience has become a major form of nonviolent confrontation. Civil disobedience does not entail breaking laws randomly. (For instance, a young person who believes that the high cost of movies is unfair and therefore sneaks into a theater without paying is not practicing civil disobedience.) Practiced as a form of nonviolent protest, civil disobedience normally involves: First, breaking only those laws considered unjust; secondly, accepting the legal penalties for breaking the law; thirdly, making a clear, public statement of intentions; and, lastly, ensuring that no harm is caused to persons. Some of the protests against the racial segregation laws that existed in the United States half a century ago illustrate classic civil disobedience. Martin Luther King, Jr., himself spent time in jail for violating laws he considered unjust.

During the era of the Vietnam War in the United States, some antiwar protesters went beyond breaking laws that they considered unjust. Instead, they also broke laws that they considered moral in order to bring to light what they saw as a grave immorality—specifically, the Vietnam War itself. For example, a group of protesters broke into a draft office near Baltimore, Maryland, and burned some files housed there.◆

The Promise of Pacifism

Does pacifism work? That is, do nonviolent conflict-resolution techniques provide ways to justice that violence does not? Given the horrors of genocide and the extreme disregard for human life under Nazism, what type of nonviolent tactics might have been employed during the World War II era? Could pacifism be applied to large-scale, global conflicts? What would such pacifism look like? Given the expense of maintaining military preparedness, would a nation such as the U.S. or Canada ever spend an equal amount on exploring nonviolent alternatives to resolving conflicts?

Many questions about pacifism remain unanswered. A writer once said that Christianity cannot be said to have failed because it has never really been tried. The same might be said of pacifism. Before we reject it for fear that it has its limits, we would do well to explore its possibilities. Certainly, especially in the past century, violence has already been tried. The results have been horrid deaths and destruction,

civil disobedience

breaking a law for what one considers just and moral reasons

blockade

preventing the transport of goods to their intended destination

◆ One alternative to all-out violence sometimes recommended in international conflicts is a **blockade**. The aim of a blockade is to prevent certain goods—perhaps all goods—from entering a country. Do you consider a blockade of all goods to be a form of nonviolence? Would restricting everything but food and medical supplies from entering a country be nonviolence? Explain your responses.

and more often than not violence has led to more violence. A new millennium offers the world community an occasion to re-examine where it is headed and what tactics would be most effective for getting there. On this point Gandhi again offered a helpful insight. He believed that, in resolving conflicts, means and ends are not separate. In other words, using violent means to attain peace is a contradiction. Only peaceful means ultimately bring peace.

A final point about pacifism leads us to the next section of this chapter. For Christians the question about pacifism is not simply "Does it work?" but "Is it faithful to the gospel?"

Review

9. What is the difference between *pacifism* and *passivity*?
10. What is the difference between *absolute pacifists and practical pacifists*?
11. Name three attitudes that can foster a climate of peace.
12. Describe the *spiral of violence*.
13. Define *satyagraha*.
14. What two principles did Gandhi hold to in resolving conflicts?
15. Define *civil disobedience*. Name the four elements of traditional civil disobedience.
16. How did some antiwar protesters take civil disobedience beyond its traditional definition?
17. What did Gandhi see as the relationship between means and ends in resolving conflicts?
18. Beyond "Does it work?" what question does the Christian ask about pacifism?

Discuss

E. A famous modern pacifist says: "To practice nonviolence, first of all we must learn to deal peacefully with ourselves" (Thich Nhat Hanh, *Living Buddha, Living Christ*, page 92). What do you think he means? Give an example to illustrate what you think he means. Do you think his statement is true?

F. Name five ways that a climate of peace does exist or could be encouraged within your school community. If you can identify ways that you believe a climate of violence exists within your school, list those as well and suggest how that climate could change.

G. Name five ways that a climate of violence exists within your country. Suggest ways that such a climate could change.

H. Name five ways that a climate of peace does exist or could more strongly exist within your country.

I. Name five situations within the world community where a climate of violence (short of all-out war) currently exists.

J. Name five ways that a climate of peace could be fostered within the world community.

K. When you visualize peace, what images come to mind? Do your images reflect a notion of peace as a calm and restful lack of conflict or as an active involvement in addressing conflicts?

Christianity and Peacemaking

Non-violent means of resistance to evil deserve much more study and consideration than they have thus far received. There have been significant instances in which people have successfully resisted oppression without recourse to arms.

—U.S. Catholic Bishops, *The Challenge of Peace,* number 222.

War and Peace in the Bible

In the Jewish Scriptures, God is occasionally portrayed as a warrior God who batters the enemy. Many biblical heroes—for example, Joshua, Samson, and David—employed violence without a hint of disfavor on the part of the author. On the other hand we can also find passages from Scripture that denounce violence. The books of the prophets provide us with images of a reign of peace and the melting of ill will between enemies. Here is one passage that ever since biblical times has stirred the imagination of those who long for peace.

> *The wolf shall live with the lamb,*
> *the leopard shall lie down with the kid,*
> *the calf and the lion and the fatling together,*
> *and a little child shall lead them.*
> *The cow and the bear shall graze,*
> *their young shall lie down together;*
> *and the lion shall eat straw like the ox.*
> *The nursing child shall play over the hole of the asp,*
> *and the weaned child shall put its hand on the adder's den.*
> *They will not hurt or destroy on all my holy mountain;*
> *for the earth will be full of the knowledge of the Lord*
> *as the waters cover the sea.* ◆

—Isaiah 11:6–9

◆ Write a "peace poem" or create some other artistic depiction of peace.

Jesus and Pacifism

Much in popular culture—and some would say our natural instinct as well—glorifies violence. In movies a frequent theme portrays otherwise peaceful people driven to their breaking point. When they finally repay with violence, the music rises in pitch and the audience cheers them on. Typically, when a U.S. president declares war on another country, his approval rating immediately goes up. Politicians and judges who promise to "get tough" win votes.

The culture of Jesus' day was equally attracted to violence. Armed Roman soldiers patrolled Israel, and some Jews, called *sicarii,* carried knives hidden in their sleeves, ready to attack unsuspecting soldiers. In the face of such violence, Jesus comes across as an unmistakable person of peace. Jesus constantly advocated peace and refused to resort to violence, even when his life depended on it. Some readers interpret the incident when he cleared the temple area and derided the money lenders gathered there to be an endorsement of violence on the part of Jesus. The actions of Jesus can also be viewed as a nonviolent demonstration to claim the temple for his teaching ministry.

Jesus met his persecutors and death on the cross nonviolently. He censured the Apostle Peter when in the garden of Gethsemane Peter cut off the ear of a soldier who had come to arrest Jesus. The early Christian writer Tertullian declared, "The Lord, by taking away Peter's sword, disarmed every soldier thereafter." All Christians must come to terms with the clear teaching of Jesus: In response to violence done to you, "turn the other cheek."

The Gospel of Peace

When Saint Paul joined the followers of Jesus, he contrasted Jesus' "gospel of peace" with reliance on military weapons and warfare. He describes the message of Jesus as one of truth, justice, and peace, replacing the old ways of violence and domination. In this passage from his letter to the Ephesians, Saint Paul's portrayal of Christians sounds similar to what Gandhi understood practitioners of satyagraha, or "truth force," to be:

> Stand therefore, and fasten the belt of truth around your waist, and put on the breastplate of righteousness. As shoes for your feet put on whatever will make you ready to proclaim the gospel of peace. With all of these, take the shield of faith, with which you will be able to quench all the flaming arrows of the evil one. Take the helmet of salvation, and the sword of the Spirit, which is the word of God.

—Ephesians 6:14–17

Pontius' Puddle

In the gospel of peace, all traces of a warrior God dissolve. Jesus preaches love of enemies, not their destruction; and enduring suffering, not inflicting it. For Jesus, God's reign signifies forgiveness, compassion, elimination of underlying causes of violence, and expansion of the term *neighbor* to include all people—thus rejecting the notion of enemy. In the "Lord's Prayer" Christians pray for God's reign to be established on earth. Through this prayer they are reminding themselves to cooperate with God in establishing a reign of peace.

The Church and the Gospel of Peace

In the early Church most Christians interpreted Jesus' rejection of violence in a literal sense. Even into the fourth century, Christians refused military service. For example, Saint Martin of Tours (d. 397) rejected his soldierly profession in these words: "I am a soldier of Christ. It is unlawful for me to fight." However, once Christianity became the religion of the empire under Constantine (306–337), Christian leaders felt that the responsibility of ruling in a sinful world required the use of force.

The reign of Constantine represents a turning point in Christian thinking about the legitimacy of violence and war. By and large writers before him tended to be pacifist in outlook, whereas those following his rise to power argued for the legitimacy of war under certain conditions.

—Louis J. Swift, *The Early Fathers on War and Military Service,* Collegeville, MN: Michael Glazier, page 27.

It was at this time that Saint Augustine first laid out the restrictions of the just-war theory. In other words violence never was meant to go unchecked. Christianity has at times had a very bloody history, especially during the Crusades. Yet even during the Middle Ages, when violence was so much a part of the feudal system, the Church enacted strict rules governing warfare. For instance:

- According to a decree called the *Peace of God,* certain groups such as members of the clergy were not to participate in war, and excommunication was imposed upon those who used violence against noncombatants.

- The *Truce of God* prohibited fighting on Sundays and specified holy days, during Lent, in seasons of harvest (August 15 to November 15), and for a part of each week (usually from Wednesday evening to Monday morning). In its final form the truce allowed only eighty days a year for war.

- In 1139 the Second Lateran Council forbade the use of "military engines" against people. ◆

The Church in the Modern Era:
A Resurgence of Pacifism

Nonviolence implies both a philosophy and a strategy which rejects force and pursues a range of alternative actions (e.g., dialogue, negotiation, protests, strikes, boycotts, civil disobedience and civilian resistance) in order to bring law, policy, government itself or other armed parties in line with the demand of justice. Although nonviolence has often been regarded as simply a personal option or vocation, recent history suggests that in some circumstances it can be an effective public undertaking as well. Dramatic political transitions in places as diverse as the Philippines and Eastern Europe demonstrate the power of nonviolent action, even against dictatorial and totalitarian regimes . . . These nonviolent revolutions challenge us to find ways to take into full account the power of organized, active nonviolence . . . As a nation we have an affirmative obligation to promote research and education in nonviolent means of resisting evil. We need to address nonviolent strategies with much greater seriousness in international affairs. In some future conflicts, strikes and people power may be more effective than guns and bullets.

    —U.S. Catholic Bishops, *The Harvest of Justice Is Sown In Peace*, 1993, pages 10–11.

    Over the course of the modern era, war has regained its bad name among Church leaders. That does not mean that modern Church statements promote pacifism exclusively. However, they do recognize pacifism as a legitimate Christian position. They also warn against using just-war principles to defend wars that do not meet the strict standards of the theory. Beyond that, in the past forty years, no organization of such size has spoken more forcefully or more frequently against use of military power than the Catholic Church. Priority is always to be given to peaceful means for resolving conflicts. Therefore, pacifism and nonviolent approaches to problems have reclaimed their position as the Christian ideal. Any use of violence falls short of the ideal, must meet strict standards, and, at the very least, requires constant reevaluation.

◆ Make a case for one of the positions below as the Christian position on violence. Is each of these positions acceptable for a Christian to hold? Why or why not?

- A Christian is a crusader, ready to take up the sword in the cause of right. To conquer evil a Christian does not hesitate to fight with whatever means necessary. The Christian crusaders, who used force to conquer the Holy Land, were heroic "soldiers of Christ."

- A Christian uses violence only reluctantly and regrettably. However, since sometimes violence is necessary, a Christian may participate in a just war, although limiting its destruction as much as possible. Great Christian thinkers such as St. Augustine and St. Thomas Aquinas laid out strict, sensible guidelines about when and how to fight a "just war."

- A Christian is a pacifist. Violence against others is evil and contrary to the teachings of Jesus. No circumstances can justify its use. In the spirit of Jesus, Christians must stand for peace. Using violence diminishes the life-affirming message of Jesus. Heroic Christians such as St. Francis of Assisi and, more recently, Dorothy Day and Pope John Paul II, have shown pacifism to be a powerful tool for combating both injustice and a culture of violence.

Peace is not just the absence of war. . . .Like a cathedral, peace must be constructed patiently and with unshakable faith.
—Pope John Paul II, "Homily at Coventry Cathedral," *Origins* #12, 1982, page 55.

Review

19. In terms of violence, how is God sometimes portrayed in the Jewish Scriptures?

20. What was the attitude of Jesus toward violence?

21. What did Saint Paul contrast with use of military weapons?

22. What effect did the reign of Roman Emperor Constantine have on Christian attitudes toward war?

23. Define the medieval decrees called the *Peace of God* and the *Truce of God*.

24. What view of pacifism has developed within modern Church teaching?

25. What warning is found in modern Church teaching regarding use of the just-war theory?

Discuss

L. With which of the following statements do you most agree? Explain your choice.

- Jesus was a pacifist. Christians in turn should be pacifists.

- Jesus was a pacifist, but Christians must exercise their own judgment about how best to address injustice and conflicts. "Turning the other cheek" to violence represents the Christian ideal. Sometimes it must be discarded.

- Jesus was not a pacifist. Circumstances of his day led him to preach against violence. Christians are responsible for responding to today's problems in whatever ways they determine to be best.

M. What specific roles would you want Church leaders and other Christians to play in our conflict-ridden world? What message would you want Christianity to stand for in relation to violence, war, and peace?

In Summary: Creative Conflict Resolution

Let us . . . find ways of resolving controversies in a manner worthy of human beings. Providence urgently demands of us that we free ourselves from the age-old slavery of war.

— "Pastoral Constitution on the Church in the Modern World," number 81, *The Documents of Vatican II.*

At this point in history, we are in urgent need of discovering new methods of resolving interpersonal and international conflicts. In the words of the U.S. Catholic bishops, "Catholic teaching begins in every case with a presumption against war and for peaceful settlement of disputes" (*The Challenge of Peace*, summary). In this chapter peace has been presented not as the absence of conflict but as creative resolution of conflicts. Jesus tells us that peacemaking is such an integral part of the Christian vocation that "Blessed are the peacemakers, for they will be called children of God" (Matthew 5:9).

Let us pray . . .

Lord, make me an instrument of your peace.

Where there is hatred, let me sow love;

Where there is injury, pardon;

Where there is doubt, faith;

Where there is despair, hope;

Where there is darkness, light;

And where there is sadness, joy.

O, Divine Master, grant that I may not so much

seek to be consoled as to console;

To be understood as to understand;

To be loved as to love;

For it is in giving that we receive;

It is in pardoning that we are pardoned;

And it is in dying that we are born to eternal life. Amen.

—St. Francis of Assisi

For further study . . .

1. Describe two conflict situations that exist in our world today. Is violence employed by representatives on either or both sides in the conflicts? What approaches to resolving each conflict would you recommend? Explain why you believe the approaches you recommend would be successful in resolving the conflicts justly. Upon what basis could you make a case for or against the use of violence in each conflict?

2. Give pros and cons of the following statement: "People who wish to overthrow or influence the government of their own country should never use violent means to do so." State your position on this issue. Use examples to illustrate why you do or do not support this statement.

3. Research the atmosphere that surrounded the end of a war that has occurred over the past few centuries. Write a report on whether or not there was concern for justice on the part of the victors.

4. Think about a real or potential conflict situation on a personal level, a societal level, and an international level. Examine each conflict to determine in what ways just-war principles and the elements of pacifism could help understand or resolve it.

5. Would you describe your nation's policies and practices in dealing with conflicts as more militaristic, just-war approach, or pacifist? Use examples to explain your answer. Which approach would you want your nation to emphasize? Explain why.

6. Research one of the following advocates of pacifism. Write a report describing their position on violence and conflict resolution:

   • Leo Tolstoy
   • Mohandas Gandhi
   • Martin Luther King, Jr.
   • Dorothy Day
   • A. J. Muste
   • Thomas Merton
   • Molly Rush
   • A. A. Milne
   • Gordon Zahn

7. If you were part of a commission set up to establish a "national peace academy" similar to the military academies, what would you include in the program of study? Design a series of courses that students in a peace academy should take.

8. Through research name three instances when a nonviolent technique has been employed during a conflict. Analyze whether or not the technique helped resolve the conflict. If so, how?

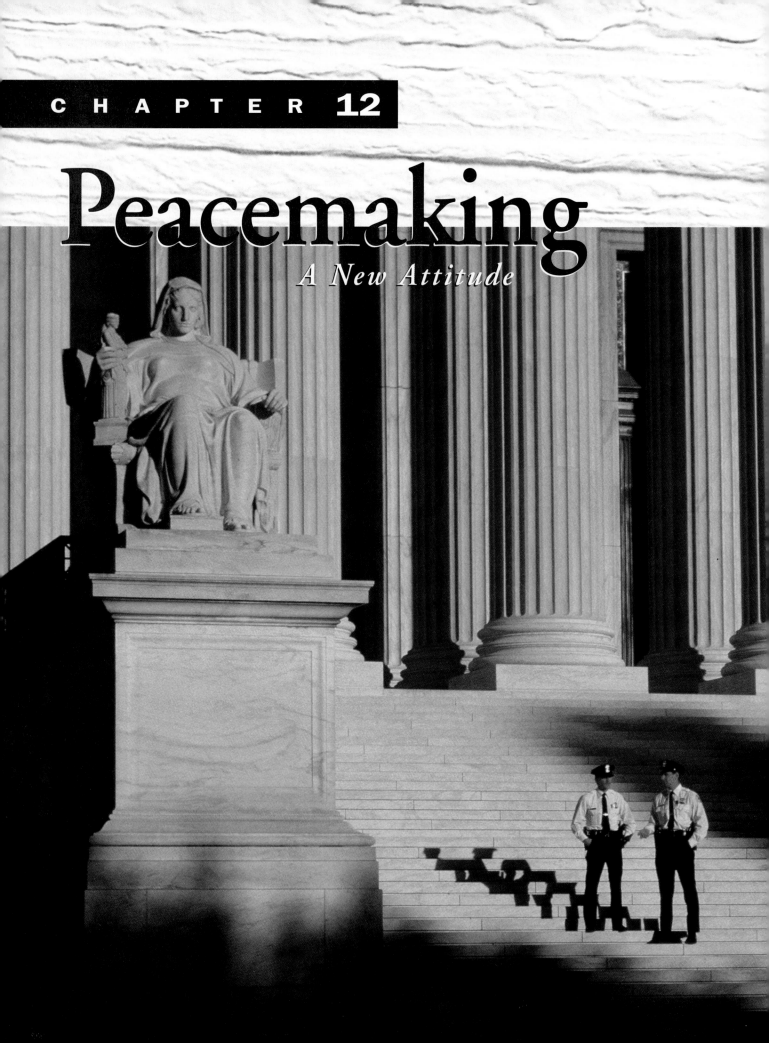

CHAPTER 12

Peacemaking

A New Attitude

...verwhelmingly, at least on a personal level, people ...re good to one another. However, violence continues ... be too much with us in our world. The biblical ...ision holds out hope that God shall be judge and ...rbitrator between people and nations. "They shall ...at their swords into plow shares, and their spears ...to pruning hooks; nation shall not lift up sword ...gainst nation, neither shall they learn war any ...ore." (Micah 4:3). Christians are called upon to ...ork with God in bringing this vision into existence, ...stering peace in a world festering with violence.

Major Concepts

A. A New Attitude Toward War

- Jesus' view of the enemy

B. Becoming a Person of Peace: A New Attitude toward Ourselves

- Meditation
- Action

C. Creating Interpersonal Peace: A New Attitude toward Others

- Assertiveness
- Respect
- Mutuality

D. A New Look at Violence in Society

- Breakdown in community
- Institutional violence

E. Nurturing Global Peace

- Nuclear weapons
- Land mines
- Healthy patriotism

Opening Prayer

God of peace and love, we seek your peace within us and among us, for our communities and for our world. When we praise you in song we say, "Let peace begin with me, let this be the moment now." May these words lead us to work for peace in our world. We pray this in the name of your Son who renounced violence and lived peace. Amen.

Before we begin . . .

Answer **agree**, **disagree**, or **uncertain** to the following statements. Choose statements that you believe to be most significant and explain your answers.

1. Teenagers, more than any other age group, engage in violent activities.

2. The United States is an exceptionally violent country.

3. When someone goes on a killing spree, I view it solely as that individual's problem.

4. If I had children, I would restrict the hours they watch violence on television.

5. The U.S. should take the lead in contributing to the United Nations' efforts in supplying military training, advisors, and weapons to insure peace throughout the world.

6. I want my country to be militarily the best equipped nation in the world.

7. Nuclear weapons are the greatest threat to the survival of our world.

8. I consider myself a peaceful person.

Viewing a War Movie Backward

In Kurt Vonnegut's science-fiction novel Slaughterhouse Five, *the main character has the ability to travel backwards and forwards in time. All of us would probably welcome the ability to reverse some things we have done or said. If nothing else, looking at events backwards gives a special view of them. Here is how Vonnegut describes a movie about World War II viewed backwards.*

Billy looked at the clock on the gas stove. He had an hour to kill before the saucer came. He went into the living room. . . . turned on the television. He came slightly unstuck in time, saw the late movie backwards, then forwards again. It was a movie about American bombers in the Second World War and the brave men who flew them. Seen backwards by Billy, the story went like this:

American planes, full of holes and wounded men and corpses, took off backwards from an airfield in England. Over France, a few German fighter planes flew at them backwards, sucked bullets and shell fragments from some of the planes and crewmen. They did the same for wrecked American bombers on the ground, and those planes flew up backwards to join the formation.

The formation flew over a German city that was in flames. The bombers opened their bomb bay doors, exerted a miraculous magnetism which shrunk the fires, gathered them into cylindrical steel containers, and lifted the containers into the bellies of the planes. The containers were stored neatly in racks. The Germans below had miraculous devices of their own, which were long steel tubes. They used them to suck more fragments from the crewmen and planes. But there were still a few wounded Americans. . . . and some of the bombers were in bad repair. Over France, though, German fighters came up again, made everything and everybody as good as new.

When the bombers got back to their base, the steel cylinders were taken from the racks and shipped back to the United States of America, where factories were operating night and day, dismantling the cylinders, separating the dangerous contents into minerals. Touchingly, it was mainly women who did this work. The minerals were then shipped to specialists in remote areas. It was their business to put them into the ground, to hide them cleverly, so they would never hurt anybody ever again.

—Kurt Vonnegut, *Slaughterhouse Five*, New York: Dell Publishing, pages 73–75.

A New Attitude Toward War

In this unusual look at war, Kurt Vonnegut makes fun of what we humans spend our time and energy on. The movie's story line is one of violence and destruction. Backwards, however, it shows tireless compassion and peacemaking. Such a fresh look at warfare reminds us that human resources are too precious and limited to waste them on destruction. Today we need every ounce of energy we can gather to counter violence and encourage peace.

Especially since the terrible devastation of World War II, Church leaders have grappled with the question of war. Reflecting on the extent of violence that has marked our modern age and also the destructive power of modern weapons, the bishops of Vatican Council II make the following timely observation:

> All these considerations compel us to undertake an evaluation of war with an entirely new attitude. The (people) of our time must realize that they will have to give a somber reckoning for their deeds of war. For the course of the future will depend largely on the decisions they make today.

—"The Church in the Modern World," number 80, *The Documents of Vatican II*.

In many respects the "new attitude" that the bishops call for resembles the topsy-turvy view of war described by Kurt Vonnegut. But in fact, this "new attitude" is as old as the Christian Good News itself. Jesus proposes that we look at violence and enemies with a new attitude:

> You have heard that it was said, "An eye for an eye and a tooth for a tooth." But I say to you, do not resist an evildoer. But if anyone strikes you on the right cheek, turn the other also; and if anyone wants to sue you and take your coat, give your cloak as well. . . . You have heard that it was said, "You shall love your neighbor and hate your enemy." But I say to you, love your enemies and pray for those who persecute you, so that you may be children of your Father in heaven. ◆
> —Matthew 5:38–40, 43–45.

◆ What are the opposites of the violence and war shown in Kurt Vonnegut's movie? Sometimes stories such as *Slaughterhouse Five* can give us a perspective on violence that we can otherwise miss. Think about books you read as a child or about movies you have seen. Name two stories or films that helped you perceive in a new way hostility between people and characteristics associated with violence. Explain why they did so.

Becoming a Person of Peace: A New Attitude toward Ourselves

In our world teens kill teens with baseball bats, and nations outbid one another to possess the most powerful weapons. On television and in movies, bloodshed is so commonplace that it frequently plays a major role in any serious plot. Women carrying their purses in public must be cautious lest they appear to be easy prey to would-be attackers. Entering the twenty-first century, human beings make more and more sophisticated communications systems; but the news from around the world is of genocide and ethnic groups killing each other with careless disregard for life.

In light of all this violence, it is necessary to focus on the words "Thy kingdom come on earth." To make a beginning at making this happen, it is necessary to strive for a personal spirituality that seeks for inner peace.

Meditation

In the busyness of every day living, it is necessary to stop and take time to think about yourself, your God, and what is going on around you. How does it all connect? How do you make sense of what happens? Without peace within ourselves we cannot live in peace with others. Meditative prayer is one source of finding this peace. The *Catechism of the Catholic Church* explains meditation in this way: "The mind seeks to understand the why and how of the Christian life, in order to adhere and respond to what the Lord is asking" (2705). ◆

Meditation leads automatically to the next step of Christian living—response or action. No one can save the world by himself or herself. Yet, each person is called upon to do something to develop compassionate communities among those who are hurting. Using our gifts and talents and the situations we find ourselves in, we are called to further the reign of God. As we broaden our views and deepen our consciousness of what is happening around us, we seek to develop attitudes, actions, and structures that build peace within ourselves, peace which overflows to others.

◆ Take the time to go by yourself to a quiet place where you can think about and journal on the following questions: Where in my life am I experiencing a lack of peace? Who or what is causing me to not be at peace? What action can I take to find peace?

Creating Interpersonal Peace

During conflicts, people have a tendency to reduce other individuals, groups, or nations to being simply "the enemy." The term carries tremendous emotional weight and short-circuits their ability to see others as human persons like themselves. Peace can never be achieved until simplistic name-calling is put aside along with the toy guns and toy soldiers of childhood. In interpersonal relationships true peace does not produce "winners" and "losers" but aims for a win-win outcome.

> "I" and "you," "us" and "them," "winning" and "losing," "victor" and "vanquished"—these are no more than the tricks of the mind exiled from the heart. The face we see before us is no other than our own, the person we see before us is ourselves in another guise. What else can we do but open our hearts, what else do we need to do?
>
> —Christina Feldman, in *Peace Prayers,* HarperSanFrancisco, 1992, page 34.

In the face of a culture that divides people into friends and enemies, good guys and bad guys, what are wholesome ways of relating to others with whom we don't get along or who rub us the wrong way? Are we left solely with giving in to their wishes? Also, since most violence occurs within families and among friends, are there skills we can work on to prevent disagreements from becoming violent?

The last chapter defined the difference between pacifism and passivity. In that discussion we examined how peacemaking actually involves putting into practice certain positive attitudes and behaviors rather than sitting back and letting things happen. Three skills that can help us in our personal relationships are *assertiveness, respect,* and *mutuality.*

A New Attitude Toward Others: Assertiveness

At first, being assertive can sound like a behavior leading to violence rather than preventing it. That's because **assertiveness** is often contrasted with passivity. However, assertiveness can also be contrasted with **aggression**. Put simply, passivity means allowing other people to invade your space while feeling no control over the situation. A passive person gives in to the wishes of others rather than acting on her or his own point of view. Aggression means violating the space of others. It disregards the needs, wants, limitations, misgivings, and outlooks of others. Assertiveness, on the other hand, is neither passivity nor aggression. Assertiveness means making known one's wants, accepting and acting upon one's feelings, and being sensitive to one's own concerns and viewpoints without intentionally hurting anyone else.

Assertiveness has been studied for a few decades now. When programs to address concerns of women began twenty-five years ago or so, studies identified many women in particular as lacking in assertiveness. But, in fact, both men and women can be more or less passive, aggressive, or assertive. One finding of studies in this area is that *both passivity and aggressiveness are more likely to lead to violence in relationships than assertiveness is.* A leading expert on communication describes assertiveness this way:

> An assertive person steers a middle course between not doing anything and doing too much. An assertive person gets the work of interpersonal communication done but does so in a way that respects both his or her own rights and the rights of others. An assertive person is one who acts, who puts himself or herself on the line, but does so in a responsible way.
>
> —Gerard Egan, *You and Me,* Pacific Grove, CA: Brooks/Cole Publishing Company, 1977, page 39.

assertiveness

to express or act out in a positive and affirming way one's wants, feelings, concerns, or viewpoints

aggression

actions which disregard the needs, wants, limitations, misgivings, and outlooks of others

Based on this description of assertiveness, one can be overly passive or overly aggressive. One can never be overly assertive. If the student sitting behind you is mindlessly tapping his foot on the back of your desk and you find this annoying, what do you do? A passive response would be to say nothing but instead to stew in anger and irritation. An aggressive response might be to turn around and throw his books across the room. An assertive response would be to let the person know that his tapping is annoying you and ask him to stop it. If he doesn't, then assertiveness would call for re-evaluation of the situation and actions aimed not at causing harm but at resolving the conflict in ways that respect both your rights and his.

A New Attitude Toward Others: Respect

In 1995 Pope John Paul II bestowed the title of *blessed* onto a man who lived most of his life on a remote Hawaiian island. In the latter half of the 1800s, Father Damien was a Belgian missionary to Hawaii. At the time many native Hawaiians were stricken with diseases introduced by the visiting Europeans—the worst of which was leprosy. The Hawaiian government decided that anyone with leprosy had to move to the remote island of Molokai. There they lived without benefit of proper medical treatment, food, or shelter. At times ships carrying newly stricken persons would not even dock, forcing those who were ill to battle the waves and

Assertiveness Scale

Rate yourself on the following assertive behaviors using a scale of 1 (never true) to 10 (always true):

	1	2	3	4	5	6	7	8	9	10
1. I talk and think positively about myself.										
2. I am comfortable receiving compliments.										
3. I compliment others freely and honestly.										
4. I say what I mean directly and spontaneously.										
5. I ask directly for what I want.										
6. I say no when I mean no.										
7. I accept no from others.										
8. I insist on fair treatment for myself and others.										
9. I take first steps in making friends.										
10. I keep in contact with others if I want to.										

Looking over this list, answer the following questions:

• In general, am I an assertive person? Why or why not? What behaviors might I work on to become an assertive person?

• Are there other behaviors that would help identify whether or not someone is assertive? What are they?

• Do you believe that assertive behaviors such as those listed here can help diminish violence in relationships? Why or why not?

surf just to get to land. Fr. Damien accepted an assignment to serve this peculiar parish of diseased and dying persons. While he realized that no cure for leprosy existed at the time, he also knew that the lepers suffered greatly and unnecessarily from lack of self-respect. During his sermons he addressed the assembly as "we lepers." Instead of the common practice of tossing the dead into shallow graves, he saw to it that burials were carried out with dignity. Within years Damien transformed the island into a community where people treated one another with respect. By the end of his life, including himself among the lepers in word became an inclusion in fact. Damien himself became sick with the disease, suffering both the physical pain and the rejection associated with it.

Another holy man of the late nineteenth century was Charles de Foucauld. Born into an aristocratic European family, he chose to live a simple life amid Bedouin tribes of Arabia. He founded a congregation of men and women dedicated to living among people usually shown little respect. He described his life choice in these words:

> Jesus came to Nazareth, the place of the hidden life, of ordinary life, of family life, of prayer, work, obscurity, silent virtues, practiced with no witnesses other than God, his friends and neighbors. Nazareth, the place where most people lead their lives. We must infinitely respect the least of our brothers . . . let us mingle with them. Let us be one of them to the extent that God wishes . . . and treat them fraternally in order to have the honor and joy of being accepted as one of them.

—In Robert Ellsberg, *All Saints,* New York: Crossroad, 1997, page 525.

respect

appreciating and valuing persons as they are

Both of these saintly men allowed **respect** to direct their lives. Literally, the word means "to look at a second time." Damien took the time to look at the people with leprosy on Molokai, gazing long and lovingly enough to see their dignity. By spending time with people who owned nothing but what they could carry through the deserts, Charles de Foucauld came to see God in them. As the word suggests, *respect* is a way of looking at people, appreciating them and valuing them as they are. However, like assertiveness, respect is shown through our actions. In 1994 when the U.S. Catholic bishops addressed violence, they called for "a commitment to civility and respect in public life and communications—in the news media, politics, and even ecclesial dialogue" (*Confronting a Culture of Violence,* page 14). They note that: "Violence is overcome day by day, choice by choice, person by person" (page 15). Father Damien and Charles de Foucauld demonstrate how a simple attitude of respect can change a culture of violence. ◆

◆ Charles de Foucauld called the everyday places where we live our lives "Nazareth"—like the little town where Jesus spent most of his life. Think for a moment about your Nazareth. Then, in a poem, a story, a group symbolic gesture, or a drawing, illustrate how respect can influence a culture of violence in a positive way.

A New Attitude Toward Others: Mutuality

A key technique for actually demonstrating respect is a third skill that cultivates peaceful relationships—mutuality. You may recall the use of this word in chapter 6 where Pope John Paul II used the term to describe the ideal marriage relationship. Mutuality means helping others realize their potential while not denigrating your own. In a sense mutuality is "respectful assertiveness." Mutual relationships are affirming relationships. They start with listening, along with caring and acceptance, even when disagreements run deep. Mutuality then takes another step—actively supporting and encouraging others. Sometimes mutuality includes confrontation, which can be mistaken for "attack" but in fact is quite different. Confrontation is a challenge but not a personal attack. It involves inviting people to examine their words or actions and the consequences of those words or actions.

For instance, a boy might tell a girl how much he cares for her and that she's the only one for him. Then, among his friends, he keeps his distance from her and doesn't communicate publicly that they are going out. An empowering confrontation on the girl's part would be to point out to him that his words say one thing but that his actions say another. Chances are, such a confrontation shows true feeling, as well as care both for oneself and for the other person. Even if a breakup results, it is an invitation to mutuality and intimacy—honest sharing—rather than violence. ◆

Two Tales of Violence

- At school Luke is often the butt of jokes. Perhaps it's his weight, his attempts to be funny—which always seem to fall flat—or just that he tries too hard to fit in. For whatever reason many of his fellow students feel as though Luke is fair game for teasing and mocking. No one thinks that they are treating Luke violently.

- Muriel's mother has a way of talking to her that always leaves her angry and baffled. When Muriel brought home a report card with mostly Bs, her mother said, "Those are very good grades—for you." When she brought home some classmates, her mother announced to all of them, "I'm so glad to see that Muriel has some friends." Muriel has recently started hanging out with a group that doesn't take school or anything else very seriously—the only group she feels comfortable in. Muriel doesn't know anything about abuse, but she does know what her mother has taught her—she shouldn't expect much of herself or of life.

◆ Think about concrete examples of the following violent situations. Describe whether or not, and if so how, assertiveness, respect, and mutuality might help to lessen the chance of violence and promote peace in each situation:

1. abusive boy-girl relationships or dating circumstances
2. violence between gangs or groups of teenagers
3. young children who are not getting along
4. confrontations between police officers and citizens
5. vandalism
6. automobile-related violence
7. sports-related violence
8. family violence

Psychological Violence: Violence Can Be More Than Physical

At first glance the stories of Luke and Muriel do not seem to be about violence. In neither case is someone physically striking or abusing another person. However, isn't it true that both Luke and Muriel are victims of violence of another sort?

Psychological violence refers to harming a person in ways other than through physical force. In chapter 7 on gender, we already looked at domestic violence, or violence that occurs within a family. It is a commonly occurring expression of psychological violence. Sometimes psychological violence within families builds to physical violence. Even if it doesn't, domestic violence leaves people damaged. For example, in the above scenario Muriel suffered because of emotional rather than physical abuse from her mother. Frequently, patterns of psychological violence at home carry over into violence at school or in other settings. As the story of Luke illustrates, the weapons of words, looks, and gestures can cut down a person as violently as guns can.

psychological violence

harming someone through non-physical means

Review

1. Explain the difference between *passivity*, *aggression*, and *assertiveness*.
2. Name the Belgian priest who worked with lepers on Molokai.
3. Who left his aristocratic roots in Europe to live a simple life in Arabia?
4. What is the literal meaning of *respect*?
5. What did Charles de Foucauld mean by "Nazareth"?
6. Why is confrontation different from an attack?
7. Define *psychological violence*.
8. In what setting does *psychological violence* frequently occur?
9. What do studies about violence in the U.S. consistently conclude?

Discuss

A. Do you believe that passivity and aggression are always wrong but that assertiveness is always acceptable? Give examples to support your position.

B. Read the following statement carefully. Would you like to see such a petition passed around your school? Would you sign such a petition? Why or why not? Explain.

I pledge to seek peace and to resolve problems peacefully. Toward this end, to the best of my ability I will:

- Reject violence, physical and psychological.
- Avoid rash judgments and listen to what others have to say.
- Tell others my wants and viewpoints without demeaning them or their views.
- Seek resolutions to conflicts, not victories over enemies.
- Remain open to new ideas and possible solutions.
- Rely on the power of reason, not that of physical intimidation.
- Focus on current problems, not on the past.
- Be honest about myself and my feelings.
- Search for good in others.

The News from Main Street, USA

Here is a portion of a news report from a major metropolitan newspaper. Has a similar article ever appeared in your local newspaper? Could such an article appear in your newspaper?

When John Montgomery heard yesterday that the youths on the footbridge planned to retaliate for the beating of Levittown teen Mike Powell, he sprinted to a police car in the Wawa parking lot in Levittown, his down coat slapping against his knees. "I heard they've got guns, so I wanted the police to know," the 15-year-old said as he flopped into a booth at Anthony's Pizza. "People have been calling Levittown the mini-Brooklyn."

On the footbridge, where drops of blood from Powell's beating Saturday night had dried on the broken concrete, teenagers from this middle-class neighborhood said, yes, they wanted to fight. "We're talking about fists, and they're talking about drive-bys," said Ed Boyce, 17, one of two dozen teens who kept returning to the bridge after being chased away by police periodically throughout the day.

Bristol Township police are focusing on several suspects, Sgt. Charles McGuigan said. Squad cars descended on strip malls and township parks yesterday, questioning dozens of teens in a search for those who beat Powell, 16, nearly senseless late Saturday with a baseball bat, rocks, fists and feet. . . .

With a fractured skull and 12 stitches in his scalp, Powell, a junior at Harry S. Truman High School, was in stable condition yesterday at Lower Bucks Hospital. His condition has left him nauseated and unable to eat solid food, said his girlfriend, Stephanie

Mahon, 15. "He gets frustrated that he can't talk straight," Mahon said as she smoked a cigarette at the swing set near the footbridge that connects two Levittown neighborhoods. "He's going to be okay.". . .

The fight that smashed Powell's skull is the latest in a series of clashes between rival teen groups in Levittown since June, police said. That's when Richard Goodbred, 17, threw a punch at 19-year-old Robert Claudio in front of a convenience store, police said. Claudio, who police say slashed Goodbred's arm to the bone with a six-inch knife, is awaiting trial on charges of aggravated assault.

In another fight, a 19-year-old's arm was split open with a tire iron and another teen was left with several stitches in his head from a whack with a baseball bat. Teens say the culture of violence has roots in an incident two years ago, when four teens beat 15-year-old Larry Morris. The youth emerged from a 12-day coma with permanent brain damage; the four were convicted. . . .(Crossing guard Cheryl Birtell stood) peering down the sidewalk at elementary school students lingering over Powell's blood on the pavement. "They really wanted to look at it," she said. "I was shocked when I read it in the paper. I didn't really think it would happen here."

—Reprinted with permission from the *Philadelphia Inquirer*, October 22, 1997, pages B1, B6.

A New Look at Violence in Society

The National Center for Health Statistics reported that in 1993 more preschoolers were killed by guns than were police officers and United States soldiers shot in the line of duty.

> —Raymond B. Flannery, Jr., *Violence in America*, New York: Continuum, 1997, page 27.

Confronting a Culture of Violence

We don't need to recount here other incidents of violence that have recently stained our national character. Nightly news reports and newspaper headlines regularly remind us of our culture of violence. Studies about violence in the United States consistently arrive at two conclusions: the U.S. is particularly violent, and violence increases when there is a breakdown in community.

Here is one psychologist's assessment:

> *The United States is a violent country. Episodes of violent crime . . . are not exceptions to the rule. Indeed, comparative statistics among nations . . . indicate that the United States out-ranks most other nations of the industrial world in violent crimes like assault, rape, and robbery. In the category of murder, we are far and away the most violent industrialized nation on earth.*

> —*Violence in America*, page 18.

Addressing the causes of violent behavior in society, the psychologist admits that many factors contribute to it. Some studies even suggest a genetic tendency toward aggressive behavior in some people. However, if such a gene exists, it is a human gene, not an American one. Therefore, it does not account for the higher level of violence in the U.S. In the documentation of violence over the past fifty years, Flannery observes a **breakdown in community** as a consistent pattern:

> *The network of stable family life, consistent schooling, and supportive services from other adults in the community was not a part of the lives of these offenders, and it is reasonable to assume that this absence of community may have contributed, at least in part, to their violent lifestyle.* ◆

> —*Violence in America*, page 22.

breakdown in community

lack of a stable family life, regular schooling, and support services from other adults

---

◆ List social factors that you believe contribute to a culture of violence, as many as you can. Then number these factors in terms of importance. Compare your list with those of other students, seeking to arrive at agreement on factors influencing violence in society. Search the Internet for organizations that offer solutions or are attempting to change these social factors.

The U.S. Catholic bishops express great regret over teen violence, over any violence. In their examination of the culture of violence, they too detect a link with the breakdown of community:

> *Our social fabric is being torn apart by a culture of violence that leaves children dead on our streets and families afraid in their homes. Our society seems to be growing numb to human loss and suffering. A nation born in a commitment to "life, liberty, and the pursuit of happiness" is haunted by death, imprisoned by fear, and caught up in the elusive pursuit of protection rather than happiness.*

> —U.S. Catholic Bishops, *Confronting a Culture of Violence*, page 2.

What would Kurt Vonnegut's "war movie played backwards" look like if applied to violence seen in society? If breakdown in community contributes to violence, then it stands to reason that building up community serves as an antidote to violence. In the illustration, look at psychologist Raymond Flannery's list of the risk factors that lead to violence. If these factors ignite violence, then eliminating or changing them in healthy ways kindles peace. ◆

> *Brandon Centerwall, an epidemiologist at the University of Washington, studied the relationship between TV violence and the growth of violence in various communities. His conclusion: TV violence is a public health problem deserving measures as practical as nutrition, immunization and bicycle helmet programs. He cites such studies as one from a remote Canadian community that in 1973 was due to acquire television. Social scientists seized the opportunity to investigate the effects of television on this community's children, using for comparison two similar towns that had long had television. Before television arrived, they monitored rates of inappropriate physical aggression among 45 first- and second-graders. After two years of television, the rate increased 160%, in both boys and girls, and in those who were aggressive to begin with and those who were not. The rate in the two communities that had television for years did not change.*

> —John W. Glaser, *Three Realms of Ethics*, Kansas City, MO: Sheed & Ward, page 138.

Factors that lead to violence

- poverty
- domestic violence
- discrimination
- inadequate schooling
- substance abuse
- easily available weapons
- the media

◆ On a scale of 1 (not at all) to 10 (very much), how connected is the teen violence described above to the type of childhood experience described in the following scenario? Explain your rating.

Mr. Dickerson has his ten-year-old son, Jeremy, and two of Jeremy's friends staying over Friday night. Wondering what to do with the three boys, Mr. Dickerson looks at the entertainment section of the newspaper. "Oh, good. A new movie is out. It's rated R, but it's science fiction. It has aliens. How bad can it be?" The review in the paper reads, "Graphic violence. Not suitable for children under seventeen." Mr. Dickerson thinks about this for a moment then says, "Well, at least it doesn't mention graphic sex scenes." He calls Jeremy and his friends together and announces, "Okay, boys, get your coats. We're going to the movies."

What Can One Person Do?

In 1988, a young man named Thomas Feeney died in a random act of violence. His family, naturally distraught, tried to make sense of his death: How could such a senseless act happen? A few years later, Feeney's niece, Meaghan, read about a movement encouraging people to do "random acts of kindness." She thought, since my uncle was killed in a random act of violence, maybe an appropriate response is to do random acts of kindness. She began a "random acts of kindness" club at her school, Cardinal Dougherty High School in Philadelphia. She even petitioned her local state representative to name the anniversary of her uncle's death as "A Random Act of Kindness Day."

Here is the result of her petition—House Resolution No. 392 of The General Assembly of Pennsylvania:

A Resolution

Designating November 1, 1994, as "A Random Act of Kindness Day."

WHEREAS, On November 1, 1988, Thomas Feeney was murdered; and

WHEREAS, All Pennsylvanians, regardless of gender, race, age or economic status, may be victims of violent crimes during their lives; and

WHEREAS, The number of murders, especially in urban areas, is increasing each year; and

WHEREAS, Crime statistics do not convey the personal tragedy and the suffering of the victim and his or her family; and

WHEREAS, It is important for all citizens of this commonwealth to remember the victims of crime and to express this remembrance through acts of random kindness; therefore be it

RESOLVED, That the House of Representatives designate November 1, 1994, as "A Random Act of Kindness Day" as a day of remembrance of Thomas Feeney and all the victims of crime in our society.

On the day he died, Thomas Feeney carried a laminated card in his back pocket that read:

ON THIS DAY

Mend a quarrel. Search out a forgotten friend. Dismiss suspicion, and replace it with trust. Write a love letter. Share some treasure. Give a soft answer. Encourage youth. Manifest your loyalty in a word or deed.

Keep a promise. Find the time. Forego a grudge. Forgive an enemy. Listen. Apologize if you were wrong. Try to understand. Flout envy. Examine your demands on others. Think first of someone else. Appreciate, be kind, be gentle. Laugh a little more.

Deserve confidence. Take up arms against malice. Decry complacency. Express your gratitude. Worship your God. Gladden the heart of a child. Take pleasure in the beauty and wonder of the earth. Speak your love. Speak it again. Speak it still again. Speak it still once again.

• What message would you want to be found in your back pocket if you were to die?

Institutional Violence

If you want peace, work for justice.

—Pope Paul VI

- Sabrina cleans houses for a living. Actually, she cleans houses when she can. Due to the uncertain nature of her work, Sabrina is not always sure she can support herself and her two children. During a recent public transportation strike, she was unable to get to two houses she was scheduled to clean. As a result the homeowners hired another person for the job, someone who owned a car. Sabrina was left with a drastic reduction in her weekly income. She receives some food and clothing for the children from a neighborhood church. She tries to remain optimistic while she searches for other employment, but it is hard for her to not feel trapped within the violence of poverty.

- Darnell, who lives with his grandmother and three other children, has skipped school for a number of days. The counselor at his school has spoken to him about the importance of his attending school, but she fears going to Darnell's home because of the violence that occurs on his block. She has spoken to the school reading specialist about Darnell. The reading specialist informed her that space is not available for all the children who need personalized assistance with reading. Since no one has pushed for Darnell to receive this help, he has not received it.

Isn't it accurate to say that both Sabrina and Darnell are experiencing violence? This type of violence should not be overlooked simply because its portrayal would not be the subject of a blockbuster action-adventure movie. If someone locked Sabrina in her home so that she could not get to work, we would immediately identify that as violence. If reading textbooks were handed out to students, and Darnell's was snatched from his hands, we would call that violence. However, Sabrina and Darnell are suffering a similar fate because of less direct, less obvious expressions of violence. We could mistakenly say that such violence exists because of a combination of bad luck, bad genes, and bad decisions on the part of certain individuals. But truthfully, individuals alone don't seem to be at fault here. In fact, the perpetrator of the violence seems to be society itself.

Pontius' Puddle

In cases such as this, the major thesis of this course comes full circle: justice, created by a compassionate community, brings peace. That is, only a just community is truly a peaceful one. Therefore, a principal way to confront violence in society is to work for justice. Violence resulting from injustice within a society is **institutional violence**. Institutional violence refers to the harm done to people through the structures of a society. This includes the way that public utilities and businesses operate, the way that schools and hospitals are funded, the types of programs made available for different age groups, the methods in place for helping families, and the way that law enforcement and the criminal justice system works. Insofar as institutions are unjust, they are violent. Injustices that make up the very fabric of society are institutionalized violence. On the other hand healthy and just institutions foster peace.

institutional violence

violence that results from injustices within a society

> *My experience has been that the poor know violence more intimately than most people because it has been a part of their lives, whether the violence of the gun or the violence of want and need.*
>
> —Cesar Chavez, *in Peace Prayers*, HarperSanFrancisco: 1992, page 83.

Review

10. Name the risk factors that Raymond Flannery identifies as contributing to a *culture of violence.*

11. Define *institutional violence.*

Discuss

C. Think about characteristics of contemporary society, especially about the various institutions that make up society. Make four lists naming strengths, weaknesses, opportunities, and threats that you perceive in society as it functions today. Based on your lists identify key changes that could lessen societal or institutional violence. Compare lists within your class.

Nurturing Global Peace

Military Power: Part of the Solution or Part of the Problem?

> *Every gun that is made, every warship launched, every rocket fired signifies, in the final sense, a theft from those who hunger and are not fed, those who are cold and are not clothed.*
>
> *This world in arms is not spending money alone. It is spending the sweat of its laborers, the genius of its scientists, the hopes of its children.*
>
> —President Dwight D. Eisenhower, in *Peace Prayers*, HarperSanFrancisco, 1992, page 23.

The above quote was spoken in the 1950s by a president, himself a former army general. It voices a concern that remains with us today. Nations have limited funds. They can build either tanks or tractors, warships or low-cost housing. The pie that symbolizes a nation's budget can be sliced only so many ways. For a majority of countries, including the U.S., military spending accounts for a large piece of the pie. President Eisenhower knew that money spent on expensive weapons systems meant that less money was available for education, health care, and other social programs. The U.S. Catholic bishops thus call the amount of money spent on weapons a "distortion of priorities."

But doesn't the armaments industry create jobs? In the first place, military spending actually creates fewer jobs than almost any other form of government expense. Secondly, most jobs created by military spending are positions for highly skilled labor. Consequently, the defense industry employs few of those people most in need of work—the unskilled and the poorly educated people who make up the ranks of the unemployed.

If justice leads to peace, then an unequal amount of time, energy, technology, research, and money given over to military matters takes away from applying these same resources to creating justice. In other words the following question demands an answer: Which is more likely to bring on peace—preparedness for war or working for justice? Unfortunately, given limited resources, "both" is not a workable answer.

Weapons of Mass Destruction: Are They Effective for Today's Wars?

ethnic conflicts

two or more groups fighting for control of the same region

A common scene in cartoons shows a character trying to kill a pesky fly with a hammer or a shotgun. The end result is a large hole in a wall or a painfully throbbing bump on a friend's head—and a fly that keeps on buzzing. The joke is straightforward: if we try to use high-tech weapons in a situation that calls for a more low-tech response, then we will end up making matters worse.

For over forty years the focus of the U.S. military was on winning or preventing an all-out nuclear war with the other super-power of the time, the Soviet Union. Since the beginning of the 1990s, there has been no Soviet Union. Unfortunately, that has not meant an end to wars. Wars continue, fired by ethnic conflicts—two or more groups from the same country fighting over control of the same area. An **ethnic conflict** can also erupt when a group within a country feels discriminated against and seeks justice. In these types of conflicts, heavy weapons are not particularly effective.

If used they are likely to make matters worse for all sides in the conflict rather than resolve the conflict itself.

Eleven-year-old Zlata Filipovic kept a diary when her Eastern European home town of Sarajevo became enveloped in ethnic conflict. Her description of the war reveals how devastating such conflict can be to people who for the most part feel trapped in other people's hatreds. The solution to wars of this nature does not lie with defeating armies, destroying roads and bridges, or targeting certain areas for complete destruction. In Zlata's case, the war was going on down the street, sometimes fought between a former baker and one of his customers. Solutions to such wars seem to demand intervention on a human scale, not high-tech weapons.

Sunday, May 17, 1992

Dear Mimmy,

It's now definite: there's no more school. The war has interrupted our lessons, closed down the schools, sent children to cellars instead of classrooms. . . .

Saturday, May 23, 1992

I'm not writing to you about me anymore. I'm writing to you about war, death, injuries, shells, sadness and sorrow. Almost all my friends have left. Even if they were here, who knows whether we'd be able to see one another.

Saturday, July 17, 1993

Suddenly, unexpectedly, someone is using the ugly powers of war, which horrify me, to try to pull and drag me away from the shores of peace, from the happiness of wonderful friendships, playing and love. I feel like a swimmer who was made to enter the cold water, against her will. I feel shocked, sad, unhappy and frightened and I wonder where they are forcing me to go, I wonder why they have taken away my peaceful and lovely shores of my childhood. I used to rejoice at each new day, because each was beautiful in its own way. I used to rejoice at the sun, at playing at songs. In short, I enjoyed my childhood. I had no need of a better one. I have less and less strength to keep swimming in these cold waters. So take me back to the shores of my childhood, where I was warm, happy and content, like all the children whose childhood and the right to enjoy it are now being destroyed.

The only thing I want to say to everyone is: PEACE! ◆

—from *Zlata's Diary* by Zlata Filipovic, translation copyright, 1994 editions, Robert Laffont/Fixot. Used by permission of Viking Penquin, a division of Penguin Putman Inc., pages 45–48, 155–56.

◆ Create a political cartoon or poster about some aspect of modern warfare.

Nuclear Weapons: Are They Still a Threat?

Since 1990 U.S. and Russian strategic forces have been cut by close to half, and U.S. nuclear spending has shrunk by 75 percent. And the Kremlin has docked most of its missile subs and locked up its mobile ICBMs in garages and railroad yards. Yet the risk hasn't gone away. The U.S. nuclear force . . . still has roughly 7,000 nuclear weapons programmed against targets in the former Soviet Union, more than ten times the number it needs to destroy its former enemy. And Russia has as many that can reach the United States.

—John Barry and Evan Thomas, "Paging Dr. Strangelove," *Newsweek*, June 30, 1997, page 56.

In the decades from the 1950s to the 1980s, many Americans feared that they would die in a nuclear holocaust. Since then that fear has greatly diminished. While people's *fear* of nuclear destruction has lessened, as the above quote points out, the *risk* of nuclear destruction remains. The U.S. Catholic bishops addressed the question of nuclear weapons most directly in their 1983 pastoral letter, *The Challenge of Peace*. There they state that use of nuclear weapons is wrong and can never be justified. They apply traditional just-war principles to the unique nature of nuclear weapons to arrive at this conclusion: "In simple terms, we are saying that good ends (defending one's country, protecting freedom, etc.) cannot justify immoral means (the use of weapons which kill indiscriminately and threaten whole societies)" (number 332).

While the bishops condemn the use of nuclear weapons, they do not outright condemn *possession* of nuclear weapons. At the time, possessing nuclear weapons was considered to serve the purpose of **deterrence**. In other words if a country has nuclear weapons available for use, then other countries would risk their own destruction if they used nuclear weapons against it. The bishops accepted this reasoning, but only hesitantly. For one, they agreed with what President Eisenhower had said: money spent on nuclear weapons is taking money from much needed social programs. Secondly, they note that: "The political paradox of deterrence has also strained our moral conception. May a nation threaten what it may never do? May it possess what it may never use?" (number 137) Thirdly, nuclear deterrence is justified so long as there is progress toward nuclear disarmament (number 188).

deterrence

to discourage an action through fear

28

Since the breakup of the former Soviet Union, the reasoning for keeping nuclear weapons has become even more clouded. For instance, what justification exists for targeting sites in a country that is no longer considered either a threat or "the enemy"? In effect the U.S. is spending money to maintain the capacity to destroy a nation to whom it now sends aid. One general formerly in charge of the U.S. Strategic Command finds that nuclear weapons become an addiction. Once we have them it's hard to give them up—even when their reason for being is unclear. Like cigarettes and alcohol, this addiction is very expensive. Nuclear weapons cannot simply be stored somewhere. They require constant maintenance and updating, the cost of which is very high.

> *The end of the Cold War still provides an opportunity to substantially reduce military spending. Diverting scarce resources from military to human development is not only a just and compassionate policy, but also a wise long-term investment in global and national security. Concern for jobs cannot justify military spending beyond the minimum necessary for legitimate national security and international peacekeeping obligations.*
>
> —Administrative Board, USCC, *Political Responsibility*, USCC Publication 5-043, 1995, page 15.

Land Mines: The Residue of Wars Past

Peter Bell is president of CARE, the world's largest international relief and development organization. In thirty-nine of the sixty-three countries where CARE works, land mines are still in place. According to Bell, the U.N. estimates that 110 million land mines are planted around the world. Each year, 26,000 people are killed or hurt by land mines. Besides this direct human suffering from mines, whole communities are effectively paralyzed by them. An organization such as CARE, which tries to help people in need, cannot work effectively where land mines exist. Staples of life—farmland, water, and trade—are cut off where mines dot the landscape.

Few soldiers actually die from land mines during wartime. Mines do their damage after the fighting stops, when children and farmers try to resume some sort of a normal lifestyle even though unforeseen danger is present. In 1996 fourteen retired generals, including Norman Schwarzkopf, who headed U.N. troops during the Persian Gulf War, wrote President Clinton to say that a ban on land mines would not lessen the effectiveness or safety of U.S. troops or those of other nations. The governing board of the U.S. Catholic bishops repeats what many recent Church documents have stated: "The United States should take a leadership role in reducing reliance on, ending export of, and ultimately banning anti-personnel land mines, which kill some 26,000 civilians each year" (*Political Responsibility*, USCC Publication 5-043, 1995, page 15). ◆

◆ Imagine that Jesus addresses the United Nations on nuclear weapons. What do you think he would say? Imagine that after his address, you interview representatives from four different countries. Identify each country and record how you think each representative would respond.

No less than 25 percent of land mine victims are children. . . .mothers in Somaliland are forced to tie their children to trees so they will not wander innocently into one of the more than one million laid haphazardly in that country during the last decade. . . .I spoke with Andrew Cooper, land mines researcher for the Human Rights Watch Arms Project in Washington, D.C. . . .A total of 4.4 million anti-personnel mines, he commented, were exported by the United States from 1969 to 1992 to countries in Asia, the Middle East and South America.

—Regina Griffin, "The Land Mine Menace," *America*, July 19–26, 1997, 117:2, page 14.

The Role of the U.S. in Global Peacekeeping and Warmaking

The virtue of patriotism means that as citizens we respect and honor our country, but our very love and loyalty make us examine carefully and regularly its role in world affairs, asking that it live up to its full potential as an agent of peace with justice for all people.

—U.S. Catholic Bishops, *The Challenge of Peace*, number 37.

The U.S. Catholic bishops are encouraging Catholics to be active in politics. They encourage Catholics to ask the country's leaders and citizens to make peace always a primary concern in policies and practices. At Vatican Council II, the world's Catholic bishops gave a fuller description of the virtue of patriotism:

Citizens must cultivate a generous and loyal spirit of patriotism, but without being narrow-minded. This means that they will always direct their attention to the good of the whole human family, united by the different ties which bind together races, people, and nations.

—*The Challenge of Peace*, number 327.

patriotism

love of country that admits its shortcomings and tries to right them

nationalism

love of country regardless of its actions, and refusing to recognize or trying to change its flaws; placing one's own country above the needs of the rest of the world; a "my country right or wrong" attitude

This description of patriotism differs greatly from nationalism. **Patriotism** means a genuine love of one's country that nevertheless admits its shortcomings and seeks to right its faults. On the other hand, **nationalism** means a spirit of one-upmanship, lording it over other countries whenever possible. According to the world's bishops, patriotism is a positive virtue; nationalism is a selfish, narrow-minded vice. Patriotism includes identifying oneself as a world citizen, not just a citizen of one's particular country. A true patriot seeks to find out how one's country can contribute positively to making the entire world a better place. On the other hand a nationalist spirit places the good of one's own country above the needs of every other country, as if one nation can exist apart from and independent of all others.

The question is not whether we will be extremists, but what kind of extremists we will be. Will we be extremists for hate or for love? Will we be extremists for the preservation of injustice or for the extension of justice?

—Martin Luther King, Jr., in *Peace Prayers*, Harper San Francisco, page 84.

12. What caution was voiced by President Eisenhower about a military buildup?
13. Describe two types of ethnic conflicts.
14. Define *deterrence* in relation to nuclear weapons.
15. Which group receives more injuries from land mines: soldiers or civilians?
16. Besides killing and maiming civilians, how do land mines disrupt communities where they exist?
17. Explain the difference between patriotism and nationalism.

Discuss

D. Evaluate the following activities from the view of nationalism and patriotism. When you have finished, describe the types of activities you would like to see the U.S. engaged in that would show "America at its best" for you.

- U.S. companies are the world's greatest suppliers of military weapons.
- A school run by the U.S. army trains military leaders from Latin American countries. Some graduates of this school have been directly responsible for repression, torture, and human rights abuses. Sometimes their victims have been U.S. citizens doing missionary work in poor countries.
- The U.S. government sends its military into a civil strife occurring in a country which is strategically important to U.S. interests. It voices concern but provides no military or economic assistance to a country experiencing civil war which is not strategically important.
- If the U.S. grants "most favored nation" status to a particular country, it would benefit some U.S. companies. However, the country is known for its human rights abuses.
- The U.S. government supplies economic aid to countries based on their benefit to the U.S. rather than based on their need.
- A group of U.S. missionaries to a Latin American country are killed by terrorists. The U.S. government does not pressure the country's leaders to investigate the murders for fear that they might involve government officials friendly to the U.S.

E. Debate the pros and cons of the position on land mines presented by the U.S. Catholic bishops.

In Summary: Where Are We Going?

On the president's chair in Independence Hall in Philadelphia is a carving of half a sun on a horizon. After the signing of the Declaration of Independence there, Benjamin Franklin reportedly remarked that "only time will tell whether the sun is setting or rising." Today, the world finds itself facing an even larger crisis. Modern weapons possess ever-increasing accuracy and destructive capabilities. Modern technologies have created a world that is more a global village than a collection of isolated nations. Some old feelings of hatred died with the end of the Cold War, but other problems continue to make war a painful everyday experience for many people. The decisions we make and the actions we take, individually and collectively, will determine whether our sun is rising or setting. Ultimately, only justice built on compassion will bring the world peace.

Let us pray . . .

God our Father, giver of life, from the beginning you planted within us the seeds of an earth on which people care for one another and where peace reigns. Your Son, Jesus, is our hope and our inspiration. Because of him we can dream dreams of a just and peace-filled world. With him, we add our voices, our eyes, our ears, our hands, and our feet to building your reign. In him and through him we proclaim that justice and peace are possible, that people who are poor or otherwise needy will be satisfied, and that those who are suffering now will be refreshed.

Lord Jesus Christ, you said to your apostles:
I leave you peace, my peace I give you.
Look not on our sins, but on the faith of your Church,
and grant us the peace and unity of your kingdom
where you live for ever and ever. Amen.

—"Order of the Mass," *The Sacramentary,* Catholic Book
Publishing Co., 1974, page 562.

For further study . . .

1. In light of this past chapter, consider the following question: Am I a peacemaker? List ten attitudes you have or actions you perform that would identify you as a peacemaker. Then, make a similar list of attitudes and actions that you could cultivate to help you become even more of a peacemaker.

2. The twentieth century has been the bloodiest in history. It also planted seeds for a new attitude toward violence and toward how people and nations get along. Draw a picture in words or images of how you see the twenty-first century taking shape.

3. Give two examples of what the U.S. Catholic bishops might have in mind with the following quote: "The celebration of violence in much of our media, music, and even video games is poisoning our children" (*Confronting a Culture of Violence*, page 2). Do you agree with their statement? Provide research to support your stance.

4. Use an almanac or other resource to find out the percentage of this year's federal budget that is to be spent on the military. Compare this portion of the budget to what is spent on education and other social programs. Also compare that portion to what was spent on military spending 10, 20, 30, and 40 years ago. Present as a chart for class viewing.

5. Look through news magazines or newspapers from the past few months to find out where ethnic conflicts are currently being fought. Write a report on one such conflict, describing the groups involved and the issues at stake.

6. Read *The War Prayer*, by Mark Twain. Write an updated version of it.

7. Write a brief science-fiction story based on the following premise: You travel forward in time 100 years when humanity has banned all nuclear weapons as being outdated, destructive, and unnecessary. Explain to a gathering of world leaders of the time why some nations of your time felt that they needed to have the ability to destroy the world many times over.

Glossary

absolute pacifists—persons who believe that all violence is wrong and violates their religious or humanitarian principles

ageism—discriminatory attitudes and practices toward people based on their age

aggression—actions which disregard the needs, wants, limitations, misgivings, and outlooks of others

Alzheimer's disease—a progressive disease that may occur in older people, leading to confusion, grouchiness, and impaired judgment

Americans with Disabilities Act—act passed by Congress in 1990 initiating changes to ensure that the rights of the disabled are not violated because of a disability

anawim—Hebrew word for the poor and the weak, those in special need of help

animal experimentation—scientific research on animals, including some questionable practices

anthropocentric—emphasizing the rights of humans at the expense of all else

assertiveness—to express or act out in a positive and affirming way one's wants, feelings, concerns, or viewpoints

barbarians—people lacking refinement or culture

blockade—preventing the transport of goods to their intended destination

breakdown in community—lack of a stable family life, regular schooling, and support services from other adults

capital punishment—the authorized killing by a nation's legal system of a person convicted of a particular crime

capitalism—individual ownership and administration of the production and distribution of goods

cash crops—crops grown to be exported in order to raise money

Christendom—ruling powers and levels of society that existed in the empire were viewed as the way God intended them to be

chronic malnutrition—constant illness caused by lack of proper amount of vitamins and nutrients

civil disobedience—breaking a law for what one considers just and moral reasons

civilization—the established social order

colonialism—one nation taking control of another nation by force

communal prayer—prayer prayed aloud with others

communities of resistance—groups who take a unified stand against an area of injustice

consumerism—the distorted desire to possess things out of proportion to our needs or normal wants

contemplation—being filled with a sense of wonder; seeing all life as a gift and acting responsibly toward that gift

continuum of conflict resolution—refers to the degree someone will accept violence as a means for resolving conflicts, ranging from absolute acceptance of violence to absolute rejection of violence

corporate farming—ownership of a large number of acres and animals by persons or organizations that oversee production but do not actually work with the land or the animals

crimes against persons—killing or physically hurting someone

crimes against property—stealing or damaging property

criminal justice—focuses on treatment of people in the judicial system

crisis of limits—the finite and irreplaceable nature of essential resources, such as oil and rainforests

critical thinking—examining with an open mind what we usually take for granted

culture of death—culture which values having over human beings

culture of life—culture which values life over all else

decision-making power—ability to make choices regarding an institution or one's life

deterrence—to discourage an action through fear

domestic violence—physical or psychological abuse within a family setting

drought—a long period with no rain

ecology—study of the environment and the relationships among the elements of creation

economic colonies—poorer countries dependent upon a few wealthy countries to purchase their limited selection of crops or products

economic migrants—people who come to a county seeking a better life for themselves and their families

empowerment—the gaining of power over one's life and within one's community

encyclical—official papal letter

energy-intensive—large-scale farming that depends more on heavy machinery, chemical fertilizers, irrigation systems, and pesticides than on people

ethnic conflicts—two or more groups fighting for control of the same region

euthanasia—killing or permitting the death of hopelessly sick or disabled individuals

famine—a long period with little or no food

fatalism—the belief that the world is out of our control and in the hands of blind fate

feminization of poverty—trend that results in more women and dependent children living in poverty than men

fixed income—income that remains much the same year after year, such as Social Security or pension payments

food crops—crops grown to feed the people within a country

global warming—an increase in the temperature worldwide

graced social structures—encourage and strengthen life, dignity, and the development of community

graying of America—the trend toward an increasingly older population in the U.S.

greenhouse effect—a warming of the earth's surface and lower atmosphere that tends to intensify with an increase in atmospheric carbon dioxide

Gross National Product—a measure of the overall wealth of a country

hierarchical—distinct levels of power and responsibilities

homophobia—fear of homosexuals or of being homosexual

hope—a virtue that envisions a better world and affirms that, with God's help, a better world is possible

income levels—comparative amounts of money earned annually by individuals or families

individualism—emphasizing personal independence and the rights of individuals over interdependence and concern for the common good

inorganic farming—farming dependent on chemical fertilizers and pesticides; produces immediate high crop-yields but depletes topsoil

institutional racism—racist actions and attitudes ingrained and generally accepted by organizations of a society

institutional violence—violence that results from injustices within a society

interdependent—reliance on others for survival and well-being

Jubilee Year—redistribution of property and wealth that took place according to Jewish law every fifty years in order to restore greater equality in possession of goods

labor-intensive—small-scale farming that depends more on people than on machines to do the farm work

liberation—the act of being set free

liberation theology—belief that the gospel message addresses today's social concerns, especially those of people who are poor

life choices—choices about living made by an individual or group

long-term solutions—answers which provide on-going resolutions to problems

low-tillage farming—farming that disturbs topsoil as little as possible, leaving some ground cover to prevent erosion, but still allowing some use of fertilizer and pesticides

malnutrition—a state resulting from a diet lacking the nutrients vital to good health

means—method or resources

middle class—people of moderate income, distinct from wealthier people and those who are poor

migrant—a person who moves regularly in order to find work

militarism—enthusiastically advocating the use of righteous violence; glorifying the use of violence to resolve conflicts

multinational corporations—companies that operate in a number of countries

mutuality—the recognition that we need each other and that the good of one person matches the good of all people

nationalism—promoting the interests of one's own country and culture over others; love of country regardless of its actions, and refusing to recognize or trying to change its flaws

near homeless—people with no savings or resources to carry them over during times of financial crisis

oligarchies—countries ruled by a few members of an elite group clearly distinct from the masses of people who make up the rest of the population

organic farming—farming without the use of toxic chemicals; can create topsoil

pacifism—conflict resolution through nonviolent means

pantheism—regarding nature or the elements of nature as divine

passivity—making no attempt to resolve conflict; not getting involved; detached

paternity and maternity leave—paid time off from work for the father and or the mother after the birth or adoption of a baby

patriarchy—a society in which most of the power is in the hands of men

patriotism—love of country that admits its shortcomings and tries to right them

personal causes—individual actions that lead to problems

personal problems—an individual's concerns

physical quality of life index—levels on this table are determined by a combination of average length of life, average rate of death for babies, and the number of people who can read

plea bargaining—pleading guilty in exchange for a lighter sentence

practical pacifists—persons who believe that nonviolence is a better way than violence to resolve conflicts

prejudice—narrow-minded judgment or opinion

prophet—one who speaks divinely inspired insights

psychological violence—harming someone through non-physical means

racial prejudice—a strong negative feeling that a person holds toward members of another race

recycling—converting waste products and other goods we throw away into usable products instead of putting them into a landfill

refugee—one who flees to a foreign country or power to escape danger or persecution

respect—appreciating and valuing persons as they are

satyagraha—truth force; soul force; belief that right makes might, not that might makes right

senility—irreversible brain damage that may occur in the aging process

sexism—discrimination or oppression based on gender

simple living—buying and using only what is needed, out of respect for people and resources

sinful social structures—discourage and weaken life, dignity, and the development of community

single export economies—budgets based on one product as the main source of income

social action—steps taken to change society's structures

social justice—focuses on discrimination and unjust social structures

socialism—government ownership and administration of production and distribution of goods

societal problems—problems that affect an entire community or nation

solidarity—a spirit of unity and mutual concern; the quality of justice that breaks down barriers between people

solitary prayer—silent prayers or prayers said while alone

spiral of violence—an injustice which leads to violence and an attempt to crush that violence with more violence; violence that builds on violence

stereotype—a prejudiced generalization, a way of thinking that is in error

stewardship—humanity's role, designated by God, to protect, care for, and sustain the rest of creation

subordination—being placed in or occupying a lower class, rank, or position

theologians—scholars of religion

throwaway society—squandering of useable materials and products

triage—the practice of placing people into one of three groups based on their likelihood of survival and treating first the two groups most likely to survive

underlying causes—ways that society is structured that affect people

undernourishment—amount of food is less than what can sustain life

welfare reform—initiated by the federal government in the mid 1990s. These changes in programs aimed at helping people who are poor shifted administration of programs to the state level, limited the amount of time people could receive government assistance, and attempted to move people previously on welfare to being economically self-sufficient.

welfare-to-work programs—government assistance programs that provide aid while individuals are trying to learn a new trade or seek employment

works of mercy—charitable actions by which we come to the aid of our neighbor in physical and spiritual ways

Index

Bolded number indicates page on which word is defined.

helping, 134–135
in America, 86–111
migrants and immigrants, 96–103
preferential love for, 70
women and children, 145–146
Pope John XXIII, 4, 58, 150
Pope John Paul II, 9, 10, 18, 21, 59, 63, 102, 123, 150, 151, 214–216, 224, 226, 235, 263, 272
Pope Leo XIII, 58
Pope Paul VI, 59, 129, 280
Pope Pius XI, 58
Pope Pius XII, 58, 100
population,
changing in the U.S., 96, 186
growth, globally, 122–123
and older people in the U.S., 186
poverty (see also the poor)
the real issue of, 101
in America, 86–111
1998 guidelines, 91
and children, 104–105
and homelessness, 94–95
and immigration, 98–103
and the Church, 92–93, 104, 127–130, 134–135
and the elderly, 105
eliminating, 107–108, 135
global, 112–137
and international development, 133–134
and military spending, 133
and overconsumption and waste, 132
and sinful social structures, 101, 120–126, 130, 132, 133–134, 145–146
and world hunger, 116–119
of whole countries, 116
the feminization of, 145–146
power and change (see social action)
powergap,
and sexism, 146–147
and racism, 169–171
practical pacifists, **251**
prayer, 80–81
prayers, 1, 22, 25, 44, 47, 84, 87, 110, 113, 136, 139, 156, 161, 180, 184, 193, 199, 204, 212, 218, 221, 238, 241, 264, 267, 288
preferential love for the poor, 70, 127
prejudice, 161–164, 165–171, 172–179, 186, 189, 195, 201, 202, 206–207, 209
Bible and, 172
characteristics of, 161–163
Church and, 175
Jesus and, 173
responding to, 176–179

roots of, 164
prisoners, and justice, 204–211
and captial punishment, 209–210
and Christianity, 209, 210
and compassion, 209
and plea bargaining, 207
and prisons, 208–209
and social structures, 211
and the criminal justice system, 206–207, 208–209
and types of crime, 206
in relation to poverty, 206–207, 209
problems, personal and social, 11
Promised Land, 30–33
prophet, *33*
prophets, the
characteristics of, 34
and justice, 33–36
message of, 35–36
protein-deficiency diseases, 117
Protestant Reformation, 55
psychological violence, **275**

R

race, 158–179
a social construction, 167–168
and prejudice, 169–179
and racism, 169–179
discussing, 164
racial prejudice, 160, 161–163, 166, 167–168, **169–171**, 172–179
racism, 158, 169–179
in the biblical view, 172
and Jesus' radical love, 173
and the Church, 175
as a function of society, 170
as fact and as sin, 175
as subordination based on race, 170
institutional, 171
responding to, 176–179
recycling, **230**
Reformation, the, 55
refugee, **100**
reign (presence) of God, 38–40, 41–42, 69, 260, 270
relationship between
age and health problems, 186–188
age and prejudice, 186–188
ageism and suffering, 186–189
attitudes and peace, 252–260, 269–289
attitudes and poverty, 98–99
availibility of guns and crime, 211
childhood/old age and poverty, 104–105
colonialism and poverty, 120, 125
compassion, justice, and peace, 287

corporate development and poverty, 123
culture and sexual identity, 141
disabilities and rejection, 195
disabilities and special needs, 196
distribution of goods/services and poverty, 123
environmental destruction and world hunger, 224–232
homophobia and injustice, 202
humanity and disability, 196–197
injustice and institutional violence, 281
lack of education and poverty, 101, 115
literacy and poverty, 115
media and crime, 211
migration and poverty, 96–101
military power and war/peace, 282–286
poverty and capital punishment, 209
poverty and homelessness, 94–95
poverty and hunger, disease, and death, 116–119
poverty and imprisonment, 207
poverty and infant mortality, 113
poverty and length of life, 115, 117
poverty and population growth, 122
prejudice and injustice, 158–179
race and capital punishment, 209
racism and abuse, 176
racism and isolation, 158–179
racism and poverty, 169–171
racism and power, 169–171
sexism and domestic violence, 152–153
sexism and family roles, 153
sexism and injustice, 141–148
sexism and poverty, 145–147
sexism and power, 141–148
social change and eliminating poverty, 107
social evils and violence, 278
social justice and criminal justice, 204–211
social structures and poverty, 98–99
social values and abortion, 214
social values and crime, 211
social values and destruction of the environment, 224–232
social/political climate and poverty, 124–126
the earth and all its creatures, 226–237
work availability and poverty, 91–92
work location and poverty, 92
relationships, 29, 39–40, 152–153, 154, 271–275
relieving suffering, 66–83
through social action, 72–76